THE LAST OF THE OLD BREED

THE LAST OF THE OLD BREED

AN ORAL HISTORY OF THE FINAL MARINES FROM WORLD WAR II

★ ★ ★ ★ ★ ★

SCOTT DAVIS

ST. MARTIN'S PRESS
NEW YORK

First published in the United States by St. Martin's Press, an imprint of St. Martin's Publishing Group

EU Representative: Macmillan Publishers Ireland Ltd, 1st Floor, The Liffey Trust Centre, 117–126 Sheriff Street Upper, Dublin 1, D01 YC43

www.stmartins.com

The Library of Congress Cataloging-in-Publication Data is available upon request.

ISBN 978-1-250-42993-3 (hardcover)
ISBN 978-1-250-42994-0 (ebook)

First Edition: 2026

10 9 8 7 6 5 4 3 2 1

To the veterans of World War II
who came home and suffered in silence

My friend was blown up at Iwo Jima,
you told me, 92, gripping your walker.
Right next to me, his back
was blown away, I could see his lungs,
I could have been killed.

You never talked about this the years
I was growing up. But when I was nine
you had a nervous breakdown
and wouldn't get out of bed.
For months we drove every Saturday
from Palmer to Anchorage so you could
see a doctor.

There's a scar at the corner of your jaw
where the bullet passed through. You think
it causes your headaches and stiff neck.
When my sister visits, she says
you cry out in the night. You say
you can't shake the loss of your friend.
You say you couldn't tell his family
the truth.

You were twenty-one, a Marine on a ship
with your buddies, gliding toward
a deadly island
in the dark night sea
waves rising and falling.
Silently you slid into the water.

They asked for a volunteer
someone to walk in front of the tank
on enemy ground. You'd learned
to jump out of airplanes.
You jumped in front,
leading the way.

Some of your friends lived, came home.
Some of your friends died, never left.
Every one of you lost your self
one way or another,
winning the war.

—Marcia Rutan,
daughter of Iwo Jima survivor Bertram Rutan

CONTENTS

AUTHOR'S NOTE

This book is not intended to act as a comprehensive account of the Pacific Theater, a sweeping tome of military strategy, or an in-depth study of squad-level tactics. This is a story of memory. And because memory is often unpleasant, the sentiments that follow may be offensive to a modern audience. I have decided, for the sake of transparency, to report the stories exactly as they were told. Topics such as killing or war crimes have not been censored, nor have I altered any derogatory racial language, including the term "Jap." While I do not condone some of the views expressed, each veteran was encouraged to speak openly, lest we romanticize or glorify the past. Any mistakes in historical accuracy are mine and mine alone. The text was edited for clarity, but the unique speech pattern of each veteran has not been touched. I would also like to note that twenty-one US Army divisions served in the Pacific between 1941 and 1945. To maintain some semblance of brevity, I elected to document Marines, but in no way wish to diminish the Army's sacrifices during the island war. This is their story too, unfiltered and raw. Additionally, a select number of veterans have been quoted under pseudonyms for the privacy of their families—the rest are listed in the rear of the book, alongside their assigned company, battalion, and regiment. For simplicity's sake, each person is introduced only by their division and age. The age noted for each veteran reflects their age when interviewed. As of this writing, only a few participants are still alive, the youngest rapidly approaching the century mark. Soon enough a new generation will be born with no firsthand connection to World War II, and their perceptions will be painted by movies, miniseries, and social media. For better or worse, they will remember the war in a way unique to the context of their society. This book, I hope, will help span the chasm of time and memory.

THE LAST OF THE OLD BREED

1 ★★★★★★

THE GREAT DEPRESSION

On Black Tuesday, October 29, 1929, the stock market crashed, and the United States plummeted into an unprecedented economic downturn that left millions of Americans destitute. In major cities across the country, shantytowns—known as Hoovervilles, after President Herbert Hoover—blossomed as national unemployment peaked at nearly 25 percent. Severe drought in the southern plains only exacerbated the problem as millions more fled apocalyptic dust storms in search of safety and greater opportunity. Amid such widespread despair, the country elected Franklin Delano Roosevelt in 1932. Armed with a bevy of new legislation, the statesman from New York wielded his voice over the radio to pledge a "new deal" for the American people. Thousands went to work on public projects: the Hoover Dam was constructed and dedicated in 1935, the Lincoln Tunnel was unveiled in 1937, and the Civilian Conservation Corps (CCC) planted more than 3.5 billion trees. But it did little to help. For perhaps the first time in American history, young men and women were facing the prospect of growing up with fewer opportunities than the preceding generation.

Mike Ladich, 96: I was born in Superior, Wisconsin, in 1923. My father had tuberculosis and was in a sanitarium. We were on relief—*welfare.* We had it rough, it was tough; that was the goddamn Depression. I can remember unemployment lines: Under Roosevelt, they gave out free food and the whole line was three blocks long. People waiting to get a handout. They won't admit it today, but they were there, waiting for a goddamn relief handout. Everyone was a little bit ashamed of standing in that line. I used to have my younger brother stand in line for me—and I'd stay out of sight. He was naïve and young. Then I would pick up the groceries and take them home.

I grew up in an immigrant neighborhood, basically Scandinavian and Polish. I'll describe the gang: We were pretty big, an immigrant population from below the tracks, if you know what I mean. The uptown kids—*the sissies*—were afraid to play football against us. We were a bunch of tough Polacks. One kid who lived above the tracks, I've forgotten his name, ran when we came to play football against them. I had a light complexion, but the Italians caught hell. That's no bullshit. If you were a little bit on the darker side—*look out*. But I tended to be blondish. And my brothers were too, so we didn't take any crap. But a lot of them did.

Having a father in the sanitarium was hard, damn hard. My mother had to do everything, so there was no fun. I was the oldest and working. Instead of playing football in high school, I went down to the docks and worked as a longshoreman at sixteen years old. The football coach got mad at me—*that lousy bastard*. When I saw him, I punched him out. He called me a goddamn quitter. Can you imagine that? Calling *me* a goddamn quitter. He didn't even ask me why I quit the fuckin' football team. But doing that job at sixteen taught me a work ethic. It had a good effect: I've been a good worker ever since. I had to be.

Luther Hendricks, 96: Without sounding bitter, it wasn't a very happy time to grow up. I was born in Denver, Colorado, in 1925, and, back then, things were really bad. My father was from the old country and my mother was from Louisiana. She was a full-blooded Indian and my father was Irish. But she had one-eighth Negro in her, so she was a Negro. You never get used to being called "boy," "uncle," or "you people." I've seen things done to African Americans: hangings, burnings, decapitations, people being dragged through the streets. You'd get off the sidewalk when you saw a white person coming; hold your head down. I never could do that. When I saw something that I didn't like, I just couldn't be still. It's a wonder I wasn't one of the people that got hung. But I survived it—I think I'm doing well not to be really bitter. I've kept my sanity. But when you've seen things like that, you don't forget them.

John Marx, 97: As a kid, I didn't notice the Great Depression. I would take my wagon and go pick up food: bread, potatoes, and stuff like that for the family. I always helped the neighbor ladies with their groceries; always carried their groceries. I mowed lawns and cut hedges for a quarter, the whole backyard and front. I always had a job. Sold newspapers for three cents on the street, going car to car, yelling, "Get your *Evening Herald*!" I worked at a pottery place, a drug store, and I was a bouncer at the movie theater (to keep the kids in line). We always went to the beach, all the neighborhood kids. Sometimes we'd stay four or five days. It was safe then. My dad worked for Chevron and my mother was a housewife. Later, she worked at a jewelry store. Dad was okay, but he was kind of ornery—wasn't too good to my mother. He was in World War I, a forward observer. I don't know if that had something to do with it or not, but he was always getting into fights.

Francis Stanger, 92: I was born at Turtle Lake, Montana, on December 19, 1927. My mother went out to clean herself and she caught pneumonia and died. My grandfather and my dad raised me. Frank Stanger, my dad, was a bronc buster. He was a tough guy—and my grandfather was the same way. Grandpa only had one leg. He fell into a river once and his cousin pulled him out; he lost his leg to frostbite. But he was a bronc rider too, and he used to carry pistols like in the Western movies. He taught me how to shoot. When we had a hard time getting food, I would go up into the hills with a .22 and shoot grouse.

Ray Garland, 96: My father was kind of a harsh man. He believed in the razor strap. But he was doing hard work in the mines and that's the way he was raised. My mother was only fifteen years old when they got married. She was a hardworking woman.

Donald Brown, 95: I was born in Washta, Iowa, in 1927. I grew up during the Depression—and it was rough. We had a hard time. My father—that sonofabitch—ran off and left us. My mother was raising three kids on a dollar a day by doing housework. That's what we lived on: a dollar a day.

Don Pilcher, 95: My mother had fourteen children. There were eleven of us that lived. The birth dates were from 1906 to 1930. We all went to the same grade school and high school. My twin brother and I were next to last.

Elwin Hart, 93: My biological mother died when I was nine years old, during childbirth.

Milton "Red" Cronk, 98: I was born in Iowa City, Iowa, and I was in an orphanage for a short time. The people who adopted me got me when I was eleven months old.

Eugene Jones, 94: I was sent to an orphanage and got out at fifteen.

Hattie Kelley, 98: My mother died when I was three years old. My dad died, too. He was injured very badly in an automobile accident when I was five. My sister had to go live on a dairy farm, and she never got to go to high school. Neither did my brother. I went to live with a man named Bill Pearson and his wife Ester, kind of as a foster child. I have a picture of them sitting in the living room. They were great people; they were wonderful to me. Ester was my mother, in a sense. But Bill died in a terrible accident when I was ten. He came home drinking, had a quarrel with Ester, and went for a walk. Later that evening, the train people called and said there was a body laying over the rails. Apparently, Bill tried to walk across, but he had a bad knee, and he fell and hit his head on the rail. And he died.

Richard Nelson, 98: My dad died when I was two and my mother had eight kids. Things were rough growing up: We were always hungry, always had to pay rent somewhere, living in the west side of Chicago. Everything was bad there. I had to get paper routes, sell stuff, and go looking in the alleys for empty bottles to cash in.

Les Anderson, 97: During the Depression, we all worked in the fields picking berries: strawberries, raspberries, cherries. Made enough to pay for our school clothes. Dad had been a cook in a forest camp, then he was a sawyer in a lumber mill, before he started his own business as a painter and paper hanger. Most of the kids helped him with that. Momma grew a big garden and canned everything.

Robert Hall, 95: We lived on a farm, and like many people in those days, during the Depression, were pretty self-sufficient. We hardly ever went to a store. We had a big garden, a few cattle, chickens, and that sort of thing. My mother put together about three hundred jars of fruits and vegetables every year. My father was a butcher for a while and eventually became a farmer and a cattle dealer.

Don Pilcher, 95: My father was a tenant farmer, but he lost the farm.

Ernie Ferguson, 98: We left Oklahoma due to the dust storms.

Bill Gropp, 97: My folks decided, in 1928, that they'd come out west. We ended up in Clarkston, Washington. I was only four years old, so I don't remember a heck of a lot about it. But that's where we grew up. The major business in the valley was the Potlatch Forest, as I recall. I started working with the Forest Service when I was fifteen years old.

Ray Garland, 96: I went to Butte High until my sophomore year, then I joined the CCC when I was sixteen. We fought forest fires and took care of trees.

Francis Stanger, 92: I became a sawyer at twelve years old with a crosscut saw. We'd dig out big yellow pines and knock them down for lumber in the spring. My dad would make me saw them and they were huge! I went to school in Polson for a while, but I couldn't talk very good English because my first language was Salish. I flunked a couple grades. Then I went to Chemawa Indian School in Oregon, north of Salem. A lot of us went to school down there. I was about fifteen or sixteen, I think. I worked in a dairy and went to school part-time.

Tom Charlton, 95: I quit school when I was in the eighth grade and went to work building butter boxes for a local creamery. Dad wanted me to go to school in the worst way, but I hated it. I'm self-educated.

Art Perez, 96: Things started to get better about '37 and '38. I could tell a difference in school by the way the kids dressed.

Clyde Lacquement, 95: By the time I was eighteen, things had picked up a good bit. But I never even thought about going to college.

Glenn Ferguson, 99: I jumped a grade prior to high school, so I graduated when I was sixteen and went off to college. They were filled up in chemistry, which I was supposed to take my first year. Instead, they put me in physics, which was for second-year students. I was sixteen in sophomore level classes, and I decided I didn't like that. I wanted to travel, so I joined the Marine Corps in 1939.

Ray Garland, 96: I had never seen a Marine before, but there were pictures of them in a copy of *Life* magazine. I liked their blue uniforms. Not long after that, I opened our local paper, and it said that the Marines were going to interview men at the Finlen Hotel. The next day, I went up and I think I was the first man to join the Marine Corps from that station in Butte, Montana.

Billy Hall, 98: A recruiting sergeant came down from Amarillo and he was talking to the boys around Hereford, Texas.

My mother had passed away a little over two years prior and my dad had remarried. So, I was kind of a "third wheel" in his new family. The Marines had a beautiful uniform; I had never seen anything like that before. I was quite impressed and decided to enlist. People ask me if I lied about my age (because I was fifteen). I say, "No, I didn't. But the recruiting sergeant sure did." He knew how old I was, and he was more than willing to falsify the records so I could go in. Five of us were supposed to go to Amarillo for induction—but that Saturday, I was the only one that showed up.

Tom Baker, 98: I was sixteen years old when I enlisted. That's the way it was in those days. I was big and husky and that's all they cared about. I wanted to join the Navy, dadgummit. I always have. I went to Aberdeen, Washington, to talk it over with a friend who was a recruiter for the Navy. But when I walked in the door, there was a Marine inside with a fancy uniform. My buddy said, "Which branch are you going to join today?" I said, "I don't know. Who's gonna take me the quickest?" My Navy buddy looked at his calendar and said, "Well, it will take us about a month." The Marine looked at his watch and said, "Will you be ready in ten minutes?" Away I went!

Ray Garland, 96: Boot camp wasn't easy, but I knew about hard work from the CCC. After that, I was lucky: in those days, if you looked good in your uniform and were about six feet tall, you had a chance to go to Sea School. There were probably sixty guys in one platoon but only ten of us got to go. Sea School was as rough as boot camp, if not rougher. After that, I joined the USS *Tennessee* at the end of October of 1941.

Eugene Jones, 94: I went to work on the *Washington Times-Herald* as a copy boy in 1940. One of my jobs was, once a week, to bicycle five blocks to the White House and pick up the exposed picture plates for our cameramen stationed there. Of course, I saw FDR many times. The fellas on the paper said, "Look, kid, there's gonna be a big war coming and you're gonna be in it."

2 ★★★★★★

PEARL HARBOR

While America struggled to emerge from the Great Depression, momentous events were unfolding across the globe. Spurred by rising nationalism and a desire for territorial expansion, Japan was perpetrating a brutal war of conquest in China that would ultimately result in the deaths of nearly twenty million people (including 200,000 to 300,000 in the city of Nanjing alone). Wary of further aggression in the region, President Franklin Roosevelt imposed a series of economic sanctions and trade embargoes intended to cripple the Japanese war machine. For a trade-reliant nation that received 90 percent of its oil from the US, this left two options: withdraw from China or go to war with the United States.

The answer came without warning on the morning of Sunday, December 7, 1941, when a formation of 183 Japanese planes arrived over the American Pacific Fleet moored at Pearl Harbor, Hawaii. Among the unsuspecting servicemen on duty was a young Marine from Butte, Montana, named Ray Garland. Private Garland was standing on the fantail of the USS *Tennessee*, preparing to raise the American flag as a member of the color guard, when the first flight descended.

Ray Garland, 96, USS *Tennessee*: I happened to look over my shoulder and I saw these planes coming down. The corporal in charge said, "Turn around, Private Garland, we're getting ready to make colors." About that time, a Japanese Val dive-bomber dropped its bomb on Ford Island and started coming down "Battleship Row." The rear machine gunner was shooting as he came by. He was close enough that I could see his goggles. I ran to my station, but we couldn't shoot our five-inch gun because Ford Island was next to us. Then a one-ton bomb hit one of the fourteen-inch guns and killed some sailors there. I went up and—*it was a mess*. We mopped up pieces of people. It was not good to look at.

After that, I was assigned to a fire hose on the quarterdeck to keep burning oil away from the ship. Someone opened up a hatch and a sailor and I went down the ladder. I glanced over and saw what I *thought* was a fire. So, I turned the hose on it. But it wasn't a fire—it was a sparking electrical cord. That's the last thing I remember. The electricity hit me, and I ended up in sick bay. I couldn't see for a couple of days. That was the end of Pearl Harbor for me.

At the same time, across the international date line, Japanese forces struck American bases at Guam, Wake Island, and the Philippines. On Guam, a small bastion of Marines and sailors offered several days of paltry resistance before Naval Governor George McMillin surrendered the island. A mixed defense force of Marines and civilians on Wake Island repulsed an invasion on December 11, but eventually surrendered when further opposition became untenable. In the Philippines, American forces mustered a desperate defense but were also crushed by the Japanese juggernaut. Back in the United States, news of the Japanese attacks spread rapidly across the country.

Burt Withee, 95: I was up at the Laurelhurst Playfield in Seattle, playing football. The ball went across the street, and I went to retrieve it. Suddenly, a guy stuck his head out the door of his house, and yelled, "The Japs just attacked Pearl Harbor!" I said, "Where in the hell is Pearl Harbor?"

Donald Brown, 95: We didn't even know where Pearl Harbor was. Never heard of it before.

Howard Rieckers, 100: I was milking cows in a barn in Chewelah, Washington. Dad and I thought the world was coming to an end. We walked out the door and looked up.

W. Lee Robinson, 97: I'd been out skiing with a friend, and we were on our way home when we heard that the Japanese had bombed Pearl Harbor over the car radio. It was very surprising because I'd grown up in a calm atmosphere with very little fear. I had lived a mellow life. That kind of shook me into reality because I was seventeen at the time.

Donn Thompson, 95: That December, we were all in shock when the Japanese hit Pearl Harbor. We all, as young men, looked at each other and said, "Well, it won't be long before we're in it."

John Marx, 97: I was excited. I don't know, as a kid, I was excited.

Luther Hendricks, 96: I was in school in Los Angeles when they attacked. I went down the next day, wanted to join up. I was sixteen. The response I got: "We don't take coloreds in the Marine Corps." What the hell have I been living here for? This is America. This is my home. But they don't want me to fight?

I went back home and said, "Must be something I could do." I went to Vallejo to work at Mare Island. I worked there from '42 until August of '43. Then I went back when I found out they were taking Negroes in the Marine Corps, and I joined up.

Les Anderson, 97: There were about a dozen Japanese kids in my high school graduation class. The school took the salutatorian and valedictorian titles away from the Japanese kids and gave them to white kids. My Japanese friends from school were all interred in a—I call them concentration camps, at the Puyallup fairgrounds. I was amazed that the kids weren't terribly upset at our government. They were born here, and they were as American as I was; and they proved that later in the Nisei military groups.

Raymond Lewis, 95: I was in the ninth grade at a high school in Clarksdale, Mississippi, on December 7, 1941. They broke into the auditorium and said that Japan had bombed Pearl Harbor. I was fifteen at the time and that enraged me. I had a homelife that I'm not particularly proud of—my dad was an alcoholic. So, I got my mother and him to sign papers saying I was seventeen, and I joined the Marines.

Harold Rediske, 94: I graduated from school in 1942. Billings, Montana, was our nearest recruiting station, so I went down there to join the service. They told me to go home and grow up. I was fifteen.

Tom Shields, 93: I was only seventeen years old. My mother and dad had to sign for me.

Bob Ehrlich, 94: I wanted to get into the service so bad, but my mother made me finish high school first. Once I was seventeen, I was in.

Robert Brutinel, 100: My mother said, "No way!" She said, "I don't care how mad you get, I'm not signing!" My dad said, "For God's sake! Sign that thing! I'm tired of hearing you and him arguing all the time!"

Francis Stanger, 92: I came out of school and worked at a dairy farm in Ronan, Washington, but I got bored. I thought I might as well join up. I was only seventeen. They called me "Chief" because I was the only Native American there.

Milton "Red" Cronk, 98: I could have stayed home on the farm—*I had the chance.* But I didn't want to. I wanted to go in with the Marines and do my patriotic duty.

Eldon Cedergreen, 96: Me and my brother were deferred from the draft because we were farm boys. But we saw all our high school buddies going, and that kind of got to us. We asked our folks, "Can we go?" They let us go, so we joined up.

Clayton Narveson, 99: Mother had seven children: six boys and one girl. All six of us went into the service and all six of us served overseas. I went into the Marine Corps in October of 1942.

Melvin Gribble, 95: I was working for the Forest Service when they called me up for the draft. I came out of the forest, went to Spokane, and enlisted in the Marine Corps. I wanted to get over there and fight; didn't have sense enough to know it was dangerous.

Les Anderson, 97: My brother was in the Army, and he didn't like it. A good friend of mine was in the Navy, and he didn't like it. So, I picked the Marine Corps. I figured you had to have a college education to be in the Air Corps.

Elburn Cooper, 95: Like a lot of other kids my age, I received a draft notice while I was still in high school. I was afraid I might not be able to finish school, so I bid a hasty retreat to the center where they enlisted people. I went to the Air Force first: "No, we can't take you because you don't have enough math." Then I went to the Navy: "No, we can't take you because you don't have enough math." Then I went to the Army: "No, we can't take you because you don't have enough math." Then I went to the Marine Corps and—*bang!* They just wanted cannon fodder, I think.

Wallis "Wally" Hamlin, 100: Nobody seemed to know anything about the Marine Corps, so I said, "I'm going to join that." And I did. I signed up in Orofino, Idaho.

Jack Becker, 99: I was riding home on a bus and there was a Marine sitting in the back, all decked out in his dress uniform. I thought, *Oh fuck, this guy looks good! I want to look like that!*

W. Lee Robinson, 97: If I could blame it on anything, it would be the uniform. I thought that uniform was great.

Elwin Hart, 93: My stepmother was influential because she loved the Marine Corps for some reason; the uniform or whatever it was.

Gordon Black, 94: I don't know why I joined the Marine Corps. It must have been Tyrone Power or some other actor that played a Marine in the movies. My buddy, who went into the Air Corps, said, "Why'd you pick the Marine Corps?" I said, "I don't know, must be the uniform."

Marvin Strombo, 95: I wanted to join the Marine Corps because I saw a movie. When I went into the service, a lot of the other guys had seen the same movie. That's the reason we went in.

Frank Wright, 96: The scuttlebutt was, if you got in the Marine Corps, you could get duty aboard ship and wear those beautiful dress blues. I was really excited about it. There was a movie out—I can't remember the name of it—that was a recruiting type of movie. But they wouldn't take me because I was too young and too light. I only weighed 128 pounds. So, I went over to the Navy. I figured that was close to the Marine Corps. Same thing—I was too light and too young. I figured I could increase my weight quickly, so I bought a lot of food; bananas and stuff like that. I got my mother and her sister to agree to give me a delayed birth certificate. Then I went back to the Marine Corps and got ahold of a different recruiting sergeant. By that time, it was January, and I'd gained enough weight. A few weeks after Pearl Harbor, I was accepted and quit high school.

W. Lee Robinson, 97: On my way home from Coeur d'Alene, Idaho, I happened to pass down Main Street in Pocatello. There, on a second story window, I saw this fellow in a blue uniform with a white hat. And he yelled, "Semper Fidelis!" I thought he said, "Seventy-five dollars!" So, I went in and signed up to become a Marine.

Jim Palmieri, 103: I did not want to fight Italians in Europe. So, when I was drafted, I picked the Marines. I didn't like the Navy because I wasn't too happy with the water.

James Shriver, 98: There was a Civil War veteran in a small hotel up in Portland, Oregon, where my mother was working as a telephone operator. He and I would sit in the lobby of the hotel, and he would tell me stories about the Civil War. One day, he told me, "Why don't you go into the service!" I said, "My mother won't let me." A couple of days later, he talked me into walking across the street to the courthouse, up to the Marine Corps recruit office. I signed up.

John L'Abbe, 97: I tried to sign up with the Free French before Pearl Harbor, when the Germans still had France. But the Japanese bombed Pearl Harbor, so I thought, *Hell, I'll join the Americans.* My mom said, "Oh, yes! That's better!" I ended up enlisting in the Marine Corps. I had to stand in line to get in.

Walter Spuck, 95: I was in the merchant marines for about six months, but I couldn't take it because I was seasick most of the time. I came out and lived with my two sisters for a while. But that wasn't working out either, so I tried to get into the Army. The Army said, "Try the Marine Corps, you're too young."

Mike Ladich, 96: When I got back from the merchant marines, like an idiot, I joined the Marine Corps. I thought, *Enough of that shit, getting torpedoed over there!*

Robert Hall, 95: I was so "Gung Ho" that I wanted to join the best fighting outfit that the US had. I've never regretted it. I still think they're better than other service. But we're all prejudiced, of course.

Chuck Meacham, 96: I understood that the Marine Corps was the best, from what little studying I did. Therefore, I chose the Marine Corps.

Frank King, 100: I was scheduled to go into the Army Air Corps as an Air Cadet. But when I was taking my final exam at March Field, the interviewer asked me about my medical history. "Have you ever had TB, diabetes; anything like that?" I said, "Well, when I was a kid, I had hay fever." That was the end of the interview—they kicked me out. Oh, I was pissed! The next day, I went down to LA and signed up with the Marine Corps. They gave me a departure date of February 9, 1942. I went home and told my parents. My dad broke into tears; just sobbed. He said, "My God! Do you want to get yourself killed? Do you know what Marines do?"

Robert Evans, 97: I wanted to work at Farragut Naval Training Station, but the guy in charge said I was too young. I said, "Oh no, I'm old enough to work!" I was seventeen. He said, "I can't hire you. You're too small." I said, "Well, the hell with you." I went and joined the Marine Corps. There were fourteen of us that went in, but only two passed the exams. The other guy—his folks wouldn't sign for him. But mine would, mine signed for me. They were glad to get rid of me.

Milton "Red" Cronk, 98: When I went into the Marine Corps, my mother told me: "I hope, if the Japs get you, that you can kill yourself before they torture you."

John L'Abbe, 97: The last thing my father said: "Don't ever surrender."

Elburn Cooper, 95: My mom was sad that I was leaving, but everyone else was going. They sent us off to what was called a V-12 program, which was a pathway for future officers. I went to a little college called Gustavus Adolphus in the Minnesota River Valley. I took trigonometry the first term and I passed that fine. But the second term was solid analytical geometry, and I flunked that. I immediately packed my seabag, and I was on my way to boot camp.

Walter O'Malley, 98: I graduated from high school in June, then went up to Dartmouth College for the V-12 program on July 1. We were supposed to be in for sixteen months, four semesters. But after about two months, going into September, this fella from Worcester said, "You know, I'm passing on my books. If we stay here, this war's going to pass us by." Guess what we did? We flunked out on purpose. They sent us to Parris Island for Marine Corps basic training. But it was full, so they put us on a train, sent us out to San Diego.

3 ★ ★ ★ ★ ★ ★

PREPARING FOR WAR

In the months and years following the Japanese attack on Pearl Harbor, the country witnessed a mass migration of American youth as volunteers from across the country headed for Marine Corps boot camp in San Diego, California, or Parris Island, South Carolina. Boot camp lasted up to sixteen weeks (the duration fluctuated during the war to meet manpower needs) and stressed physical fitness, marksmanship, and discipline.

Ken Brown, 95: My parents encouraged me to get into a branch where I wouldn't be in too much danger. I went to Pocatello, Idaho, signed up, and was sworn into the Navy. From there, I got on a troop train for Camp Farragut in northern Idaho. But when we got to Boise, the guy in charge came through and called off our names, maybe about thirty people. He told us to get out and wait on the platform. While we're standing there, the train pulled out and left us! We didn't know what was going on. A jeep finally came up and a Marine Corps sergeant came out. He was dressed in a fancy blue uniform. He called us to attention and said, "Congratulations, men. You've just volunteered to serve in the United States Marine Corps." Of course, we protested. Then we found out that the Marine Corps was a branch of the Navy. *They had us!* Instead of going to Camp Farragut, we got on a bus and headed down to San Diego for Marine Corps training.

Roy Mays, 99: We left Texas on a bus and the only stop we made was in Palm Springs, California. We got the windows down and climbed out. We all got oranges out of the trees. It was kind of fun.

Howard Frye, 95: I got on a train in Mansfield, Missouri, and I went all the way through to California. I never was on a train before. Then we hopped off in San Diego.

John Haney, 98: When I got there, I thought, *Oh, boy! I'm going to be greeted and welcomed.* Instead, it was just the opposite! They treated me like a dog!

Lucien Jandreau, 99: When we arrived in Parris Island, our drill instructor got us young eighteen-year-olds together and said, "Your soul belongs to God, but your ass belongs to me!"

Howard Rieckers, 100: Boot camp was like the movies. The old sergeant walked up and down, saying, "I'm your mommy!" and that sort of thing.

Gordon Black, 94: I'll never forget when I got off the train. We were issued bedding, pillows, and blankets. Then Corporal Foster said, "On the double!" I didn't know what that meant, so I walked up to him. He grabbed me by the shirt and said, "When I say on the double, I want you to run!" That was my first introduction to our drill instructor.

Elwin Hart, 93: I was one of the "Feather Merchants," which is what they call the little guys. The line started with the tallest guys, and I was one of the last two or three of about thirty or forty from our platoon.

Howard Rieckers, 100: We lined up by a table and they threw clothes at us. They all didn't fit. A sergeant hollered, "If your clothes don't fit, trade with someone else!"

James Shriver, 98: When I was in line getting my gear, I happened to use the word "pants." And the guy in charge said, "You dumb son of a bitch! Women wear pants, men wear trousers!"

John Haney, 98: Our drill instructor was kind of a harsh guy. He had a big ole swagger stick with a .50 caliber shell on one end and a bullet on the other. When we were out there in the heat, marching around, he'd come by and whack you on the peak of the helmet with that swagger stick.

Raymond Lewis, 95: The first day we fell out, the drill instructor looked at me and said, "Did you shave this morning, boy?" I said, "No, sir. I don't shave" (at fifteen, I didn't shave yet). He said, "Do you have a razor?" I said, "Yes, sir, my daddy packed a razor for me." He said, "Go get your razor." I got my razor and came back. He said, "Did you put a new blade in?" I said, "Yes, I did." He said, "Good!" Then he opened the razor up, dropped the blade on the sand, and rubbed his foot back and forth on the blade. Then he picked it up, put a handful of sand on my face, and dry shaved me. I've been shaving ever since. Later, I got caught with my hands in my pockets and they filled my pockets up with sand and sewed them up. I had to march with pockets full of sand. Anyway, they taught me discipline.

W. Lee Robinson, 97: That was a different kind of discipline: that was discipline without love.

Marvin Strombo, 95: It was probably one of the worst periods of my life. They didn't treat you very good. Ordering you around, so strict. We weren't used to it.

Keith Tucker, 100: It was very strict and strenuous training: marching, running obstacle courses, running bayonet courses.

Robert Beale, 97: My first week in boot camp, I cried every night in my bunk. I thought, *Why did I join such a maniacal group of sonsabitches?*

Lester Penney, 98: Boot camp was no problem for me because I was an orphan. I had no trouble being there. A lot of kids were unhappy: it was their first time away from home and they were missing their parents and family. I didn't have that problem. I was glad to get away from the farm. And I didn't have any trouble with the physical end of training because I'd just spent four years working on a chicken farm. It was very heavy work, and I was in good shape.

Bill Gropp, 97: I could do almost anything from working on our farm. And, of course, working with the Forest Service. You had to be able to chop, saw, and be in pretty good shape to put out fires. I was in pretty good shape for the Marines.

Howard Frye, 95: A lot of guys would fall out, but I would just a-keep a-going 'cause I was from a farm. I already had the endurance.

Melvin Gribble, 95: A lot of the training was pretty tough. Some of the guys that went in there couldn't take it. There was a piano player, and he was always passing out from walking and swimming. It took a few of those guys a while to get toughed up, but it didn't bother me because I'd been working.

Donald Brown, 95: Boot camp was tough in the Marine Corps. A lot of kids didn't make it, but I didn't have any trouble because I was used to doing hard work. I had quit school and started firing steam engines with the Illinois Central Railroad when I was sixteen.

Elburn Cooper, 95: Boot camp was not hard for me. Not like it was for some guys.

Paul "Bill" Town, 95: They said it was tough, but I didn't think it was very tough.

Clyde Lacquement, 95: They rushed us through, so it wasn't a bad experience at all.

Don Browning, 95: When I went through boot camp it was pretty rough. A lot of the guys shed weight, but I gained ten pounds. I wasn't used to getting three meals a day, all you can eat.

Clayton Narveson, 99: When I went to boot camp, I weighed 125 pounds. After eight weeks, I weighed 160 pounds, and grew five inches.

Luther Hendricks, 96: They would not take us at Camp Lejeune because that was for the "white Marine Corps." They kept us over in the boondocks at Montford Point: substandard buildings, forty or fifty people to a barrack, one stove in the middle. Up in the morning, five miles out and five miles back, even before you ate. Then we'd take a shower and go out for the day's drill. We got everything thrown at us.

Ben Carson, 96: We didn't even have real weapons. Somebody was turning out replicas of the 03A3 Springfield rifle, but none of the parts were moveable: it was just a hunk of wood to carry. About two-thirds of the way through training, we were issued real Springfields. The bolt didn't work on the one I had, but at least I had some weight to carry. That's how tough times were at the beginning of World War II.

Wallace "Wally" Hamlin, 99: In those days, they didn't distinguish between left- and right-handed people. I'm left-handed and they were trying to teach me to shoot right-handed. That was a "no-go." I couldn't shoot for beans. But I could mount the rifle left-handed and outshoot anybody there.

Tom Shields, 93: I was a damn good shot because I came from Kentucky and had a rifle since I was seven. I learned to shoot squirrels with that damn thing. When you only have one shot, you got pretty accurate. We went to the rifle range at Camp Elliott and fired "Expert."

Burt Withee, 95: A lot of the guys came from troubled backgrounds—they got in a lot of trouble. That's what kept the brigs going in the Marine Corps. But they were good Marines: put a rifle in their hands and they did their duty.

Louis Bourgault, 97: The average age was probably twenty. We had four or five guys in their upper twenties, but anybody over twenty-five, we called them "Pops." War is a young man's business.

Robert Beale, 97: At the end of twelve weeks, I would have followed my drill instructor all over hell and half of Georgia. I really admired the man. Those twelve weeks were a total indoctrination—changed a boy into a Marine. I'll say this: the Marines is a cult. They warp your mind and make you a Marine whether you like it or not.

Elburn Cooper, 95: They wanted to make you devoid of any human qualities and turn you into a killing machine. They do a pretty good job of that.

Eldon Cedergreen, 96: We were given a choice of what we'd like to serve in. Most everyone put down orderly aboard a ship. But that was always full. My next choice was tanks, rather than infantry. I was given a position as a tanker.

Howard Frye, 95: I went right into artillery after boot camp.

Eugene Jones, 94: I wanted to be a flamethrower, and that's what I was.

Howard Rieckers, 100: Most of them went into the infantry, but I didn't want to go into the infantry. I ended up serving with armored tanks and got three more weeks in the States. More training, more training. That's how I got into the Second Armored Amphibian Battalion.

Burt Withee, 95: I went into cooks and bakers training, but they were short of help, so they put me in a naval gunfire outfit called the Second Joint Assault Signal Company. A really good outfit. It was brand-new. It coordinated the Air Corps, the Navy, and the Marines, all under one command. We would go in and land on the beaches, set up a radio, and radio targets to the Navy ships. That proved very successful, very successful.

Bill Gropp, 97: They asked me what I was interested in. Ordnance School was a choice, so I was assigned to Ordnance School. It was twelve weeks, I think. We went to San Francisco and stayed on Treasure Island.

Richard Nelson, 98: When I was in high school, they said, "You're shy one credit, you can't graduate." So, I decided, on my own, to go to summer school and get a diploma. When the Marine Corps saw my transcripts out of boot camp, they said, "You took a lot of math courses. We know what we're going to do with you." I got assigned as a forward observer, telling the guns where to shoot.

Don Pilcher, 95: I went from there to Camp Pendleton for infantry training. That was a horrible place. They did a lot of foolish things. For instance, there was a parade ground covered with little rocks. We'd go out each morning and clear it off. Then the road grader would come by and put them back on. And the food was awful. We ate standing up, over outdoor tables. One time, we were called to go fight fires in the mountains. We had a full day of that, which we didn't expect. The tents had no floorboards, just dust, terrible dust. On occasion, we'd go on a march and do a little training, but it was pretty haphazard. At the time, we didn't have enough officers to do anything more than that.

Bert Rutan, 95: I had never done anything difficult or dangerous in my life before, so I volunteered for the paratroopers.

The Marine paratroopers. I'm sure my parents were a bit alarmed. Or, at least, my mother probably was. But I appreciated the training. It helped me grow up a lot. I did okay, made my jumps. In the Army you could get your wings after five parachute jumps, but in the Marine Corps you had to make at least six jumps. So, I made my six jumps and got my wings.

W. Lee Robinson, 97: I went through boot camp, then went through parachute school, and became a paratrooper. I thought that might be an exciting experience.

Chuck Meacham, 96: I really wanted to go into the paratroopers, but there were no more openings. They had another unit called "Marine Raiders" that was a small, all-volunteer unit. I wanted to find out what that was. I played football and basketball, so I understood small groups. I couldn't get my head around the "big Marine Corps." So, I went into Marine Raider training.

Ben Carson, 96: Word came out that some nutty colonel was putting together a Raider Battalion. And if you wanted to get out of boot camp and get some pretty good chow, that was the route to go. They lied like hell about most things, but I joined up with Carlson and "Carlson's Raiders."

Frank Wright, 96: They sent a platoon sergeant to the Tongue Point Naval Air Station looking for volunteers for the Raiders. I had been stationed there for not quite a year, so I wanted to get into the action. I was interviewed and the guy said, "Private, you're a badass Marine. I think we'll accept you." And they admitted me as a member of the Fourth Marine Raiders. My commanding officer was Major Jimmy Roosevelt. I thought, *It can't be too bad if the president's son is in there. They ain't gonna put him in harm's way.* I was badly mistaken.

Joe Harrison, 98: I trained as a scout and sniper. As a kid, I did a lot of hunting in the Ozarks. When I heard that the Raiders needed volunteers, I volunteered.

Chuck Meacham, 96: We got a seventy-two-hour pass every two weeks. They would haul us out to the highway and dump us off. You had to be back Monday morning for muster, at seven thirty, which was a three-mile walk back in.

Robert Brutinel, 100: We graduated, and they gave us our first liberty. They wouldn't let you tuck your pants into your jump boots because they didn't want you to look like the Army; they wanted you to look like Marines. But as soon as we got away from the gate, we'd slip our pants into our boots. We really thought we were something else! The girls sure liked a Marine; especially when they'd see our parachute wings. They knew we got fifty dollars extra for jump pay, that's what they could see!

Bert Rutan, 95: I remember coming home: I had on my Marine greens, and I had my pants tucked into my boots. But nobody was home! I was a little disappointed. I went back to my outfit, and life went on.

Howard Rieckers, 100: We had a weekend pass, and one guy said, "I'm going home." I said, "You can't do that!" But he took off and went home. I don't know how many days he stayed. When he got back, he walked in and got in all kinds of trouble. He said, "Well, I got to stay home for a few days, anyway."

Tom Charlton, 95: When I went in, I was green as grass. I didn't know anything. When we were in Los Angeles, on leave after boot camp, I couldn't believe the things I saw. The different types of people: They were on soap boxes and had pink hair. I was in a different world. But it seemed like I adjusted easily. The only problem I had were with southerners. We had a couple in our company, and they couldn't say anything nice about Negroes. Even at that time, it bothered me; it just bothered me.

Luther Hendricks, 96: We'd go out on leave, but we couldn't go into any of the restaurants unless we went in the back door. Our white counterparts could go into any nightclub and eat at any restaurant. They said, "We're not going to miss out on the fun just because of you people." Even in the fighting areas, they used to call us the N-word, and "you people."

Bob Ehrlich, 94: I wanted to get overseas so bad, but they put me in a guard detachment at San Clemente. I stayed there a whole year. When they finally came out and told me I was going to be transferred, I jumped down a whole bunch of stairs. I was so happy! What a dummy I was.

Don Pilcher, 95: We went down to Oceanside and got on a ship. We were only out to sea about thirty minutes, and I got seasick. And I was seasick every time we went anywhere. The trip lasted about nine or ten days. It was excruciating.

Don Browning, 95: After I got out of Sea School, we boarded a converted cruise liner with bunks stacked six high. I got the top one. Praise the Lord for that! Nobody could throw up on my head. I had guard duty, but I spent most of my time hanging over the rail to vomit.

Donn Thompson, 95: A lot of those young men had never been on a ship in rough seas before. Most of them were seasick. When they came into the cafeteria, we'd put a plate down in front of them, and they'd get sick and vomit on the tray. At the end of every day, I was cleaning up vomit. I kept most of them alive by taking them apples and oranges because they *really* got sick. I didn't have time to get sick.

Milton "Red" Cronk, 98: We knew we were going to be fighting the Japs. We didn't join the service to play tiddlywinks or something like that. We *knew* what we were getting into. Of course, after we got into combat, we lost some guys; it was tough.

4 ★ ★ ★ ★ ★ ★

SAMOA AND MIDWAY

Following the Japanese attack on Pearl Harbor, the Second Marine Brigade was established and transported to Samoa to defend shipping lanes between the United States, Australia, and New Zealand. The five-thousand-man detachment joined the Seventh Defense Battalion and a small native reserve unit known as the Samoan Marine Brigade, or the "Barefoot Marines."

Dean Ladd, 101, Second Marine Brigade (Eighth Marine Regiment): I was attending a scout sniper school when the Japanese attacked Pearl Harbor. They stopped it immediately. The first thing we did, in a matter of just a few days, was start performing guard duty along the coastline of California. There were all kinds of rumors going around and changes in orders; it was a time of organization. Within one month we were aboard ship on our way to American Samoa to hopefully prevent the Japanese from capturing the island. That would have cut off our pipeline from the United States to Australia and New Zealand.

It was a wonderful environment: very mountainous, with coconut trees all around. And the natives were so friendly. They were concerned, too. The Japanese could have landed at any time. But they immediately took a liking to us and the kids were always playing little tricks. Sometimes they'd come up and say, "Ai tae, Marine!" We thought it meant "Hello, Marine!" No, that meant "Eat crap, Marine!" Then they'd laugh about it. When you'd tell them something, they'd answer, "Pepelo." That meant "Bullshit." We didn't catch on right away. They were so quick, pulling these pranks on us. Most of the girls wore a long dress called a lavalava. We found out pretty fast that if you said, "Vaai i susu," which meant, "Look at the breasts," they'd throw up their dress and pat themselves on the rear. You can imagine how that went on for a while.

Elwin Hart, 93, Second Marine Brigade (Eighth Marine Regiment): The natives evacuated all their huts (they called them fales) and turned them over to us, until we could get a tent city built. It took a couple of months, but we had a nice fale with rolldown flaps on the side and a wooden deck two or three feet off the floor. I was in one with several other Marines from my platoon. I had two or three jobs on Samoa: I was on a patrol boat for a while. In one instance, we had a few Marines get wounded because (as a prank) someone set off a hand grenade under a bunk. We had to go around to the other side of the island and evacuate them.* There were a whole lot of different chores in that little town.

They had an observation post on one end of the island, up in a tall tree. Someone had constructed slats to get up there, and a platform on top. Usually there were about five of us up there—and we'd take turns cooking food. I'd never

* During World War II, it was a common prank to remove powder from a hand grenade to frighten unsuspecting victims with a loud, harmless explosion. In many documented instances, the pranksters failed to remove enough powder and the grenades remained lethal, resulting in injury or death.

cooked in my life. I was seventeen then. So, when my turn came, I made some kind of a chili. But I must have accidentally put a whole bottle of hot sauce in it. After one taste, no one would eat it. I was relieved because I didn't have to cook anymore.

Sometimes the privates and PFCs would get together and have a beer party on the beach. I think it only happened once or twice. We'd go out and start a bonfire—but the beer was always hot. To fix that, we'd run down the beach, dig a big hole in the sand, and cover it up. Then we'd go back around the bonfire and wait for it to get cold. One time we went back and couldn't find the beer; it wasn't there. We dug up half a mile of beach, I think. I don't know how many years later it was, but I ran into a master sergeant named Posey, Warren Posey. He'd been my communications chief on Samoa. He asked me about it. He said, "Do you guys remember the beer parties you used to throw? And how you lost your beer and couldn't find it?" I said, "Yeah, I remember that." He said, "I'll tell you what happened: the sergeants would stand behind the trees and watch you bury it. As soon as you turned your back, they'd run out and dig it up. That's why you couldn't find it."

Thomas Fitzmaurice, 100, Second Marine Brigade (Second Defense Battalion): In that time, we were preparing for one of the early invasions by the Japanese. But they went further north and hit the islands of Wake and Midway instead.

In the summer of 1942, the Japanese renewed their offensive in the Pacific by dispatching an assault force for Midway Atoll, roughly thirteen hundred miles west of Pearl Harbor. Prized for its central location, the capture of Midway would supply a debarkation point for future operations against the Hawaiian Islands. But unbeknownst to the Japanese, their communication codes had been broken by American analysts and the US Fleet was waiting in ambush. On June 4, 1942, while a major naval battle came underway at sea, a small bastion of Marines settled into their bunkers to defend the shores of Midway.

Edgar Fox, 100, Sixth Defense Battalion: In June of 1941, I decided to get out of the National Guard and join the Marines to get closer to the action. I was assigned to Camp Pendleton with the Tenth Marines as a grunt. After Pearl Harbor, they needed a detachment to relieve the people on Wake Island. But by the time we boarded the ship, the Japanese captured Wake Island so they changed our course and sent us to Midway. At the time, we were young, "gung ho," gutsy, and invincible—*bring them on, let us get at them.* On June 4, 1942, they sent me into an underground position. I was a machine gunner assigned to protect the beach from anyone coming ashore. From the back of my bunker, I watched as the first Japanese planes arrived, dropping bombs and strafing. That lasted about seventeen minutes.

When they left, we were ordered to pull our guns out and mount them as antiaircraft. But we were very disappointed because the Japanese never came back. That was it, it was over. They had destroyed some airplane hangars, killed several people, and took out our communications at the power plant. We didn't even know about the naval engagement for four days because communications at that time were pretty slow. But a few days later, we held formation, and they told us that the Japanese would not be returning to Midway; their ships had been sunk. I don't remember any celebration—but I think we got an extra beer ration.

The Japanese suffered a calamitous defeat at Midway, losing four aircraft carriers, one cruiser, nearly three hundred planes, and roughly twenty-five hundred servicemen. American losses were comparatively small, with the destruction of one aircraft carrier, one destroyer, 145 planes, and 307 men killed in action.

5 ★★★★★★

GUADALCANAL

Following the victory at Midway, the United States prepared to launch its first major ground offensive of the war by seizing Japanese possessions in the Solomon Islands to protect shipping lanes to Australia. The First Marine Division received orders to capture an incomplete airfield on Guadalcanal, a humid, ninety-mile-long island comprised of multilayered rainforests, sandy beaches, palm trees, and rugged coral ridges.*

Prior to the assault, numerous Marine battalions disembarked to neutralize Japanese bases on nearby Tulagi, Gavutu-Tanambogo, and Florida Island. Only two miles in length, Tulagi encompassed a diverse terrain of low hills and heavy vegetation that housed several structures due to its former designation as the seat of the British Solomon Islands Protectorate. The assault force—consisting of the First Raider Battalion and Second Battalion, Fifth Marine Regiment (2/5)—began landing at 0800 on August 7, 1942.

* The original directive handed down from Admiral Ernest J. King called for the seizure of "Tulagi and adjacent positions." It made no mention of Guadalcanal. It wasn't until July 5, 1942, a month before landing, that Guadalcanal was marked for capture.

George Poppe, 100, First Marine Division: On Tulagi, we waded to shore a short distance because the boats couldn't get up far enough. We were under fire—light bombardment and machine gun fire. I was a member of the 81mm mortar platoon, but we didn't shoot any mortars. Tulagi was only a very small island with a couple caves in our sector—*that was it*. It was a nice-looking place with a residential area, and I understand that the governor lived there. Most of our trouble came from Japanese snipers hidden up in the trees. Anyway, the fighting on Tulagi had its good points and its bad points and a lot of people suffered misery there. But we were only there for a very short time—a very, very short time before it was all over.

The day after Tulagi was captured, the First Parachute Battalion, supported by elements of the Second Marine Regiment, seized the nearby islets of Gavutu-Tanambogo. In total, 122 Americans died in the opening battle of the Solomon Islands campaign.

Across the sound, the First Marine Division began landing troops on Guadalcanal at 0910 on August 7, 1942.

Harmon Hunter, 101, First Marine Division: It was like landing on Coney Island in the summertime: nice sunny day. As I remember, it was a Friday. They shelled the place, and we went ashore. When we got there, the Japanese were having their breakfast. They had these big, long benches made out of boards, probably ten feet long and six feet wide, with long bench seats, so they could eat outside. When we got there, their breakfast was still warm. We caught them just as they were having breakfast.

Donald Bishop, 98, First Marine Division: When we hit the shoreline, I got up on the gunnel and waited until the water receded so I wouldn't have to jump in and get my feet wet. There were no Japanese, and everyone was milling around on the beach. Some people were sitting on the bank with their boots off, wringing salt water out of their socks and trying to dry their feet in the sunshine. We finally got squared away on shore and made a big, long line going through the coconut groves. Somebody decided that they wanted a coconut, so they shot one out of a tree. But when they shot, the whole damned First Marine Division hit the dirt! That was funny.

Raymond Rice, 98, First Marine Division: The first day was a day of action—for everybody. We did very well that first day, being a bunch of boots. The Japs were up in trees and hiding in bushes. We didn't know that, of course. We were just marching along when a couple of guys got hit. But we wised up real quick. We killed probably five or ten up in the palm trees. Once we got sight of them, we just nailed every tree as we were marching.

Donald Bishop, 98, First Marine Division: We dug holes all over the place and made fortifications. Then we'd go out in front of our positions and cut grass, bushes, and whatnot to make clear fields of fire. But nothing happened. The next day, we patrolled out a little further and nothing happened. The third day, we went out a little further, but we still couldn't find the Japanese. That's the way it was for the first three days.

Harmon Hunter, 101, First Marine Division: Around then, the Navy jumped before we could get our supplies unloaded. They took off because the Japanese fleet came in. We had no ammunition, no food, no nothing. A lot of times we didn't eat. We didn't look very good when we got relieved. You could always tell apart the guys from the First Division because we looked like scarecrows. We were on the chase for a long time—or being chased. They came over every day at twelve o'clock with twenty-five or thirty bombers. Every single day at noontime: You could set your clock by it.

Raymond Rice, 98, First Marine Division: We didn't get much sleep because it was all new to us. It was new to me anyway. But I didn't chicken out, I stayed right in there. I don't remember anybody folding up—it didn't happen that way, like you read in the books.

Donald Bishop, 98, First Marine Division: We'd find bunches of Japanese here and there and have little skirmishes. But it wasn't a problem because the Japanese had this "banzai charge" thing going. Who goes to a gun battle with a knife? But *they* would do that. Of course, they didn't do much damage with it. I don't think I aimed my rifle the whole time I was there, because if you saw someone to shoot at, he was right in front of you. Word was that the Japanese had to die in battle in order to become a war hero.

Harmon Hunter, 101, First Marine Division: I'll tell you something and you won't believe it: When you've been there long enough, you can smell the Japanese. You'd go along in the jungle, out on a patrol, and you'd notice an odor. And you hope you're wrong. Marines go looking for trouble, but we hope we don't find it. You'd have to be a damn fool to want to bump heads with something that has a fifty-fifty chance to kill you; you wouldn't want that. The Japanese were very brave people. They were cruel and they were mean, but they were very brave. You don't hear people say it very often. They were really under control: If you told them to jump off the roof of a building, they would. And if you think that they always lost, and we always won—*that's bullshit*. Plenty of times we had to retreat. If you went out on a patrol with twenty guys and ran into two hundred Japanese, you were in trouble. You would stick it out until you beat them or, if you were outnumbered, you would take off. They had every trick in the book, those guys. They were really experienced. They'd been slaughtering Chinese for practice for the last five years.

George Poppe, 100, First Marine Division: I never really had any bad feelings about the Japanese. I had many opportunities to meet them face-to-face, usually while marching prisoners. I also had the opportunity to kill a lot of prisoners, like some guys would. But I never did. Everybody had different opinions on what should happen to them.

On August 8 and 9, the US Navy suffered a major defeat offshore in the battle of Savo Island and withdrew to open sea, leaving roughly eleven thousand Marines trapped on Guadalcanal. By mid-August, the Japanese were preparing to launch their first major ground offensive to recapture the airfield, now christened "Henderson Field" after Lofton Henderson, an aviator killed during the Battle of Midway. The engagement began in the early morning hours of August 21 and resulted in the deaths of more than eight hundred Japanese soldiers and forty-four Americans. It would later become known as the Battle of the Tenaru. A second major thrust to retake the airfield occurred three weeks later, on September 12, 1942, when Japanese troops attacked an exposed saddle overlooking Henderson Field. The following night, to the southeast, a detachment of Japanese hit a strategically valuable trail manned by the Third Battalion, First Marine Regiment (3/1).

Donald Bishop, 98, First Marine Division: At about midnight, somebody sent up a bunch of flares and here comes—*oh, God!*

> It must have been a battalion of Japanese. When they broke through our lines, our orders were to stay in our holes so we wouldn't hit our own men and to shoot up at them. We were loaded with ammunition, mortars, machine guns; everything. And they had nothing: they hit us with bayonets and hand grenades. The way they fought—they'd come out six abreast, *"Banzai!"* Boy, they were close enough you could have stuck them with a bayonet. Every time we came into contact with the Japanese, those poor guys didn't have a chance, they had no chance at all. We lost three men that night, and they lost hundreds.

The fighting around the Third Battalion's perimeter, christened the Battle of Overland Trail, killed roughly three hundred Japanese soldiers. Elsewhere on the line, men from the First Raider Battalion and First Parachute Battalion (supported by the Eleventh Marines) thwarted a concentrated attack over a feature that would become known as "Bloody Ridge" or "Edson's Ridge." Raymond Rice, 99, an artilleryman with E Battery, remarked, "The 75mm and the 55 packs—they were like machine guns. They were throwing shells in that chamber, and they were going off like firecrackers. We killed a lot of them."

Relief for the battle-weary men arrived in mid-September with the landing of the Seventh Marine Regiment, fresh from garrison duty on Samoa. The Army's 164th Infantry Regiment, a National Guard unit from South Dakota, followed three weeks later, raising American strength on the island to more than twenty-three thousand. On the night of October 13, the Japanese Navy welcomed the new arrivals by releasing two battleships to shell Henderson Field. The event would become known simply as "the Bombardment." H. Lloyd Wilkerson, 100, would recount, "If you like noise and fireworks, you would have enjoyed the show. First the flares, then the salvoes! The coconut palm plantations along the beach and Henderson Field were essentially destroyed; looked like pictures I had seen of World War I in France." More than nine hundred shells fell during the barrage, killing forty-one Americans.

After a series of engagements fought along the Lunga perimeter in late September and early October—known collectively as the Actions Along the Matanikau—the Japanese prepared to launch another full-scale offensive on Henderson Field. The multi-pronged attack would utilize roughly twenty thousand Imperial troops from the newly arrived Japanese Seventeenth Army. It began at dusk October 23, 1942.

Donald Bishop, 98, First Marine Division: We got hit by nine Japanese tanks on the Matanikau. They were old ones, looked like they were from World War I. Little-bitty tanks. To stop them, if you were close enough, all you had to do was jam a rifle in the sprockets and they would break. Three of them tried to get across the river. Someone shot off the front end of two of them, made them useless. One of them got across the river, but we happened to have a half-track with a seventy-five cannon mounted on it. He took aim and—*boy!*—it went right through the top part of the tank. A hatch opened up and a Jap tried to come out. They fired another shot, right through him.

George Mason, 98, First Marine Division: On October 24, we were sitting on a fence line with our 37mm gun, with an outpost about a thousand yards ahead. That night, while I was listening to the field telephone, I heard "Chesty" Puller say, "Well, if you think the Japanese have the outpost surrounded, keep as calm as you can and get back in." Some of the Marines from the OP crossed right in front of my gun. Captain Buckley, the company commander, had us change our anti-tank ammunition to canister for an infantry attack.

I fired the first shot when the enemy came in, and I'm

pretty sure I killed everyone in the formation. They hit us for the next four or five hours, all through the night, one wave after the other. I went out the next morning and—I've never seen so many dead people in my life. I think I broke a record for killing people. Each Jap had a sack of rice tied to his belt. I went around cutting off the rice, so they couldn't sneak back and get it.

We knew they were still out there. They would holler at us, "Marine, you die!" My people would yell back, "Come get it, you yellow son of a bitch!" They hit us again the next night, the same way. They kept coming, and I kept firing. We really fought the Japs face-to-face.

Richard Russell, 100, First Marine Division: We were on "Bloody Ridge" with the First Battalion that October. It wasn't long before someone noticed a bunch of Japs coming down and we were ordered to another ridge, where the enemy was expected to hit. It was quite a battle. F Company was hit the hardest. After the Japs penetrated the American perimeter, Major Conoley gathered a bunch of cooks and reestablished the line. One of the platoon sergeants in the machine gun company received a Medal of Honor. His name was Mitchell Paige. I didn't personally know him, but I heard a lot about him.

Known as the Battle for Henderson Field, the assault ultimately failed to seize the airport and cost more than two thousand Japanese lives. American casualties were comparatively light, with roughly one hundred killed or missing, a kill ratio of twenty to one. It was a striking victory for the battered defenders. Amid the ground combat and naval engagements offshore, October would also prove to be a decisive period for aviators locked in a desperate struggle in the skies over the Solomon Islands.

Frank King, 100, VMF-112: After graduating from radio school, they sent me to Miramar, and I joined VMF-112. Within two weeks, we were on an old ocean liner—the SS *Lurline*—to New Caledonia in September or October. We were based there for about three weeks. But on Nouméa, I got really sick. While I was in the naval dispensary, my squadron left and went up to Guadalcanal. When I was discharged, all I had were the clothes on my back and a few minor possessions. My gear was in my seabag. Even my rifle was gone. They flew me up to Guadalcanal on an old C-47 airplane. When we got up to ten thousand feet, I about froze to death. All I had was my fatigue jacket. A damned Air Corps colonel was sitting there with a big Army overcoat and a blanket—and he wouldn't give me a piece of his blanket. I was sitting there shaking like a shittin' dog. I lost all respect for the Army after that; I didn't want anything to do with the Army. When I got to Guadalcanal, I went to the squadron office, and they outfitted me with tropical gear.

Billy Hall, 98, VMSB-141: I was in a cargo ship, and we had a big web rope hanging down the side. We climbed down with a seabag and a bedroll, into a Higgins boat. We filled it up and headed for the beach. When the ramp dropped, we came out with our rifles ready to fire, bayonets ready to go. We had line company and aviation guys onboard. The line company guys started heading for their units and we had our people move up to Henderson Field. But I got put on a work party, unloading cargo coming off the ships. Pretty soon, the Japs discovered our position and started bombing us. The bombers were at—*I think*—four or five thousand feet; they were pretty low. My first taste of combat was digging a hole in the sand and looking up at the planes. I wanted to watch—but I was scared. So, I hid my head down. Every once in a while, I'd sneak a peek. One bomb dropped pretty close to where I was: twenty feet or more. It caught a guy, and he got a piece of shrapnel in his leg. Eventually, I got up to Henderson Field later that night.

Tom Baker, 98, VMF-112: When I first landed, all we had was Henderson Field. Then they scraped out a piece of land for our fighter planes. That's where I went—*Fighter 1*. They were flying Grumman fighters, F4F Grummans. They were tough old airplanes. It would take a lot of shooting to put them down. Joe Foss was there. He was in VMF-121. I wasn't in his squadron, but he flew with us.*

Frank King, 100, VMF-112: We had a couple famous pilots in our squadron. A guy by the name of Captain John Maas. I know he had quite a few kills. We even had one Congressional Medal of Honor winner in VMF-112: that was Jefferson DeBlanc. He was a lieutenant from Louisiana, and I think he shot down five airplanes in one flight. Another one I remember was an enlisted pilot named Bill Wamel. They called him "Wild Bill." When we were on Fighter 1, he was in an accident and hit his head. He was "punchy" for a long time; his behavior kind of changed after that. But he could fly like the devil!

Billy Hall, 98, (temporarily attached) VMF-121: I interacted with Foss—and all the other pilots. My job was to meet the planes as they came in, find out what was wrong, work on them, and make sure they were fixed so they were ready to fly when the pilots came back. I also helped the guys put on their helmets and get the radios tuned so they could talk to each other. That's what I did: I was constantly meeting flights

* Joe Foss became famous for shooting down twenty-three Japanese planes over Guadalcanal and would ultimately receive the Medal of Honor for his actions.

coming in or taking off. If a plane came in and it was too shot up to fix, we just pushed it over to the side and left it there. If you needed a part—because we didn't have a lot of parts—you went over and scavenged off the planes that couldn't fly. Our job was to keep the fighter pilots in the sky, as much as possible.

Frank King, 100, VMF-112: We were on short rations all the time: two meals a day. We'd eat at about ten o'clock in the morning and four o'clock in the afternoon. It was usually a stew made out of corn, canned peas, and canned potatoes. We spent evenings in a foxhole because "Washing Machine Charlie" would come over every night.

Tom Baker, 98, VMF-112: The Japanese bombers would come over the airfield, but they usually wouldn't hit anything; it didn't bother us very much. But the fighters would strafe us a lot. A very good friend of mine got killed about the third day. We were out working on the planes, and he got strafed by a fighter. He was a good friend of mine—I'd known him quite a while. I don't remember how many people we lost altogether. I imagine it was a lot. We kept getting replacements all the time.

Frank King, 100, VMF-112: There was a Japanese breakthrough one night. I remember that very clearly because we all grabbed our weapons. When I got to Guadalcanal, they issued me a new rifle—it was a Garand, not a Springfield. I hated it, I hated the Garand! I wanted my old rifle back, but it was already gone. For a couple of nights, we had to set up a perimeter. We were right next to Henderson Field, on Fighter 1. At that time, the front line was only about fifteen hundred yards away from us.

Tom Baker, 98, VMF-112: After a while, Fighter 1 was getting too hot because the Japanese had a gun emplacement in the hills. They could shell us, right down our throats. The Seabees came in and cleared off another runway. We went into the jungle and lived back in the hills like animals. One of the scariest memories I have was waking up in the middle of the night because a Japanese patrol had slipped into the valley. Everybody jumped up and cut loose. I was sitting on my cot with a submachine gun—I let it go! A few dead Japanese were laying on the ground the next morning. It wasn't a big patrol: probably twenty or twenty-five men in the bunch.

Did it bother me seeing the dead? Not in the slightest. They were the enemy, and I was a Marine. When I was seventeen years old, I was ten feet tall! It never bothered me. I had no second thoughts about it. One of my other jobs, besides being an aircraft mechanic, was to man a water-cooled .50 caliber machine gun. During the air raids, I'd run out and jump on it. I tried awful hard to hit them. But when they're coming at you like that, you don't know who's hitting what.

Billy Hall, 98, VMSB-141: We were constantly short on radio personnel, so I was usually pulled away from my original unit. I eventually got back to my squadron and did some flying, like I was supposed to, in the back seat of a dive bomber. Normally, when we came in for a landing, I just stowed our guns inside the aircraft. The pilot would put the wheels down, put the flaps down, then throttle back. But when you do that, you're at your most vulnerable. Pretty soon, the Japanese found out and would sneak a fighter plane over the hills to attack us as we landed.

Orders came down: From now on, gunners need to keep their guns up, charged, ready to fire, to protect the plane's tail. During one landing, I was sitting there, ready to shoot, when our pilot touched down really hard on the runway. Well, the catch on my guns came loose and it popped back, down into the storage position. Of course, I'm hanging on to it, finger over the trigger, pulling back. Well, it went off—*bbbbrrrrrpppp!*—right through the plane's tail. After that—*jokingly*—the guys gave me credit for shooting down my own airplane.

Tom Baker, 98, VMF-112: Anytime our aircraft left on a mission, we'd all get together and go on patrol and hunt the Japanese. At first, we could go out in ones or twos, but they finally said there had to be ten of us. We were young Marines out for blood. We'd hunt until we found a Japanese patrol, then cut loose on them. In most cases, we were very successful. Sometimes the line company guys would let us know they'd seen something, then we'd take off in that direction. We were aircraft mechanics, and we weren't supposed to do that. But we did.

On one particular trip, I got nicked by a bullet, and my buddy got killed right alongside of me. He got hit in the head. I remember that. Jeez, that's a hard memory. Another one of my buddies got killed: We were standing together alongside of an airplane, talking, when a Japanese sniper cut loose. They hit him but didn't hit me. I don't even remember the kid's name. But you learn quick: If your best friend gets killed today, you forget about him tomorrow. That's the way it was done back then. That's the only way you could survive. I've seen people who couldn't do that, and they went nuts; they couldn't stand it. That was one thing we all understood: If it happened to you, that's too bad. If it happened to your buddy, you're lucky. That's just the way it was.

In early November, men from the Eighth Marine Regiment landed on Guadalcanal and joined the First Marine Division and several Army units in offensive operations against the Japanese.

Many of the newly landed men still wore obsolete World War I–era helmets and carried bolt-action Springfield rifles, issued in the weeks and months following the Japanese attack on Pearl Harbor.

At the same time, the Second Raider Battalion landed roughly forty miles west of Lunga Point at Aola Bay. They soon received orders to pursue more than two thousand Japanese troops fleeing an American encirclement on the Metapona River. The movement, later known as "the Long Patrol," would span thirty days and kill 488 Japanese. All told, the fall and winter months on Guadalcanal would bear witness to extensive fighting along the American perimeter, particularly in the Point Cruz and Matanikau area.

Dean Ladd, 101, Second Marine Division: I landed there in November of '42. It was unopposed, of course, because the First Division had already landed and was in heavy combat. They were young people, just like me. They all hadn't shaved in weeks and weeks. They were tired and looked about ten years older than they really were.

Elwin Hart, 93, Second Marine Division: We were scared as hell because it was our first time in combat. We didn't have landing craft that lowered ramps, so you had to jump over the side. The water was about two or three feet deep, so you got a little wet going in. Before we got off the beach, we noticed a fleet of Japanese bombers flying overhead. I thought, *Oh, God! What is this?* We started digging foxholes in the sand. That's pretty difficult because it collapses in on you. We were halfway through digging when, all of a sudden, we hear explosions way down the beach. *Boom! Boom! Boom!* And it keeps getting closer. The closer it gets, the faster we dug. Come to find out—*later*—they weren't bomb explosions. It was our own antiaircraft guns shooting at the bombers. But we sure expended a lot of energy trying to dig those holes!

Keith Tucker, 100, Second Marine Division: That first night, we heard the air raid sirens from Henderson Field. Nobody had told us to dig foxholes—*nobody!* The truck tracks were down in the mud, below the ground, so we laid in that.

John L'Abbe, 97, Second Marine Division: I remember looking up in the sky—and I never saw so many bombers. You could hear them coming, dropping bombs on the airport. When you're in your foxhole, you get your head down!

Robert Evans, 97, First Marine Division: I landed there as a replacement, and we were bombed the same day. I had stolen a can of pineapple from the ship, but the damned Japs dropped a bomb and threw sand in it. I just cleaned it up and ate it anyway. The Jap subs and battleships were right out there and really blasted us. Seemed like they had bigger guns than we did. There were some real sea battles going on.

Dean Ladd, 101, Second Marine Division: In November, the Japanese made their final attempt to retake the island and that became the Naval Battle of Guadalcanal. We saw ship after ship firing at each other at night—*hits*. You could see the red-hot shells going back and forth. You couldn't tell friend from foe at night. Well, we couldn't from where we were, and I don't think the combatants knew either. The next morning, after the battle, there were three Japanese transports that had beached. The troops got off, but they couldn't get their equipment off.

Richard Russell, 100, First Marine Division: Our battalion was asked to go out ten to fifteen miles to meet a Japanese force expected to land on a nearby river. We went out and dug in by nightfall and waited. At midnight, we could hear the ships coming in and the Japanese officers shouting. Unfortunately, they landed on our flank, right beside F Company. We withdrew and went inland, crossed the river, and came up on the other side of the Japanese. Finally, we engaged them on a riverbank; had quite a rifle fight. Our platoon leader said, "Okay men, we're going to cross the river!" He stood up and—*bang!*—he went down. Our platoon sergeant took over and we crossed the river and hit the Japanese. We suffered a large number of casualties, but we won the battle.

Dean Ladd, 101, Second Marine Division: This one time, we were assaulting a ridge that was held by the Japanese. We saw where the bullets were coming from, but we couldn't tell exactly where the position was. I was squatting between my squad leader and one of the men. We were throwing hand grenades at the ridgeline. When the Japanese fired again, the guy to my right said, "I see them!" Just about that time, a bullet hit his neck and he was killed instantly. The squad leader to my left—a bullet went through the magazine of his rifle while he was shooting; all the bullets dropped out. He said, "Well, I'll be a dirty name!" He never cussed. He said, "Well, I'll be a dirty name!" And here I was, right between those two guys, with all these bullets flying, and I didn't get hit. That was one of my close calls.

Not long after that, we were moving along a ridgeline on the flank of our unit, looking towards the beach, when a sniper started plunking away at us. Some cocky lieutenant I didn't know came strolling by and said, "You don't have to worry about that guy!" Just then, he got hit in the upper arm and disappeared. I laid down in some shoulder-high kunai grass and spotted the sniper's leg. But he spotted me at the same time because I was looking through my field glasses. The sniper took a shot and threw dirt into my face. I had a

Springfield '03 rifle ready, just in case I wanted to shoot snipers, and I killed him. I killed the sniper, right after he almost hit me in the face.

We didn't know what to think about the Japanese. We knew they were going to be a very worthy opponent, that they were highly motivated. And we knew that they would fight to the death. In fact, they would never surrender. It was a dishonor to their ancestors and their emperor. That was true, they were worthy. They'd usually fight at night, and they were good at it. The Japanese would sneak through our lines, anywhere there was an opening. Usually, the attack would start in the early morning hours, between midnight and three or four o'clock. Once they started, there was no turning back. They just kept coming. We would machine gun them all down. That was their drawback: Once they were given orders, they would keep attacking until everyone was killed. We just couldn't believe it.

Elwin Hart, 93, Second Marine Division: One of our S2 guys would go out beyond our front lines to collect intelligence for our operations. He came back through one time with a young Japanese prisoner, tied around the ankle with a rope, dragging him through the command post. At the time, it didn't seem unusual, but later in life, as you think about it: *Oh, God. Were we that cruel?* Probably.

John L'Abbe, 97, Second Marine Division: This poor Jap was sitting there and a southerner with a World War I hat took a bayonet and tried to knock his teeth out. The poor bastard was still alive. I thought, *What in God's name?* This Marine was kind of goofy. I think he'd been in the company when I joined it. There was another Marine who was goofier than hell, too. His comrades said he turned really Asiatic.* But he got killed—I don't remember the circumstances.

Harmon Hunter, 101, First Marine Division: You'd have to be a pretty cool customer to do something like that, there's something wrong with you. It is true though: Americans make up an awful lot of different personalities. As far as knocking people's teeth out for the gold? I can't even imagine doing it.

Ben Carson, 96, Second Raider Battalion: We had a lot to learn there. Hell, we were Iowa farmers and Minnesota farmers in the middle of the tropics, trying to live like the natives. And the natives thought we were nuts to fight a war in that area. The jungle was wet and there was a lot of respiratory diseases. It would hit your lungs like whooping cough or pneumonia. A helluva lot of people got sick that way. If we had a price on our head, it would have been about fifty cents.

Don Bishop, 98, First Marine Division: A bunch of us got malaria and they put us in a big dugout. When we had an air raid—*immediately*—all the guys I knew got up, got out of the dugout, and walked up the street. They had one thought in mind, *Maybe this time they'll get me,* because malaria is a bad thing to catch. There isn't one square inch of your body that doesn't ache. It's bad stuff. The corpsman used to come running out, grab them, and drag them back into the dugout. We had a lot of guys who caught malaria.

* "Asiatic" is a term commonly used by Pacific War veterans to describe eccentric people or those suffering from psychiatric ailments. Marines, soldiers, sailors, and airmen who spent too much time in the South Seas were often said to be "going Asiatic."

Robert Evans, 97, First Marine Division: I got sick, but they couldn't take us back to E Company medical because they didn't have anything to haul us with. I was sitting down alongside the road when some officers came by in a jeep. They stopped and picked me up, took me back to a doctor. Then we went aboard ship: I had blood poisoning, malaria, and some type of dysentery.

John L'Abbe, 97, Second Marine Division: There was one guy from Chicago; he was a prick. On Guadalcanal, we went through a battle, and he survived. He went back, wrapped bandages all over himself, then got aboard ship and went back to New Zealand. Of course, they found him. When they looked at him, there was nothing wrong, so they put him in the brig.

By December of 1942, the battle-weary First Marine Division began withdrawing to Australia, leaving the Guadalcanal campaign to the Second Marine Division and various units from the United States Army. Intense fighting would continue into early 1943 around Mount Austen and on several formidable hills known as the Galloping Horse and the Sea Horse.

Don Bishop, 98, First Marine Division: The Army was taking over, and they came down to our position with six or eight guys. They asked us if we would mount a patrol to show them where the Japanese were. We said, "Are you out of your mind? Go back out there? They're taking us to Australia!" Someone said, "Go that way. You'll find them."

Elwin Hart, 93, Second Marine Division: I remember being in a stable position for—it seemed the last two or three months of the operation. It really quieted down. In battalion headquarters, we didn't get into combat except for a few mortar attacks. Our communications chief got hit in the stomach once. We took ponchos and loaded him up. But to get off the ridge, we had to go straight down seventy-five or one hundred yards, then back up. That was tough.

Dean Ladd, 101, Second Marine Division: We were exposed to malaria in that time because there were a lot of mosquitoes. Men started coming down with it very fast. But a lot of men already had it from duty in Samoa. They were also coming down with filariasis, where your glands swell. It would usually affect your testicular area or your arms; anywhere you had a gland, you would swell up. We noticed some of the natives had monster legs. They called it elephantiasis.

Tom Baker, 98, VMF-112: I had malaria awful bad. All of us did. I've suffered from it all my life. The fevers would hit you hard and there was no warning. *Boom!* You're down. You'd be out working, then turn around and your buddy would suddenly drop. You'd pull him out of the way. But next thing you know, you're lying alongside him. They tried their damnedest to keep the pilots from getting malaria, but the ground crews all had it.

Keith Tucker, 100, Second Marine Division: We started taking Atabrine tablets for malaria aboard ship after we left New Zealand for Guadalcanal. The corpsmen were always right there, watching during our meals. You wouldn't get served your ration until he saw you take the pill. In about ten days, we still had fifteen guys out of our company come down with chills. We had to drag them back to their foxholes. Most of them got sent back to New Zealand where they had a hospital for malaria patients. Those guys eventually went back to the States.*

John L'Abbe, 97, Second Marine Division: Another guy and I got sick at the same time from malaria. They yelled, "Everybody out! Everybody out! Get into air raid shelters!" But I was too sick. I said, "Audie, are you going?" He said, "No, damned if I can get up!" We were so sick we were hoping the Japanese would hit us.

On February 9, 1943, Guadalcanal was officially declared secure. In three major ground battles, seven sea battles, and thousands of small-unit engagements, American forces lost roughly 7,100 men. The Japanese suffered the loss of 31,000 troops and a strategic defeat that would turn the tide of the war.

* Atabrine was a medication commonly used during World War II to treat malaria.

6 ★★★★★★

AUSTRALIA AND NEW ZEALAND

In February of 1943, following months of sustained combat, the Second Marine Division boarded troop transports and arrived on the shores of New Zealand for a period of rest and recuperation. At the same time, the First Marine Division, replenished by replacements from the United States, was enjoying a bucolic stay around the bustling city of Melbourne in Australia.

Carl Scott, 98, First Marine Division: We shipped out from San Diego on a troopship and zigzagged all the way to Melbourne, Australia. They divided us alphabetically: The first group was assigned to the First Regiment stationed in downtown Melbourne at the cricket grounds. The next group went to the Fifth Marines. The last group went to the Seventh Marines. I was assigned to B Company, First Battalion, Seventh Marines at a place called Mount Martha, fifty miles outside of Melbourne. I was put in a tent with men who had been on Guadalcanal. Most of them treated me okay, but there were a couple that gave me a bad time. Those guys would steal anything they could—they even stole my dress shoes. But Australia was probably the best time I had in the Marines. I loved Melbourne. The people treated us really well.

Harmon Hunter, 101, First Marine Division: Australia is a beautiful country with the finest people on earth. It's wonderful. If you've got an Aussie friend, you've got a real friend. Wonderful, wonderful people.

Elwin Hart, 93, Second Marine Division: New Zealand was a walk in the park. There were five hundred females on the pier to greet us when we arrived. Boy, we were waving like hell! We stayed there ten months, as I recall. We were at Paekakariki, which I think was about thirty miles north of Wellington. We had to ride a train back and forth when we went on liberty. We had a pretty good tent camp set up there.

John L'Abbe, 97, Second Marine Division: You'd get on a train and go on down to Wellington. Get off, go to a bar. It was like America.

Dean Ladd, 101, Second Marine Division: They were so friendly, and they were so glad to have us there. We'd go on a ten-day leave and we'd stay with the families. They'd even have a cow to make sure we had all the cream we wanted. It was incredible.

Clayton Narveson, 99, Second Marine Division: The people were so good to us there. They'd invite us into their houses and give us a meal. They were short on food, but they were glad to share what they had. I learned to love mutton. I'd never had mutton in Minnesota.

Wallace "Wally" Hamlin, 99, Second Marine Division: They talked kind of funny. It was English, but it was really blubbery English.

John L'Abbe, 97, Second Marine Division: They'd stop at teatime, close things down, and have their tea. I went to a barber once and was getting my hair cut when the barber took a time-out and walked away. I asked him, "What's going on here?" He said, "It's teatime." After his teatime was over, he finished my haircut. That was funny.

Wallace "Wally" Hamlin, 99, Second Marine Division: I will never forget tea and crumpets. If you stayed overnight with somebody, you stayed until they invited you to have crumpets before you left. You couldn't leave—and if you did, you weren't invited anymore. Oh, it was weird.

Don Bishop, 98, First Marine Division: There was a nun's convent in Brisbane and all the nuns moved out and they made it into a hospital for the Marines that had malaria. That was pretty nice. They assigned two men to a room—and my room already had a guy in it. We were shooting the breeze when he said, "Watch it in the morning; when the nurse comes in, she'll grab your feet to wake you up." I said, "Oh, Jesus. Tell her not to touch me." He said, "Yeah, I know what you mean."

The next morning, the nurse came in and saw my feet sticking out from the bottom of the bunk. She grabbed me by the ankle. In the field, I always slept with a .45 or knife, so when she grabbed me, I came up looking for my knife. I hit her once and knocked her into the cubby of a desk. She got up to run past me, and I backhanded her right across the jaw; I really hit her hard. Then she got up, into the hallway, screaming her head off. I was just starting to come to a little bit, and I ran after her. I wanted to tell her I was sorry, but she kept running. They immediately transferred her to another ward. I was thinking, *How am I going to get in contact with that woman and apologize.*

Pretty soon, here came two great big guys carrying a canvas restraint jacket with great big buckles. They sat down on the bed, on each side of me, and said, "Do we need to use this?" But my roommate told them what had happened. One of the big guys said, "Jeez, I wouldn't dare wake you guys up. I'd rather poke you with my rifle." Afterwards, they went around and put signs on all the doors: "Make sure both men are up and talking before you enter the room."

Robert Evans, 97, First Marine Division: I was in the hospital most of the time there. But we'd sneak out the back, hop the fence, and take our pick of the ladies. My brother came to see me once and asked the nurse where I was. She said, "Well, we'd like to know, too." You could ride the electric trolley back from town. But it wouldn't stop at the hospital, so we had to pull the emergency brake. Then we'd all bail off. One time, a major grabbed ahold of this West Virginian and said, "I caught you!" The kid hauled off and knocked the major on his butt and said, "You *had* me!" We had a lot of fun in Australia.

Carl Scott, 98, First Marine Division: We went to Melbourne every ten days. I got a girlfriend—almost everybody had a girlfriend. The Australian men were over fighting in Africa, so there was a shortage of men. If you found a Sheila—that's what they called girls—and asked her for a date, you could go get steak and eggs for thirty-five cents. When some of the Australian men came back from Africa, there were a lot of fights. A few of the Marines had been sleeping with someone's wife or girlfriend. If they caught a Marine by himself, they would beat him up. Marines would usually go around in pairs to make the fight even.

Robert Evans, 97, First Marine Division: They weren't very good fighters. One time I was out in a back alley gambling with some Aussies, throwing dice. I was winning all the money and they decided they wanted their money back and tried to take it. I whipped all three of them; one I didn't even hit. He swung at me, I ducked, and he hit the brick wall behind me. That was the end of him.

Russel Nelson, 98, First Marine Division: They had a paddlewheel boat you could ride with your friends and have dinner. It went up the river and back, probably held one hundred people. I had a real nice girlfriend. I was kissing her, sitting on the porch, and I accidentally pinched my legs between the railing and got two big bruises. But I didn't want to let her go and stop. After the kiss, I couldn't hardly stand on my legs. She said, "What did you do?" Of course, I was too embarrassed to tell her what happened. Kind of funny—that was a fun "hurt."

Keith Tucker, 100, Second Marine Division: I was told one time we had fifteen hundred married. Probably should have been fifteen thousand!

Robert Evans, 97, First Marine Division: They sent us a newspaper after we left Australia: Apparently there were five thousand American babies born there.

Elwin Hart, 93, Second Marine Division: We had half a dozen marriages in our unit. Of the older guys, I knew two or three that got married.

Wallace "Wally" Hamlin, 99, Second Marine Division: I only knew two guys who got married in New Zealand.

John L'Abbe, 97, Second Marine Division: I never had a girlfriend, not over there. They were nice people, very generous, but there was no romance by any means.

Dean Ladd, 101, Second Marine Division: A lot of men married New Zealanders. They left a lot of widows there, too.

7 ★★★★★★

NEW GEORGIA, VELLA LAVELLA, CHOISEUL, AND BOUGAINVILLE

In the summer of 1943, American forces prepared to capture key islands in the New Georgia group, ninety miles north of Guadalcanal. The operation was part of a larger Allied scheme to advance along the Solomon chain, in conjunction with operations in New Guinea, to neutralize the Japanese base at Rabaul and prepare for an eventual return to the Philippines. In the middle of June, the Fourth Raider Battalion received orders to land on the southern portion of New Georgia at Segi Point to capture strategic airfields and harbors in support of the main assault on Munda scheduled for July. Frank Wright, an eighteen-year-old from Arkansas, was languishing in a field hospital on Guadalcanal when the Fourth Raider Battalion began to assemble for departure.

Frank Wright, 96, Fourth Raider Battalion: My company and squad were going to leave for duty, so I went AWOL with a bout of malaria. I was still kind of sick when I got over to New Georgia. It was an eye-opener for us, being in combat. At the time, my squad had a .55 Boys anti-tank rifle. It took one man to carry the rifle, two to carry the ammunition, and a scout. When we got there, I was scared. In bayonet training, they didn't fight back. If you did something wrong, the trainer chewed you out then showed you how to do it.

On New Georgia it was entirely different. When you hear rifles, machine guns, hand grenades, and all that—it makes you scared. If you were trained properly, you'd be all right. But you can't get over the fact that somebody's going to get hurt. Part of our company got pinned down—*sniper fire*. We got surrounded. They were very good at camouflage. The snipers would tie themselves into coconut and palm trees. We had a hard time getting the Japanese out and killing them because we couldn't see them. And the mortars couldn't get them because there were a lot of trees in there. We lost a lot of men in that big firefight. Pastor Paul Redmond would go from dead person to dead person, reading them their last rites. The corpsmen went from wounded to wounded to check them out, too. They'd mark them with a tag if they were dead. That was bad. You feel lucky, and you're scared. Especially when you see someone you just talked to with a tag. But we were getting used to it. You'd think, *Thank God I didn't get tagged.* It wasn't easy for a young kid.

I shot my first enemy at Bairoko. We were posted on a road with our .55 caliber rifle. I saw a group of—I don't know how many. The first scout was out in a coconut grove. I was scared that I was going to shoot a native by accident. This guy was sneaking out from behind a tree. When he went to another tree, I shot him. He was about, oh, fifty feet. That scared the Jap squad, and they all took off. On other missions, I was more relaxed. I thought, *If I'm going to get hit, I'm going to get hit. Stay calm, stay cool.*

We left Bairoko and scooted around to Rice Anchorage. We didn't get into too much fighting there. Then we went back to Guadalcanal, and I got put back into the field hospital with malaria. I don't think they missed me.

The battle for New Georgia was a bloody slog that dragged into October and resulted in roughly five thousand American casualties. By early fall, Allied planners were already preparing for the next offensive, up the Solomon chain, on the seventy-five-mile-long island of Bougainville. To divert Japanese attention from Bougainville, the Second Parachute Battalion received orders to conduct a hit-and-run raid on Choiseul, an island located fifty miles to the southeast.

Choiseul stretched roughly seventy miles and housed three thousand to four thousand Japanese troops; a sizeable force Allied planners intended to bypass on their drive north. In preparation for the raid, the Second Parachute Battalion was transported to Vella Lavella in early September of 1943. The island, just north of Guadalcanal, had been partially overrun by the Army's Thirty-Fifth Regimental Combat Team, but Japanese holdouts remained in the jungle and still patrolled the skies above.

Robert Brutinel, 100, Second Parachute Battalion: We went by LST to Vella Lavella. Just as I stepped off the ramp, I looked up and a plane appeared straight overhead. I could see two great big red balls on the wings. It was a Jap Zero. He dropped a bomb down into the opening of an LST and it exploded. I was probably twenty feet away—and the concussion knocked me off my feet. It didn't hurt me, just shook me up. It didn't kill very many troops, but it killed some New Zealanders that were manning antiaircraft guns.

W. Lee Robinson, 97, Second Parachute Battalion: On Vella Lavella, I only had one exciting moment. We were moving through very dense jungle when I heard a noise about thirty or forty feet ahead of me. I had a .30 caliber Garand rifle at the time. I thought, *I can shoot in that direction, or I can wait until I see the enemy a little more clearly and get a clean shot.* Well, I decided to wait. Pretty soon, the enemy showed up—it was a big black cow! I had been hunkered down there for twenty minutes, waiting for him! I'm glad I didn't fire because that cow probably belonged to some native on the island. I would have hated to kill his cow. The natives were friendly, you know. And they had a lot of mistreatments from the Japanese. During the war, the Japanese were not good people. They did a lot of bad things. But that was my first taste of "combat."

Robert Brutinel, 100, Second Parachute Battalion: We cleared the island out real quick. We stayed there for almost a month. The Marines took over an airbase that the Japanese had built; we dug in, and they gave us cots with netting because the mosquitoes were so bad. When we went to chow every morning a corpsman—Corpsman Maple—would issue us Atabrine, which was a pill for treating malaria. Oh, it was bitter tasting! The corpsman was there to make sure you swallowed it. Some guys would put it behind their tongue, get away, and spit it out. I always took mine—but I wasn't very smart! But—*ooh*—it was bitter. And it turned your skin yellow; and it turned your urine yellow. But it worked, I never got malaria.

W. Lee Robinson, 97, Second Parachute Battalion: When it finally became apparent that we weren't going to use parachutes anymore, they gave us rubber boat training. That was quite an experience, too. They took us to a spot where the sea was a little bit wild, and we were supposed to paddle out beyond the breakers. But when we got to the breakers, they were bigger than a truck. We started up one and the whole boat turned over. There we were, dumped out in the sea. But we didn't have to swim very far because there was a coral reef leading back to the shoreline. The problem was, we didn't have shoes on; we were in stocking feet. And coral is really tough on bare feet. But that was our training on rubber boats—which we used on Choiseul.

Robert Brutinel, 100, Second Parachute Battalion: We went in under nightfall a week later. The Navy took us in and dropped us off, then the natives came down and carried our equipment into the jungle. Japanese reconnaissance planes would fly over, looking for us. We could see them, but they couldn't see us.

W. Lee Robinson, 97, Second Parachute Battalion: We got orders to hit the island in as many places as we could; to feign a major offensive with the idea that the Japanese would bring troops down from Bougainville. That raid was an experience: I was in a squad with ten men, and we landed in a rubber boat near the mouth of a river. We moved down this trail, and before we knew it, we were in a Japanese bivouac area. There were Japanese all around, but the jungle kind of hid us from view. We thought, *What should we do? Should we try to get back out, or should we stop and hold our own?* It would have been curtains if they had discovered us because we were outnumbered.

Finally, we asked one of our former Boy Scouts, who knew semaphore, to signal a landing craft offshore for help. He did and the landing craft operator came roaring in, as close as he could get. We jumped into the surf, ran to the boat, and got in. The driver turned around, and as we headed out we opened up with our rifles and sprayed the area; the Japanese took cover. I have always supported the Boy Scout program because of that incident. That kid had learned semaphore in the Scouts, and he saved our bacon on Choiseul.

Robert Brutinel, 100, Second Parachute Battalion: On one operation, we took off and went down south to where the Japanese were bivouacked. They were out in the ocean, bathing and doing their morning routines, when we hit them. The Marine Corps had given us some rockets—we'd never used them before.* The natives carried them for us, but they just sat on a rickety old platform with wire legs. You'd raise the board up and down, depending on how far you wanted to propel it. We tried these rockets out, but it was a hit-and-miss thing. I can remember one going clear over the camp, out into the ocean; it was so inaccurate!

We had one man killed in the battle, but we couldn't take him back; he was too heavy. I always carried a little prayer book in my pocket. So, I read over him, then we covered him up real quick. I often think, *There's no way they ever found him to rebury him when the war was over.* Anyway, we went back up to where we were bivouacked, got our gear together, and went back towards the center of the island, by the sea, to wait for ships to come in and get us. As we got closer to the pickup point, we set up a perimeter of booby traps, then moved further in and set up another perimeter, until we got into the pickup position. Finally, when it was almost dark, a converted destroyer came in; it had ramps coming down both sides, and you just walked up into the ship.

As soon as we got the last man aboard and started taking off, we heard the first perimeter booby trap go off. We knew the Nips were closing in on us! We all went back to Vella Lavella, and we went to sleep. They told us the next day: "Pack up your gear, we're going back to the States!"

---

* An experimental Rocket Platoon was attached to the battalion to employ forty fin-stabilized rockets against the Japanese. The warhead was grossly inaccurate and would see very little use after the Solomons Campaign.

The paratroopers succeeded in killing 143 Japanese soldiers and destroying two barges at the cost of nine Marine lives. On November 1, 1943, American landing craft disembarked for the beaches of Empress Augusta Bay on the western shores of Bougainville. Elements of the Third Marine Division and Second Raider Battalion would seize six landing zones along the beachhead, while the Third Raider Battalion (minus M Company) would capture the tiny island of Puruata on the right flank. The objective was to establish a perimeter, construct an airfield, and immediately commence combat missions against Rabaul. The first wave of Marines hit the beach at 0730.

Milton "Red" Cronk, 98, Third Raider Battalion: When we went into combat, we went over the side of a troopship, down these big ropes. *Jesus!* You just hung on for dear life. It was a challenge because you were dead weight, and it's straight down from the deck to the water. We made it, but it wasn't easy. Then we got into Higgins boats and away we went! We were lucky. I think most of us got in without getting hit by the Japs.

Louis Bourgault, 97, Third Marine Division: I burned out the barrel on my M1 firing at Jap airplanes. We were in the jungle—and there was nothing else to do. Might as well shoot at them. I must have put one hundred rounds through that damned M1, as fast as I could fire. All the other guys were shooting, too. You could either sit there and hope the planes don't strafe you, or you could do something to fight back.

Melvin Ogg, 100, Third Marine Division: Most of my company went ahead, but I stayed aboard ship to help finish unloading our gear, ammunition, and stuff. While we were doing that, we had an air raid. The Japanese came in and tried to sink our ships. I was on the fantail, watching these planes come in. A sailor, who was passing up ammunition to the 20mm guns, yelled, "Hey, Marine! Get down in the hold!" I looked up at him and said, "Hey! If you like it so damned well down in the hold, why don't you get down there and *I'll* pass ammunition up to the gunner!" He didn't like that idea very much. After that, I started looking for the Japanese planes coming in and saw one nosing down. I thought for sure he was going to hit the fantail of the ship. But he missed us.

Paul Frederick, 98, Third Marine Division: The ship I was on was torpedoed. There were five of us sitting around talking when I left to get a drink of water. That's when we got hit. Those four guys got killed and I didn't. I was burned on the right side of my arm and the side of my face. The first thing that hit my mind was, *Water puts out fire!* So, I went over the side. A few of us guys got together and an LST picked us up. Our ship went down in twenty-two minutes.

Joe Harrison, 98, Second Raider Battalion: After landing, the captain sent me to go find the regimental CP. I said, "How do I find it?" He said, "Follow the beach. At about thirty yards, there's an opening for a trail going inland." I went down there and found the opening to the trail. It was an old, abandoned coconut grove. But just as I stepped out, I heard a sniper shot. I looked over and our battalion chaplain was down on his knees about thirty feet away, right next to the water. I hollered over and asked if he was all right. He didn't answer me. I knew something was wrong, so I ran over, pinched his shoulder, and asked him how he was doing. He pointed to his ears—*he couldn't hear.* A sniper had shot through his helmet, right between the fiber and the steel. The bullet had gone out the other side. About that time, the sniper shot again. I told the chaplain, "Let's get outta here! The Japs are shootin' at us!" I gave him the helmet and we got down the trail.

Louis Bourgault, 97, Third Marine Division: I went back to the battalion CP to lead a wire team up to our position because we were digging a defensive perimeter. The trail split and I went to the left instead of the right because it looked a little drier. All of a sudden, I saw this Japanese guy moving up ahead. He was facing me with his rifle aimed down the trail. I immediately put four rounds into him. We drug him out of the bushes, and I opened the bolt of his rifle and pulled a round from the chamber. I've still got it—that bullet had my name on it. If I had gone to the right, he would have shot me in the back of the head as we went by.

Joe Harrison, 98, Second Raider Battalion: I was sent out to tell the lieutenant we were pulling back at four o'clock in the afternoon, but one of the guys directed me out into the jungle the wrong way. I heard some noise, so I looked through some bushes and saw a Jap about fifteen feet from me. He didn't see me. About that time, I saw another Jap about six feet closer with his back to me. I could only see the second guy from his shoulders up; he had branches on his helmet. Then the first guy looked right at me, so I shot him. They disappeared and I disappeared.

Jack Rasmussen, 94, Third Marine Division: It was just starting to get dark when word came down that all American patrols were in. Anything that moved from then on was the enemy. *Golly!* Not long after that, here comes some guys walking right out in front of us. They had to be Japanese! I told George, "You take the right side and I'll take the left side." We both shot. But as soon as we shot, someone yelled, "HOLD

FIRE! There's another Marine unit coming in!" Oh God! We thought we killed those two guys. Fortunately, we missed!

Louis Bourgault, 97, Third Marine Division: You didn't move at night. If you got diarrhea or had dysentery, you'd put a big banana leaf down in your hole, shit on it, and slide it over the edge until morning. *Then* you could get rid of it. You didn't get up for anything.

Chuck Meacham, 96, Third Raider Battalion: We secured the island of Puruata the second day and went down to the beach to set up for the night. At daylight, two really tough guys from Oregon decided to go out and take a little dip in the ocean to get cleaned up. Our platoon sergeant saw them coming in from the water and thought they were Japs. He took them both down with his tommy gun. Our corpsman—about eighteen years old, first time in action—knew they were the guys from Oregon. He jumped up to go take care of them, and he was shot. We lost three men that morning because they were out of foxholes. I'll tell you, nobody in that platoon ever had to have another lecture about staying in their hole. That was a lesson you'll never forget.

After meeting staunch resistance at the beachhead—notably in the Third Marine Regiment's sector, where a single Japanese 75mm cannon destroyed four landing boats and damaged another ten—the Marines were able to push inland, establish a perimeter, and commence construction on a new airfield. The Japanese responded to the American invasion by performing a counter-landing between Laruma River and Koromokina Lagoon. The resulting engagement would be the first in a series of bloody battles fought along the American perimeter in early November.

Chuck Meacham, 96, Third Raider Battalion: Bougainville was hell on earth, it was a terrible environment. We lost more people from the environment than we did from the Japanese. Some nights we'd lay there with our heads propped on a helmet to keep above the water. One time we had three days and nights in a row of rain. When I came out of that, I was a sponge. Of course, the temperature was about ninety-eight degrees, and the humidity was one hundred. It was pretty tough going.

Louis Bourgault, 97, Third Marine Division: The jungle was hell. On the coastal plain, where we landed, you couldn't dig in six inches without hitting water. There were wait-a-minute vines, trees, and typical jungle; it was the same, all through the Solomons. The worst thing that happened to me there: I had jungle rot from just above my knees, up to my chest; genitals and all. It's worse than any goddamned poison ivy I've ever had. And I had malaria and I had dysentery, too. Seemed like every day, at about two o'clock, the skies opened up and buckets of rain came pouring down. One time, the volcano on the island started rumbling. We had earthquakes and the ground came up and hit us in the ass.

Ben Carson, 96, Second Raider Battalion: When we got to Bougainville, we were back in old World War I–type warfare.

Milton "Red" Cronk, 98, Third Raider Battalion: One time, our corporal sat up to shoot some Jap. Turns out they were just waiting for him to poke his head out. When he did, they popped him right in the eye. That was it for him. Then the Japs threw a grenade in his foxhole, and it blew the other boy's leg off. That was pretty bad.

Joe Harrison, 98, Second Raider Battalion: The second day, they pulled us back beyond the main defense line. That night, the Japs tried a banzai charge against our defenses. There was a lot of them killed.

Chuck Meacham, 96, Third Raider Battalion: We set up one night and dug in. You could hear the Japanese back there, singing, making noises, and having a big sake party. Once you got in a foxhole, you didn't get out. That's the order—*or you got shot.* The next morning, just shortly after daylight, all hell broke loose; limbs and twigs were falling. The Japanese had set up a machine gun somewhere out there, and they just mowed and mowed and mowed.

Milton "Red" Cronk, 98, Third Raider Battalion: By the time the shooting stopped, "Gunny" and I were the only ones left. The rest of the guys had gone back. He was older than me, and he said, "You go first." So I did. I don't know how far I got, but a sniper hit me in the arm. It didn't knock me out, just stalled me. I had a rifle and a knife in my hand, but I dropped both because of the shock. I stayed there for a few minutes—*or seconds*—looking, trying to find my stuff. I never did find it, so I just kept going.

I finally got back to where the rest of the guys were. My wound was kind of bloody, so the corpsman took care of me and fixed me up. The next day, they put me on an amtrac, and it took me back down to the beach. I stayed there a couple of nights, then they put me on a ship back to Espiritu Santo.

Melvin Ogg, 100, Third Marine Division: When I got hit, our company was corduroying a road. It was mushy and watery, and our trucks couldn't take chow and ammunition up to the front lines. I was out there, all by myself, trimming the branches off a tree, when the Japanese fired an artillery shell. It hit the bottom of a tree and it came down across my left shoulder and gave me a concussion. I don't know how long I was unconscious, but the guys picked me up and took me up to the first aid station on the front line. When I came to, I noticed some guy from another company looking at me. He said, "When they brought you in here, I swore you were dead." I looked at him and said, "Are you sure you're not hallucinating—and I am dead?"

In late November, the First Parachute Battalion received orders to land ten miles east of Cape Torokina with a company from the Third Raider Battalion to disrupt Japanese troop movements along the American perimeter.

Robert Riechman, 98, First Parachute Battalion: We got into Higgins boats, drove up to the far part of the island, and went ashore. It was a big sandy beachhead, two or three football fields wide, surrounded by jungle. We landed at dawn with a company of special forces guys who had been in the war since 1942. They called them "the Raiders." They went into the jungle and got shot up—*really shot up*. The vegetation was so thick that it was impossible for us to go in and find the enemy. Even the Raiders couldn't get through. We had quite a few guys get wounded by small arms fire. I still had a silly '03 Springfield. I think I was the only guy with a bolt-action weapon there; the rest had the M1. I used a telescopic sight, but I couldn't see anything. We were shooting at Japanese up in the trees, but I don't know what the hell we were hitting.

We were dug in on the beach when mortar fire started coming in. It was the strangest thing: Every shell that exploded, exploded in the water. We couldn't figure out why they didn't adjust their fire. After a while, we knew we weren't going to be hit because they were exploding fifty to eighty yards out in the ocean. *BOOM! BOOM! BOOM!* I was on the beach from four in the morning until seven at night because the Navy wouldn't come in until after dark. We wanted to get the hell outta there. I couldn't wait to grab one of those poor wounded guys, laying down on a stretcher. Finally, one of the Higgins boats came in to get us. We filled up, then we were off.

Unable to penetrate the jungle, the raid on Koiari failed at the cost of fifteen American lives. It's estimated that the Japanese lost 291 men in the engagement. In the weeks that followed, fighting continued around the perimeter as American units dispatched patrols and battled for hilltop positions overlooking the airfield.

Blair Hyde, 103, Third Marine Division: There were a lot of raids that went on, but we mostly stayed in our perimeter. We didn't know what size enemy force was in the jungle between us and the Torokina River. One time, we sent out three patrols, and I took one. I was in the middle. The one on my right ran into heavy swamp and they bogged down and didn't get very much action. The patrol on my left ran into the Japanese and exchanged fire with them. I was lucky: We went straight through, up to the river, saw signs of the Japanese, but did not see any Japanese soldiers.

James Freel, 99, Third Parachute Battalion: Sometimes we laid down cover fire, but as far as ever actually seeing the enemy—no, just shadows and stuff like that. The Japanese were good soldiers. But that *is* where I saw my first dead Marine. After a patrol, we were sitting there cleaning our weapons; his gun went off and it killed him. It was an accident. That made the war solemn, brought you to reality.

Louis Bourgault, 97, Third Marine Division: When the Japs finally evacuated Hellzapoppin Ridge in late December, I got up there a few hours after they left. On one slope, the bamboo was so goddamned thick you couldn't push your way through it. Somebody cut little steps into the ridge. But when they got wet, it was like walking on snow and ice. God, it was a helluva thing! The Japanese had dug defenses under the trees. I don't know if I can even describe it to you: tree trunks, probably six feet in diameter, with big roots laying around. They would dig down on one side and pop out on the other, like a bunker. Artillery, mortar shells—nothing could touch them. Our regimental executive officer went up in an SBD Dauntless to show the pilot where to drop his bombs, to get some explosives in there. But the Japanese were so dug in, all the artillery hit the treetops. It didn't make a difference; you couldn't get them. They had fire lanes all laid out. Imagine going uphill, trying to push your way through thick bamboo (even the little stuff is two or three inches in diameter). The Japanese were firing down low, getting guys in the legs.

Jesse Arney, 100, Third Tank Battalion: Our tank was called up a couple of times to shoot something out. Or we'd carry a load of ammunition up to the front, for the infantry, then load the wounded back. But it was so boggy we could usually only make one trip. We didn't do a whole lot there, but we did a little bit. One time they called our tank up and said, "There's a Jap in a tree and we can't get him out." I had a high explosive shell in my gun, and I thought, *I'll shoot that, then put another canister shell up there*. So, I fired and hit the middle of the tree and cut the whole top of the tree down. I asked our commander, "You want me to fire another one?" He used a few choice words, then said, "No, you just shot the entire tree down!"

Blair Hyde, 103, Third Marine Division: The Japanese kept attacking, but they couldn't make any inroads because we had good, solid defenses. A close friend of mine was subjected to a very severe banzai attack in that period. Those were no fun when they came at you. After a while, we returned to the beach, and I was very much surprised to see that the Seabees had put up a whole new airfield.

By December of 1943, exhausted Marine units began withdrawing from Bougainville. The campaign, relinquished to various American, Australian, and Fijian Army outfits, would continue until August of 1945. Meanwhile, the bloodied Third Marine Division returned to Guadalcanal and began refitting for the next operation.

Milton "Red" Cronk, 98, Third Raider Battalion: When we went into Bougainville, there was a little island right next door—*I forget the name.* Some Marine got burned up there. When I was in the hospital on Espiritu Santo, he was there too, in a ward all by himself. His name was Douglas. I remember that. They would ask us to go in there and feed him. I told those nurses: "I'll do anything for him, but I won't do that." I couldn't do that. The smell of his burnt body was terrible, awful.

8 ★★★★★★

TARAWA

In early November, as American forces battled the Japanese on Bougainville, the Second Marine Division set sail for the Gilbert Islands. Refreshed after a long stay in New Zealand, the division would vanguard a new island-hopping campaign across the central Pacific by capturing the tiny island of Betio in the Tarawa Atoll. Measuring only one square mile in size, the deceivingly beautiful island—known to the Marines simply as Tarawa—was a veritable fortress, honeycombed by a series of coconut log bunkers and cement blockhouses, manned by roughly four thousand Japanese defenders.

The invasion beaches were divided into three sections—Red Beach One, Red Beach Two, and Red Beach Three—and assigned to various battalions within the division. Among the men destined for Red Beach Three were two Guadalcanal veterans from the Second Battalion, Eighth Marine Regiment, named John L'Abbe and Elwin Hart. Assigned to the initial assault wave, L'Abbe would charge ashore aboard an LVT (Landing Vehicle Tracked), while Hart followed in a flat-bottom Higgins boat. At 0824 on D-Day, November 20, 1943, the first amphibious tractors crossed the line of departure and headed for the beach.

John L'Abbe, 97, Second Marine Division: We loaded into an amphibious tractor aboard ship. It had a machine gun mounted on the front and a guy said, "You take care of that." I said, "I've never fired one, I don't know how." Then this guy from the South, who I think had just joined the company because I'd never seen him before, said, "I'll do it! I'll do it!" I said, "Merry Christmas." So, he got up there. As we got closer and closer to the beach, he started shooting the gun. All of a sudden—*BOOM!*—he fell backwards. But he got up again, tried shooting a little more, maybe two or three more bursts. Then he fell on me. He was dead, so I laid his body on the deck.

There was so much bombardment and so many airplanes hitting the island that we thought there was nothing to it; it would be an easy operation. But as we got closer—*bbbrrrppp!* You ever throw a bottle? A little bottle? And it whistles? That's what it sounded like when the bullets went over us. We got up on the beach about twenty yards from this great big pillbox. The Japs had a helluva time knocking us around. Everything in the world was shooting at us. I started to get out of the tractor, but this fella by the name of Charpilloz cut in front of me. I stopped—and he got killed jumping down. I got myself over the side, down to the beach. But two grenades went off by my feet and wounded me. I started crawling up to the seawall for protection.

All of a sudden, here comes this guy, jumping over the wall. I thought, *Good! It's a Marine!* But it was a Jap officer. He swung around with his sword. All I could see were other Marines aiming at him. I wasn't worried because I knew they would get him; and of course they did. When the officer went down, I grabbed his sword and beat on his head.

More amphibious tractors were still coming in and I thought,

Shit! They're going to hit me! I put my hand on the treads of one, but it stopped just in time, and I crawled up to the seawall. Nick was there, and another fella I knew was there. We sat with our backs to the wall and watched the other guys walking in, six hundred yards, under fire.

Elwin Hart, 93, Second Marine Division: We got caught on the reef and waded six hundred yards to get in. About halfway, I grabbed the back of a tank that was lumbering by. You weren't supposed to do that because the tanks were targets. But I did it and made it to the beach; it worked. There was a lot of small arms fire and a lot of machine gun fire. You could see it hitting the water and guys getting hit. I had two or three guys close to me get hit. Henry "Jim" Crowe—the battalion commander of 2/8—was just fearless, kicking people in the butt to get them off the beach. I saw him doing that. He was yelling all the time, running up and down, getting his rifle company guys on their way and moving us inland.

My unit found an abandoned Japanese mortar pit and used it for our radio station. We got all the equipment down and I got the transceiver off my shoulders. Then I found Eddie Fisher lying flat on his back. I said, "Hey! Eddie, what the hell's wrong?" He said, "I've got a migraine, I can't move." I said, "Okay, just lay there—don't worry about it. I'll get you a corpsman in a while. Where the hell is Clarence?" He said, "I saw him going that way when we landed." I said, "Okay, I'll go looking for him." I got out of the dugout and started running across the beach in the direction he pointed. I was yelling his name and getting a little gunfire every now and then. *Fortunately*, I didn't get hit. All of a sudden, I saw Clarence up against the seawall. He was waving at me. I ran over and I said, "What the hell's wrong with you, Clarence? We've got to get that damn radio on the air. Come on, let's go!"

He had a bullet wound right through his neck; went in and came right out. He couldn't talk. That's why he wasn't yelling at me. I tried to drag him, but he was pretty heavy; bigger than I was. I couldn't get much of a handle on him, so I got his radio off and put it on my back. Then somebody came up on the other side and helped me. We were moving out pretty good. About that time, we started taking machine gun fire. I was cussing really loud and boisterously, as many things as I'd ever learned. When they finally quit shooting, I wanted to see who was helping me. It turned out it was the battalion chaplain! I apologized to him. I told him that if I'd known it was him, I wouldn't have used that language. He said, "Son, don't worry about it! I was having similar thoughts!"

A disastrous miscalculation of the tides trapped the pursuing Higgins boats on the reef, six hundred yards out in the lagoon. LVTs from the first wave turned around to ferry the men ashore but were quickly destroyed by Japanese shells. Without transportation, hundreds of Americans were forced to disembark and wade ashore through a gauntlet of machine gun and mortar fire. Some units suffered up to 50 percent casualties in the assault.

By nightfall, the beachhead was in a precarious state. Of the five thousand Marines that had disembarked on D-Day, fifteen hundred were already dead, wounded, or missing; the rest were hunkered behind the seawall or burrowed in foxholes no more than a few hundred yards from the waterline (with the exception of L Company, 3/2, which had successfully penetrated five hundred yards beyond Red Beach One). Fortunately for the Marines, no Japanese counterattack materialized overnight. At dawn on

D+1, after circling in the lagoon all night, reinforcements from the First Battalion, Eighth Marine Regiment (1/8) received orders to land on Red Beach Two.

Dean Ladd, 101, Second Marine Division: Turned out it was the worst possible beach: The Japanese machine guns were just over the seawall shooting at us. I was the first one off my Higgins boat. I didn't know whether the water was going to be over my head or not; turned out it was only waist deep. But the bullets were hitting the water all around us. I looked back, and some of my men were hesitating to jump off the landing boat. I said, "Come on! Get off! Jump off!" Just about that time, I got hit. It felt like an inner tube snapped across my abdomen. One of my men stopped and grabbed me; kept me from drowning. Another one came over and said, "Where are you hit?" I said, "Somewhere in here." They found the hole and poured a little sulfonamide powder on it, not realizing that it would just fall off and float away in the water. Then they both dragged me to a landing boat about a hundred yards further out, in an adjacent company's sector. There were about fifteen of us collected at that point. The two men with me were trying to shove me over the boat's ramp, which was dropped at a thirty-degree angle to defend against incoming Japanese bullets. One of the wounded inside the boat, who was hit around the eye and bleeding like mad, helped pull me over with his last ounce of energy. They put us in a litter basket, next to each other, and lifted us up to a transport with a crane. I said, "We're going to make it now." He said, "You're going to make it"—and he died shortly after. That was a sad thing.

The First Battalion, Eighth Marines (1/8) suffered more than three hundred casualties during the ship-to-shore assault. In Dean Ladd's platoon alone, twelve men were wounded and twelve were killed. But despite the horrendous losses, momentum was beginning to shift in the battle. Scattered Marine units, bolstered by officers and enterprising non-commissioned officers, rushed forward behind offshore naval gunfire and advancing tanks.

By the evening of D+1, the First Battalion, Sixth Marine Regiment was ashore and established on the western end of the island (1/6 is often derided as "the condom fleet" because they came ashore in a flotilla of rubber boats). On D+2, with the bulk of the division committed, the Marines were on the offensive, clearing enemy positions, demolishing pillboxes, and burning out coconut log bunkers with flamethrowers. The final hours of battle would be a spectacularly violent fight to the finish.

Marvin Strombo, 95, Second Marine Division: I went into Tarawa on a rubber boat—*a raft*—and saw a lot of fighting. It only lasted three days because it was a small island, only a mile long, and half a mile wide. I remember seeing so many dead people. The Japanese were still throwing shells at us, mortars and whatnot. I was just hoping none of them would hit us. But a lot of guys got hit.

Seeing the dead didn't bother me any. Maybe it did for some people, but it's war. You don't think about it. You just took it as it came because you knew it was going to be rough. In close fighting like that, you just took it as it came. And you *never* think you're going to get killed. You think you're going to live forever—everybody did.

The Japanese were hard to fight because they had cement dugouts. They'd fire for a while then hide inside. They were hard to get out; you almost had to pull them out. We didn't take very many prisoners; only about seventeen, I think, on the whole island. They knew they couldn't live through the battle and go home, so they fought until death. The Japanese put up an awful good fight, you know? Hard fighters. They fought until they died.

Clayton Narveson, 99, Second Marine Division: I only saw one guy surrender at the end of the fighting. He was wearing a loincloth, no shirt, and he had his arms up in the air. It was a Korean laborer.

Thomas Fitzmaurice, 100, Second Defense Battalion: The cleanup took another two days or so. The Japanese were imbedded in palm tree, sand instillations. To be perfectly honest: When you fire, you can never be sure that you hit anybody. You hoped—but really, you were relying on satchel charges, hand grenades, and flamethrowers firing into emplacement ports. Yeah, I would say seeing Japanese dead bothered me. Of course, you felt worse about the guys in the water who didn't make it ashore; your own men. I waded in past bodies—and the odor, by about the second or third day on the island, was really bad.

Charles Pase, 99, Second Marine Division: By the time that we got to them, they were pretty rotten. Skulls and . . . it was disgusting.

After seventy-six hours of battle, the island was finally declared secure. American casualties were staggering: More than a thousand men killed and another two thousand wounded. Corpses in various states of decomposition lay across the shoreline, bloating in the hot Pacific sun. The stench was so powerful that pilots reported vomiting in their cockpits as they circled in the air above. The nearby island of Makin was captured by the Twenty-Seventh Infantry Division, along with several other smaller islets in the atoll. Remnants of the Second Marine Division loaded aboard transports in a flurry of rumors that they would be returning to New Zealand. Instead, the division steamed to Hawaii and established a new base that would become known as Camp Tarawa. The injured slowly matriculated back to the division and began preparations for the next invasion, while the severely wounded and old-timers rotated back to the United States.

John L'Abbe, 97, Second Marine Division: We went to the hospital in Pearl Harbor. They worked on me for a while, then put me on a hospital ship called the *Solace*, back to San Diego. After eight or nine months, I was released and transferred as an invalid for guard duty.

Dean Ladd, 101, Second Marine Division: The doctor patched up the hole in my stomach, took out part of my punctured intestine, then hooked it back together again. When they got through, I didn't even have to wear a colostomy bag! I was back on active duty again within another two months. After the surgery, the doctor said that I probably wouldn't live very long; that I'd be fortunate if I lived past the age of fifty.

Elwin Hart, 93, Second Marine Division: When I left Tarawa, we rotated back to Hawaii up under Mauna Kea on a cattle ranch. They sent me to Pearl Harbor, and I joined an artillery unit that hadn't deployed yet. I guess they saw that I had enough time overseas—thirty months, or whatever it was. They sent me back to the States from there.

Thomas Fitzmaurice, 100, Second Defense Battalion: I was sent to Hawaii with a new battalion because I was on the verge of going home, having already served two and a half years. But when I was transferred from Kauai to Oahu en route to the States, I tried everything to stay overseas. I even tried to get on the baseball team in Oahu. By that time, the Marine Corps was home for me—and I didn't have any desire to go back to the United States. But the Corps had its orders, so I went back and ended up down at Parris Island on the rifle range as an instructor before my second deployment.

9 ★★★★★★

NEW BRITAIN, EMIRAU, AND THE REDUCTION OF RABAUL

In the fall of 1943, the First Marine Division departed Australia for staging areas along the New Guinea coastline. After several months of training on LCTs (Landing Craft, Tank), LCIs (Landing Craft, Infantry), and LSTs (Landing Ship, Tank), the division arrived offshore of Cape Gloucester, New Britain, in late December. Located in the Bismarck Archipelago, New Britain encompassed 370 miles of jungle, mountainous terrain, swamps, and a formidable monsoon season that typically spanned from December to March. The objective was to capture two airfields and intensify attacks on Rabaul, located roughly three hundred miles away, at the island's northeastern tip. On December 26, 1943, elements of the First Marine Division splashed ashore at two beachheads east and west of a narrow peninsula.

Harmon Hunter, 101, First Marine Division: Cape Gloucester is mostly all jungle, right down to the beach.

Richard Nelson, 98, First Marine Division: When you came off the landing craft, you were wet, wet all week.

Richard Russell, 100, First Marine Division: It was a quiet landing, there was no action.

Gilbert Berg, 98, First Marine Division: We had been in Guinea for a couple of months or more, and I was very, very ill with malaria. I was constantly coming down with attacks of malaria. My combat in New Britain was a nightmare from day one until the day I left. When we stepped off the end of our landing barges, we stepped off into deep water and went in over our heads, lost a lot of equipment.

Russel Nelson, 98, First Marine Division: We had LSTs that opened in the front, so the tanks and amtracs could drive out. I went off in a jeep, but we had so much ammunition loaded in the back that we dropped into the water and sank. I swam back to the ship about fifty feet. That was kind of scary.

Carl Scott, 98, First Marine Division: The Seventh Marines landed in a swamp, and it was terrible. The water was up to our chest, and you had to hold your weapon over your head. They took my M1 and gave me a BAR. I've always accused the Marine Corps of giving its heaviest weapons to its littlest guys. Our objective was Hill 440—and they expected heavy casualties. When we got to the base of the hill, I looked up: I saw the muzzle of a machine gun and thought, *Uh oh. This is bad news.* Around that time, my assistant BAR-man had the pin pop out of a white phosphorous grenade in his pocket. It went off and started burning him—and he started rolling down the hill. When he got to the bottom, a corpsman stuck him in the mud to get the fire out.

We started climbing, but nobody was shooting at us. At the top, we saw a machine gun and a few other weapons. The guys started looking at them and someone said, "Those are

American weapons! They must have got these in the Philippines!" We lucked out there. Then we moved to our right and it started raining and I was wet for thirty days.

Our next objective was Hill 150. They picked a scout from all three squads, and all three scouts were killed there. My best friend, Harold Harnden, was killed by a sniper on the other side of the hill. He was shot in the back of the head. The sniper was in a hollow tree, and he killed eight Marines before they found him. Around the second night, "Chesty" Puller spoke to the Marines in B Company. He came up to me and said, "How you doing, old man?" I was nineteen.

Richard Nelson, 98, First Marine Division: I was with a guy out on patrol, and he said, "I see Marines out there!" I said, "There aren't any Marines out there now." He got up and he was going to holler to them. But he got shot right in the throat. I still think of that guy. I can't remember his name—*I wish I could.* I often think of him, but there are so many guys to remember.

Gilbert Berg, 98, First Marine Division: I remember one of the guys in our unit being found in the morning as we advanced. The Japs had gotten ahold of him; he was a messy dead Marine with a wire wrapped around his neck. But the *first* dead Marine I saw was under a tarp, laying on the beach. I went over and pulled the tarp back and there was a Marine with no face. That was my first encounter. It angered and saddened me. But it was the opposite feeling for the dead Japanese. In my mind, there was no feeling of remorse or no feeling of sorrow. Just, "Thank Christ he's dead."

James Rosenmiller, 100, First Marine Division: Our trucks and cannons couldn't keep up with us because of the mud.

We used to throw Jap bodies into mudholes for the trucks to get some kind of traction. That I can tell you we did—just threw their bodies into real bad spots in the trail. That was our way of getting our tanks and trucks and equipment inland.

Robert Evans, 97, First Marine Division: At one point, we got in a firefight with fourteen Japs. I remember Corporal Bellis was off to the left, and the automatic riflemen were back a ways, having it out with a machine gun. I tried to drop a hand grenade on the Japs, right before they got me.

When I got hit, it felt like a big explosion. It blew my helmet twenty feet, or that's what they told me after. A bullet had hit me in the head, one in the neck, and one ripped my jacket off. In other words: I was dead and didn't know it. A kid named Al Dhieux was dragging me out of there, and I was dragging my BAR. I wouldn't leave it.

I thought I was dead because one bullet was laying between my ribs. Every time my heart beat, it hurt something terrible. But the doctors didn't seem to think it was that serious because my blood pressure was good, and they could hear my heart beating good. I guess they knew the bullet wasn't buried in my heart. But I didn't know that, and I thought, *Son of a gun, they got me!* But I lived through it.

Don Bishop, 98, First Marine Division: Private Knight and I were going down a trail, carrying a wounded man on a stretcher, when we discovered that a big tree had fallen across the path. We started climbing through the branches, trying not to dump the injured guy.

When the tree went down, it took its roots with it and left a big hole in the ground. There were five Japanese hiding in that hole. When they saw us, they came out, whooping and hollering. A funny thing happened: When I get mad, I get *really* livid. Almost out of my mind. If the Japanese had stuck me with a bayonet just then, it wouldn't have stopped me. Boy, I was mad! The idea that they would attack men who were out of the fight, carrying a wounded man . . . oh, they just didn't care! If it had been a stretcher full of babies, they would have attacked. They had no remorse!

Anyway, one of the Japanese started running towards me, and I started running towards him. There was a big limb from the tree blocking our path, so he stopped and climbed up on top. When I got there, he dove at me. I caught him midair with a shot in his side. It spun him around and he hit me hard and both of us went down. I was trying to get out from underneath him when three more Japanese ran right past me, towards Knight. He shot two of them.

When I got up and ran back to Knight, one was lying beside the stretcher and banging a hand grenade on his helmet (that's how they set off their hand grenades). I stepped on his hand, took the grenade, and threw it into the underbrush. He was laying there, folded up, shaking. I thought: *Well, I'll put him out of his misery*. So, I shot him. I looked at Knight and said, "There were five of them. Where's the other one?" He said, "Yeah, where did that guy go?" I said, "I don't know. I think, maybe, he's behind that big tree, hiding in the roots. I'll throw a grenade in there, and when it goes off, we'll rush him." We did that.

I tossed a grenade in there and *boom!* Both Knight and I rushed in—but he wasn't there. I said, "Where the hell did he go?" Knight yelled, "In back of you, Deac!" I turned around—and there's a Japanese major standing there with a samurai sword over his head. He had plenty of time to lower that sword on me, but he didn't for some reason. He just stood there. I guess he wanted to go to his ancestors as a hero, so I just helped him along the way. I caught him with my bayonet and pulled the trigger at the same time. He went down. Knight said, "When I first saw him, he was dragging the sword," so we figured he must have been wounded pretty bad; that's why he didn't hit me.

Afterwards, I took his sword and his pistol, which were no good. The sword was bent, and the pistol wouldn't fire. We got all our stuff, picked up the stretcher, then took the wounded man down and put him on a boat. Then we took the stretcher to the ammunition dump—filled it up with bandoliers and other ammunition to take back to the front.

Richard Russell, 100, First Marine Division: On the ninth day, a bunch of Japs snuck up and charged us with bayonets. They were about twenty feet away, firing wildly from the hip. We killed the last one about ten feet from my hole. That was the most exciting part of the whole trip for me. Right after we repelled the attack, they shot a bunch of mortars at us. I was in a foxhole with my head between my knees when one of the mortars landed close and caught me in the leg. That was it: I spent about five months in the hospital.

George Mason, 98, First Marine Division: The other guys decided not to dig a hole one night. They said, "Oh, the hell with it." But I had a feeling we were going to get bombed, so I dug a big round hole, the size of my body, maybe a little bigger. Pretty soon, four Jap bombers came in. I jumped in the hole and ducked my head down. Suddenly, three other guys jumped in on top of me. Thank God the strafing was thirty meters off to the right! If it had been on target, it would have killed all of us.

Carl Scott, 98, First Marine Division: I was getting shot at one time and the bullets were hitting in front of me, knocking dirt into my face. But I couldn't see the Jap. A sergeant came along and said, "Shoot over there!" He pointed to a spot in the jungle, and I fired twenty rounds. I don't know if I hit anything or not, but he quit shooting at me.

Gilbert Berg, 98, First Marine Division: A guy and I were stringing out a sound power line to an artillery outpost, running through the jungle, when the Japanese found the two of us and opened fire. The guy I was with got hit by a bullet. We flopped down on the ground, and he said, "Jesus, they hit me." I said, "Where?" He said, "Hit in the arm!" But he was pleased: it was a way home. Stuff like that, I think about. I think about laying in a foxhole, praying to God to make it through the night.

Ernie Ferguson, 98, First Marine Division: We eventually set up a line across the island and left the Japs up at Rabaul. We sent patrols into the jungle, keeping the enemy at their end of the island. I saw a few Japs, but it was very seldom. It was mostly mosquitoes and jungle rot and dysentery. I was taking Atabrine, but it didn't do any good. I got malaria—and I still get flareups every so often. I had a flareup last month. Atabrine turns you yellow and, when you're dead, that yellow becomes more prominent.

Russel Nelson, 98, First Marine Division: We slept in hammocks. Can you imagine me with my radio and my little carbine, laying in a hammock, trying to get comfortable? They had a lot of wild boars and snakes, so we had to get up off the ground. If a wild boar got in our way, we'd shoot it. Then we had to tell our officers so they could tell the natives to come get their dinner.

Richard Nelson, 98, First Marine Division: When I got back to the ship, they threw a rope down to haul me up. I had jungle rot on my hands and feet and couldn't climb the ladder. Everybody else put their rifle over their shoulder, while the guys up on top tried to help us aboard.

The Japanese waged a formidable defense of Cape Gloucester, bleeding the First Marine Division in a series of intense battles at Suicide Creek, Hill 150, Walt's Ridge, and Hill 660. In March, the Fifth Marine Regiment boarded transports and completed the campaign by landing at Volupai in the central part of New Britain. After four months of fighting, the division had suffered more than a thousand casualties. Wet and exhausted, the First limped back to the Solomon Islands and set up camp on a former coconut plantation called Pavuvu.

Around the same time, the Marine Corps elected to disband all raider and parachute battalions. Most Paramarines and raiders were rotated home or folded into the reconstituted Fourth Marine Regiment gathering on Guadalcanal. The Fourth Marines, after a brief period of training, were rapidly ordered to seize Emirau Island north of New Britain. Emirau was a rugged, densely jungled outcrop that stretched eight miles and possessed a small harbor and an airstrip that lay within striking distance of Rabaul. The assault began on March 20, 1944.

Chuck Meacham, 96, Fourth Marine Regiment: The Japanese got out of there the night before we landed. When we hit the beach, there was nobody home. We thought, *Oh boy! We're going to be out here in the sun!* Oh no, we went right into training. We spent the next, I don't remember how long it was, working night and day.

Tom Shields, 93, Fourth Marine Regiment: There wasn't a Jap anywhere around. We dug in on the island, then brought up a few battalions of Seabees and they built two airfields.

Joe Harrison, 98, Fourth Marine Regiment: We landed on Emirau for about ten days and there wasn't any fighting, so they sent us back to Guadalcanal. We trained and got different equipment—*better equipment*. Then we started preparing for Guam.

With substantial airfields secured throughout New Guinea and the Solomon Islands, Marine and Army aviation units began aggressively attacking Rabaul and its adjacent shipping lanes. Bivouacked in relatively austere locations, subject to periodic bombings, horrendous disease, and unending boredom, ground crews and pilots waged a thankless air war in the western Pacific.

Robert Bennett, 100, First Marine Air Wing: I was in the Headquarters Squadron assigned as a ground operator on Emirau. It was all jungle; it wasn't cleared or anything. We established a camp there and, at the beginning, all we had were jungle hammocks, strung between two palm trees. But the jungle hammocks had mosquito netting all around them so we wouldn't get too many bugs on us. Then we'd dig a foxhole underneath for protection. When the Japs would come over with bombers, we'd just unzip the mosquito netting and roll out into a foxhole. They finally put up some sleeping quarters after a while. But when we were first there, it was a real primitive area.

Bob Carlson, 96, VMB-433 (Tailer Gunner, PBJ Medium Bomber): When the Coastwatchers noticed a buildup of Japanese, we'd go in at low level, sometimes ahead of the invasion troops; the Australians, Americans, or whoever they were.*

* During the war, Australian and New Zealander Coastwatchers were stationed through the South and Southwest Pacific to warn against Japanese troop movements, deliver intelligence reports, and recover downed airmen.

A fighter plane would usually go in first and drop a smoke bomb, then around three planes would go in abreast and break off every five seconds or so. That gave us three or more seconds of delay so the bombs wouldn't go off directly under us. Then I'd get my twin fifties going. Everything went under you so damned fast; it was kind of a blur until you got away. Then you could see a lot of equipment blowing up, almost as high as the planes. I saw a truck rear end tossed in the air—looked like it went higher than we were flying! And we were just above the trees!

If you went in on a real low-level pass, you could see everything. There was a good purpose for doing that: The enemy couldn't fire on you. In fact, you could go in at times and there wouldn't be any ground fire. If you were up in the sky a ways—the highest we flew was, I think, ten thousand feet—you would get quite a bit of ground fire.

Richard Kolodey, 97, VMTB-233 (Radio Operator/Gunner, TBM-Avenger): Flying is fast. It's not like on the ground; it ain't drug out. Everything happens in one or two or three minutes. Your typical bomb run only lasts about two minutes because you come down at three hundred miles per hour. Then, when you release the bomb, you get right on top of the water or the jungle and get out of there. We sank a troop transport once: put a two-thousand-pound bomb right in the side of it. And we all—*collectively*—shot up planes and ships. It was a group endeavor; one person doesn't do all of it. Now, the fighter planes soloed on some missions, but we flew in groups of six or twelve or eighteen or twenty-four, flew like geese fly, in a "V" shape.

In our dive-bombers, we had a pilot, a turret gunner, and a radio/belly gunner. The radio/belly gunner could open a window in the back and roll a machine gun down underneath the tail and shoot behind us as we left. I remember my crewmate was in the turret one day (we took turns most of the time, depends on the situation) and he got shot in the leg. He didn't get hit too bad; it went right through the fleshy part of his left leg. But he was bleeding pretty good. I took my belt off, put it around the wound, and helped him out of there. Then I got up into the turret and started shooting.

On one run to Rabaul, we were carrying four five-hundred-pound bombs instead of a two-thousand-pounder. We opened the bomb bay and dropped the ordnance on some buildings. But one of the bombs didn't drop; it got hung up on the shackle. We had to fly more than three hundred miles back to Bougainville with the bay doors open and the bomb hanging out. We couldn't close the doors, because if we hit the pin, it would blow up. Of course, we couldn't ditch in the sea either—if we hit the water, it would explode. So, we circled around trying to shake it loose. We were about to run out of fuel when the pilot called back and said, "Boys, get your parachutes on. I'm going up to about three thousand feet and I'll head the plane out towards the sea. We'll bail out and they'll pick us up." He started climbing higher and higher, got up a little ways, then said, "Hang on, boys, I'm going to try one more time, see if it'll come loose." He gave the plane a great big lurch and pressed the button—the bomb came loose. He quickly closed the bomb bay doors and we landed. We only had about four or five minutes of fuel left when we got back. That was about as close a call as you can have! Well, unless you call having your radio shot out a close call.

That happened while I was sitting on a bench seat in the back of the plane. A Jap Zero got through our formation and shot my radio, about a foot in front of me. It just destroyed the thing and punched a hole almost all the way through the plane. But those planes were tough: they flew when they shouldn't fly. I remember in March of '44, the Japs tried to retake Bougainville's Piva strip. We flew nine missions in three days: morning, noon, and afternoon, dropping hundred-pound scatter bombs on the Japs in the jungle. In January, February, and March of '44, I got sixty-five missions in those three months. A lot of it was kind of tough because we always had guys getting shot down. I watched my best friend—a boy from Milwaukee, Wisconsin—go into the jungle at the end of the runway on Bougainville.

In March of 1944, Allied forces had successfully encircled and neutralized Rabaul. More than a hundred thousand Japanese troops, one of the largest concentrations in the Pacific, would be bypassed and left to wither on the vine.

10 ★ ★ ★ ★ ★ ★

KWAJALEIN AND ENIWETOK

In January of 1944, the untested Fourth Marine Division departed the United States to spearhead the next phase of the central Pacific campaign. The division's main objective was the interconnected islands of Roi-Namur in the Kwajalein Atoll of the Marshall Islands. Small, flat, and littered with palm trees, Roi-Namur possessed an airfield strategic to neutralizing Japanese bases in the surrounding atoll. On January 31, 1944, a day before the invasion, Regimental Combat Team Twenty-Five disembarked to seize several neighboring islands.

Roy Earle, 96, Fourth Marine Division: I landed in the second wave on Albert Island with the Twenty-Fifth Marines. We set up a switchboard, then didn't need it because we overran the island so quickly. My God, we just shot across! It was a good-sized island, but not too big. I suppose, if you really tried, you could hurl a baseball from the lagoon to the sea. It had been a storage area for the Japs. One of our planes must have dropped a bomb near a warehouse because torpedoes lay scattered all over. We wanted to find Japs, but there weren't any. The rest of the Third Battalion landed on the next island over, Abraham, and they had the same thing; there was nobody there. All the Japs were on Roi-Namur.

The following day, on February 1, 1944, the main assault began.

Harold Rediske, 94, Fourth Marine Division: When our lieutenant went down the ramp on Namur, he was shot and killed. We had to jump over him to get out of the boat and get spread out. We went straight across the island and there was nothing there. We said, "Boy this is really a lark!"

James Boutin, 97, Fourth Marine Division: I had to go over the side of a Higgins boat, down into the surf on Roi. One guy fell into the water with a radio strapped to his back and couldn't get up—and he drowned. I wasn't very close with the radiomen, but I remember this guy. He was from Syracuse. His mother worked in a typewriter factory. I met her after the war and told her how her boy died. She thanked me. She was glad that he didn't suffer.

Anyway, we met resistance for the first few hours, but not for very long. Roi was an open airfield with tunnels dug underneath. I was carrying a Springfield '03 rifle because my unit didn't have the carbine yet. Every time something moved, I shot. That's where I got my first kill. Two Japs came out of a tunnel underneath the airfield. I was with three or four Marines, and we yelled, "Drop your weapons!" One of them did and one of them didn't. The Jap started raising his gun and I shot him. I was so proud of what I did! I went up there, and he had something sticking out of his pocket. It was a picture of a girl. I took it, some Japanese money, and his rifle. I felt sorry for the Japs sometimes, but it was them or us.

Kenneth Luttrell, 99, Fourth Marine Division: The primary thing I remember about the battle is a blockhouse blowing up. It was a storehouse for all the Japanese ammo on the island. An engineer threw a backpack full of explosives through a slot and blew the ammo up. We were maybe fifty yards from the beach when it blew and chunks of concrete as big as refrigerators or small automobiles were flying all over. Fortunately, we didn't get hit by one.

Roy Earle, 96, Fourth Marine Division: We were still on the island next door, and for about five minutes, we had to put our helmets back on because it was raining cement. We had to keep looking up and dodging pieces as they were coming down. It could have killed you!

Harold Rediske, 94, Fourth Marine Division: We got to the other side of Namur, and that's where we bivouacked for the first night. Every time a flare went up, it looked like the stumps were moving. All night long, we were shooting at those posts. They called us the "stump shooters" for a while. It gets pink when the sun comes up every morning, a beautiful pink color. But that morning, we heard a rooster crow. We thought, "How on earth could a rooster live under all that blasting?" It was a signal. Somebody hollered, "Here they come!"

The Japanese came running out of the water from Roi Island, screaming, and headed right for us. We could pick them off as they came, but there was just too darn many of them. One of the weapons we had was a twelve-gauge shotgun. At close range, a shotgun was a vicious machine. You don't have to aim it. You just point the gun and pulled the trigger; you'll hit somebody. The Japanese were screaming and hollering and waving swords. If anybody says they weren't afraid, they're lying.

Later that day, I crawled into a hole with seven wounded guys. The Japanese knew where we were and aimed a machine gun right down on us. Somebody had to do something, so I crawled out. There were a bunch of logs knocked down from the shelling, almost like they'd been mowed. I crawled through them and went back to the beach and gathered a bunch of Marines. Then we went out and got rid of that machine gun. Three of the wounded had to be carried—they couldn't make it—but the others were mobile.

At the time, I didn't know I was wounded. You get going on something like that and you don't pay attention to yourself. We went down to the evacuation area, and they said, "You're coming, too." I said, "No." They said, "Get in here!" I was bleeding all over the place, but I didn't go.

After the battle, my buddy came along carrying bottles of sake across his arms, like it was a load of wood. "You better have a drink, Ski." We hadn't eaten in seventy-two hours, so I took a big snort of that. I was happy and drunk when we headed for the ship. The sailors felt so sorry for me because of my wounds and helped me aboard. Then they laid me down on the operating table. The doctor came in, leaned over, sniffed, and said, "We don't have to give this guy any painkillers. He's already fixed up." I had shrapnel in my wrist, and my legs were full, too. The doctor had a silver dish on the floor. He'd drop shards in, and they'd go *clang!* I can still hear that. They went in my wrist and got the bullet out. It went through my canteen, but the cup slowed it down. If it hadn't been for that, it probably would have blown my hand off.*

---

* For his actions on Namur, Harold Rediske was awarded the Silver Star. The citation is listed in the appendix.

Roy Earle, 96, Fourth Marine Division: Within four or five days they put the Twenty-Third and the Twenty-Fourth Marines back on ships and they returned to the rest base. They left the Twenty-Fifth to secure the whole area and make sure no Japs were hiding. I never fired a shot because I was so busy with the telephone equipment. Then we went back to Hawaii and another group of Marines came in—*garrison troops.*

The Fourth Marine Division lost 313 men killed and 502 wounded during the battle. Some 3,500 Japanese lost their lives, sealed in bunkers, shot in spider holes, or cut down while moving between positions. The next objective in the Marshall Islands lay in the Eniwetok Atoll, northwest of Kwajalein. Similar in physical appearance to Roi-Namur, Eniwetok was defended by roughly 3,500 Japanese, entrenched in a series of bunkers and well-fortified positions on three main islands: Parry, Engebi, and Eniwetok. The Twenty-Second Marine Regiment, garrisoned in Hawaii, was tasked with the landings in conjunction with two United States Army battalions.

Donn Thompson, 95, Twenty-Second Marine Regiment: On January 3, 1944, we left for the assault on the Marshall Islands aboard the USS *President Monroe*. Those ships were refitted to take troops because they were originally cargo vessels. We were down in the hold on bunks, five high, hung by chains and made of canvas. I was a non-smoking, non-drinking Marine; not that I thought I was better than anyone else, I just didn't care about it. If you went down into the hold of the ship, the airflow was not good, so you can imagine trying to sleep in all that smoke. Once I went aboard ship, I always put my equipment down there, then went topside.

February 17 was D-Day for Eniwetok Atoll. We landed on Engebi Island. If you ever want to see a wonderful July Fourth celebration, with all the fireworks, watch some battlewagons and cruisers fire their big guns. The ships would jump back on each shot and flames would come flying out: blue, green, everything. The Navy said, "Don't worry, guys, there won't be anybody alive when we get through!" The night before, the Navy always fed us liver because that had a tendency, so we were told, to coagulate wounds if we were hit. Whether it was true or not, I don't know.

We got ready in the predawn hours and planned to land at eight o'clock in the morning. We had to go over the side, down hemp ropes, into the landing craft. You had to be very careful because the rope was always wet. The ships were going up and down and the Higgins boats were going up and down, too. A lot of guys around me were scared to death. I thought, *If you start getting scared, you're going to lose sight of what we were trained to do—which is to stay alive and get rid of the enemy.* That was basically my philosophy. Why? I don't know. I just had that.

When we first landed and hit the shore, one of my buddies, who was right near me, got hit in the chest and I thought it killed him. But later on I found out that the bullet went through his body, out his back, and barely missed his heart. Moving inland we saw a chicken with no feathers; the concussion had blown the feathers right off. I thought, *Somebody's going to have you for lunch today.* I was lucky on Engebi. At one point, I walked down a trail and, a little while later, a buddy of mine from Missouri walked down the same trail. He stepped on a land mine, and it blew his leg off from the knee down. The fighting on that island was unique because it was from shell hole to shell hole. At night, the destroyers would come in and fire flares connected to parachutes. Because of the motion of the shadows, you always thought someone was sneaking up on you. It was kind of eerie.

After securing the island the next day, we were pulled off.

They said we were going to Parry, which was right next door. The fighting there was almost on top of each other. The Navy thought the cruisers and battlewagons would destroy the enemy, but the Japanese still came out from under their coconut log bunkers. They were pretty shaken up, but it hadn't killed them. Seeing people get killed—I don't like that feeling, but I never got upset about it. In fact, there was one officer who was killed right near where I was. His last name was Blood (which is a phenomenal thing). He had a beautiful wife and two young children, and I thought to myself, *They don't know that their dad is gone.* That hit me a little. But the rest of the time, I didn't get that upset; you can't. Someone might say, "You're too calloused, Donn." That's not true. I'm a very sentimental guy, but I wouldn't allow myself to be sentimental on those occasions.

Robert Rakestraw, 100, Twenty-Second Marine Regiment: I was in the regimental band, so our job was to dig a ring of foxholes around Headquarters Company every night. Then my buddy and I would take turns staying awake. But during the daytime, I had another job: we would go looking for Marines that had been killed by shells and were covered over with dirt. People would recount when the Marine got hit, and our assignment was to go searching for their bodies near where the shell had dropped.

One time, my buddy and I were digging when a mortar shell fell thirty or forty feet from us. It didn't cause any damage, but we sure ran back to Headquarters Company! That's the closest I ever got to being injured. But at night, we'd hear bullets zinging by. Somebody was shooting at us—*snipers*. But they never hit us. We never kept any lights on; wouldn't dare smoke or anything. Another job we did: the engineers would dig a trench and we'd haul the dead Japs over, then stuff them inside so they could be recovered after the war.

Donn Thompson, 95, Twenty-Second Marine Regiment: We came off Parry Island, and the next day was my birthday. I spent it aboard the USS *President Monroe*, which had originally brought us down there. We transferred to the USS *Neville* and left for Pearl Harbor. On March 4 and 5, travelling in the great calm of the Pacific Ocean, the water was like a plate of glass. You could see little flying fish coming up in the distance.

In the following weeks, select units from the Twenty-Second Marine Regiment and elements of the Fifth Amphibious Reconnaissance Company would continue the conquest of the Marshall Islands as part of Operation Flintlock Jr.

Loyd Brandt, 98, Fifth Amphibious Reconnaissance Company: In the Marshall Islands, we reconned thirty-four islands in twenty-three days. For most of them, we went in by rubber boat at night. But on a couple we went in before the infantry. The one I remember the best: We were transferred into an amphibious tank, then we drove down into the water through an LST's big front doors. Suddenly, the motor quit. We floated over to where an American heavy cruiser was shelling and got caught right under that cruiser's guns. Three eight-inchers fired all at once and it almost submerged our tank, just from the concussion. It pushed us down so fast that water was coming over the sides. We had to take our helmets off to bail to keep from sinking. The coxswain finally got the tank's motor started, and we went on into the island. That was pretty chilling. We all couldn't hear for a couple of days after that.

Faris Tuohy, 96, Twenty-Second Marine Regiment: I don't like to get into the blood and guts of it because I wind up in tears, but one island from that period that I remember was named Ailinglaplap. It didn't amount to much. My group also looked over the island of Bikini—wasn't anybody there but the natives. One interesting thing happened: We were waiting on the beach for our boats to pick us up. And we waited. And we waited. Then we saw this pregnant native woman walk by, carrying a big basket on her head. She disappeared into the coconut grove, and we didn't think anything of it. She came back six or seven hours later with two big green coconuts in the basket and a baby wrapped up in her lavalava skirt; she'd had a baby while we were waiting.

One of the last islands we fought on was the main Japanese headquarters, with a big coconut grove on it. The naval gunfire played havoc with the Japanese emplacements and knocked down hundreds of coconut trees. The scuttlebutt was that all the coconut trees belonged to the Lever Brothers British soap company. As the story goes, we had to pay for every coconut tree we knocked down. I don't know if there's any truth to it or not—but it was all on fire. The coconut leaves dried for two or three days, and the naval guns just set it ablaze. When the fighting was over, once again, we were laying on the beach, counting our numbers, and seeing who got wounded. After a while, an Army unit landed. Their commanding officer came up to us, pointed to the island, all on fire, and said, "My God, you didn't leave us much!"

After one of the battles, we went back to the ship, climbed up the rope ladder, got to the railing, and two Coast Guardsmen helped us over. Then everybody went down to the sleeping deck, threw their gear on a cot, and moved down to the galley and tried to get some coffee. One of the photographers was running around and took a picture of me and two other guys. I've got both hands around a big ole white mug of coffee. Steve Garboski is across from me, with his shirt off, with a third Marine we never knew. That picture made such an impression on people: We're filthy, we're unshaven, we're nasty and dirty; we're pretty near the end of our rope. It's odd to think about it. My mother wrote me and said that that picture was blown up in tremendous size and was hanging in Grand Central Station in New York City. We were just ragged and worn out, scared to death and sad from losing friends.

The final tally for American losses in the Eniwetok Atoll amounted to more than one thousand killed, wounded, or missing. The Japanese garrison, in contrast, was virtually annihilated. Just over a hundred defenders, many of them Korean laborers, surrendered to American forces. Once secured, naval construction units, known as the Seabees, splashed ashore in the Marshall Islands and went to work scraping out airfields across the scarred landscape. When a workable landing strip was completed, Marine Corps aviators populated the island to fly antisubmarine, reconnaissance, and air cover missions over various enemy-controlled locations across the atoll.

Jonathan de Sola Mendes, 102, VMSB-151: We were ordered to fly three thousand miles from American Samoa to the Eniwetok Atoll with a squadron of twenty-four planes. We made it in three or four days and were stationed there. Engebi Island was a piece of dirt, just over a mile across. There was nothing there but sand and blasted out trees from the bombings. We had tents set up to live in and we flew daily antisubmarine patrols. But we never found any submarines. I only found one and it turned out to be an American! Hell, we never even saw a Japanese aircraft.

At the very beginning they did come over and bomb us at night and did a little bit of damage. One bomb landed so close to my foxhole that it collapsed. But I didn't get hurt. The boredom of patrolling the sea-lanes daily and not finding anything—it was just a boring experience.

11 ★ ★ ★ ★ ★ ★

SAIPAN, TINIAN, AND GUAM

In the winter and spring of 1944, American aircraft carriers launched a series of raids on Japanese bases in the central Pacific, preparatory to a major landing in the Mariana Islands. Capture of the Marianas would place American heavy bombers within range of mainland Japan in a vital step toward the reduction of Japanese industry. Assault plans were devised and set for the summer of 1944: The Second Marine Division, the Fourth Marine Division, and the Army's Twenty-Seventh Infantry Division would land on the island of Saipan on June 15, 1944, while the Third Marine Division, the First Provisional Marine Brigade, and the Army's Seventy-Seventh Infantry Division hit Guam on June 16. But just days before departure, in the early morning hours of May 21, 1944, a series of LSTs filled with equipment exploded under mysterious circumstances in Pearl Harbor, Hawaii.

Burt Withee, 95, Second Marine Division: The LSTs started blowing up—*it was a mess*. We jumped into the water and one guy was yelling that he was drowning. I grabbed him and I said, "You can't drown, you've got a goddamn life jacket on! Get onto the raft." There were guys all over in the water. They didn't publicize the story because that was before the landing

> on Saipan, and they didn't want the Japs to know we were in trouble. It took a lot of troops out of action and destroyed a lot of our landing craft. We were shorthanded going into Saipan. I spent three days in the hospital after that. We used to listen to Tokyo Rose, and she would call us "her poor orphans from the Second Marine Division." That night she said, "My poor orphans from the Second Marine Division. After what happened at West Loch . . ." She knew all about it. She said, "The Second Marine Division will be able to hold roll call in a telephone booth."

An estimated six LSTs were destroyed, and 163 men were killed, in what would become known as the "West Loch Disaster." No clear cause of the explosion has ever been determined; some sources point to Japanese sabotage, while others cite a carelessly discarded cigarette. Despite the catastrophe in Hawaii, American leaders elected to proceed with the operation. D-Day on Saipan was set for June 15, 1944. Two Marine divisions, the Second and Fourth, would land abreast on a series of beaches on the western side of the island, while the Army's Twenty-Seventh Division waited offshore in reserve (they would land the following day).

Saipan itself emerged from the ocean in a series of jutting peaks, softened by layers of dense jungle, surrounded by an expansive patchwork of flat cane fields. From the high ground, the defenders possessed a commanding view of the landing zones and preregistered the area with devastating artillery and mortar fire. Inland from the waterline, pillboxes and sniper positions speckled the marsh-strewn landscape, creating a network of intricate defenses. Some units would face the prospect of urban combat, securing the town of Charan Kanoa and its sugar factory beyond Blue Beach One and Two. Unlike Bougainville or Guadalcanal, American planners intended to avoid a prolonged campaign by swiftly seizing all forty-six square miles of the island. The first waves ground ashore under a hail of fire at 0840.

Burt Withee, 95, Second Marine Division: I'll never forget when we landed: we were somewhere between the second and third wave. That was a nasty deal because we had to go over a coral reef, which was five hundred yards out from the beach. Of course, the Japs were zeroed in on the reef, so the minute our tractors stuck their nose up, they started taking fire. We were lucky that they missed us. Boy, some of the tractors took terrible shots! A lot of the guys had to wade or swim in because their tractors got shot up. There were a lot of wounded too, mostly from shrapnel. There was a lot of it floating around—I mean *a lot* of shrapnel. You could hear it whistling and whirring.

Anthony DeMarco, 98, Second Marine Division: The ramp dropped down and we dashed out into the ocean and the water depth was chest high as we hurried to the beach. In spite of the heavy gunfire, we made it to Green Beach One, as shown on the invasion map while on the ship's deck. We hunched down and fired at anything that moved; hand grenades were thrown into houses, through windows and doors.

Clyde Lacquement, 95, Second Marine Division: Our lieutenant was a greenhorn, and our sergeant was an old-timer. After we landed, they both started up a clear alley in the shrubs. We were going to follow them, but the lieutenant and the sergeant were both shot right there. One of our other sergeants was put in charge and we didn't have a lieutenant the whole time.

Burt Withee, 95, Second Marine Division: Guys were going back and forth all along the beach yelling, "Where's Third

Battalion?" "Where's I Company?" trying to get reorganized. If the Japs had come down and hit us then, we would have been swept back out into the sea. But they waited until that night, and it was too late. That night, we wiped them out. We were already settled in.

Dean Ladd, 101, Second Marine Division: That first night I was ordered to take out a reconnaissance patrol and find the unit to our right. We had a gap between our line with the adjacent regiment—*a big gap*. I took two men with me. As it was getting dark, we went down a couple hundred yards or more. But nobody was there. We passed an air raid shelter going back, and a Japanese came running out at us. I backed up, but something tripped me. I fell over. The guys behind me shot and killed the Japanese. That night, back at our position, we had a couple others almost step in our foxholes.

Melvin Gribble, 95, Fifth Amphibious Reconnaissance Battalion: We tried to keep the Japs as far away from us as we could. But at night, you never knew how far away they really were. Hand-to-hand combat—that's bad business. We'd always sleep two guys together; one guy would stay awake all the time. I got pretty close to hand-to-hand combat one night when a Jap snuck up with a knife to kill us. But he didn't make it. Two of my buddies were there and they knifed him.

Charles Pase, 99, Second Marine Division: One night, I was in the machine gun foxhole, looking for potential targets. I'd been on guard for . . . I don't know how long at that point. I dozed off and—*suddenly*—I felt cold steel pressed against my back. I yelled and whirled, thinking a Jap was going to stab me. But it was a big land crab! They have claws like daggers, and I thought it was a bayonet! I yelled so loud that the whole company heard. Boy, did they kid me! They said, "Don't let the crabs get close to Corporal Pase!"

Harold Rediske, 94, Fourth Marine Division: We went out on patrol and started going through some heavy timber and brush. I could see a big log—and a Jap was looking over the top, bobbing up and down like a turkey. The kid with me said, "Let me shoot him! Let me shoot him!" So, I handed him the BAR. The next time the Jap peeked up, he shot—*bbbrrrppp!* The tracers glanced off the Jap's head and the kid said, "They're bouncing off his head! They're bouncing off his head!" But when we got up there, that guy didn't have any head left.

Wallace "Wally" Hamlin, 99, Second Marine Division: I was on a patrol with one of those groups. The Japanese were dug into the hills. You couldn't get at them to shoot them. We'd find a spot, then just throw hand grenades into their hole.

Charles Pase, 99, Second Marine Division: We had to sweep cane fields to flush out any Japs. They were burying themselves under fallen cane, waiting for a chance to kill somebody. We had to make a line, close together, then we'd move forward. We caught quite a few Japanese that way.

Howell Wheaton, 100, Second Marine Division: They kept me busy stringing telephone wire and dodging damned snipers. That was a big problem for me, personally. I had to traipse back to battalion headquarters or one of the other companies; and we soon realized they'd bypassed a bunch of snipers. I escaped them—but they were there.

Melvin Gribble, 95, Fifth Amphibious Reconnaissance Battalion: Those Japs were a funny race of people. They'd get up in a tree and tie themselves in as a sniper. Then you'd shoot them, and they'd be hanging there by one leg. I've seen a lot of them hanging. I never could figure out why they did it that way, but that's the way they did it.

Augustus Rogers, 100, Fourth Marine Division: I was climbing up a tree, trying to string communication wire, when I got shot by a sniper. I landed on the wire spool and broke my elbow. Two guys rushed over and picked me up; my buddies wanted to help me as much as they could. They carried me back and I remember getting aboard a hospital ship. When I woke up in the morning, I was laying with my arms tied to the ceiling in traction.

Frank Smith, 100, Fourth Marine Division: I was delivering a message to regimental headquarters when the Japanese laid down an artillery barrage that caught me. I was hit mostly in the stomach area and the hip. It was minor—they didn't even put me in the hospital or anything.

James Boutin, 97, Fourth Marine Division: The captain called me up and said, "I want you to go down to shore. We have a boat coming in with the rest of our equipment." I went down to the beach and all hell broke loose; we came under heavy mortar and artillery fire. Everybody was running all over the place, and I got blown up by a mortar and spent nine months in the hospital.

Burt Withee, 95, Second Marine Division: Pretty soon, you get wary about doing anything. Orders would come down and you'd be pretty apprehensive. But you had to do your duty. The thing about combat was, as scared as you were, you'd see somebody else being brave and you'd think: *Hell, if he can do it,*

I can do it. That carried a lot of guys through combat, because things could get pretty nasty.

Melvin Gribble, 95, Fifth Amphibious Reconnaissance Battalion: After a while, you get to thinking that you're not going to get out alive anyway, so you get over being scared. Pretty soon, you decide that you're just alive until you die. That's all.

Harold Rediske, 94, Fourth Marine Division: I never thought about it. If it was my time, it was my time. Why worry about it?

Clyde Lacquement, 95, Second Marine Division: I was in a squad on a 60mm mortar. We were at least thirty yards behind the lines. So, in all that time, I didn't get a scratch. I think that was a big element in not getting hit.

Burt Withee, 95, Second Marine Division: It comes down to circumstance and luck. A lot of people discount luck, but as a lot of the guys used to say, "I'd rather be lucky than good."

Marvin Strombo, 95, Second Marine Division: Martin Dyer knew he was going to die. When we got to Saipan, he put his arm on me and said, "I ain't gonna make it. But I enjoyed my time taking this little ocean cruise with you." One day our lieutenant called him up and told him to take a squad down into a little valley. There were some Japanese seen there. That's where he got killed. I didn't see that happen, but I heard about it right away. It kinda hurt because we got along so good. He told me things he wouldn't tell anyone else. And he knew he was going to die. And I don't care what you say, if you know you're going to die and you still go—that takes a lot of courage. You have to be awful brave.

Burt Withee, 95, Second Marine Division: There were some guys willing to "stick their neck out," so to speak. For example: We were in trouble one time, so we called up a tank to help us. The tank came up and our leader said, "Somebody's gotta tell the tank commander where to fire." The tanks had phones in the back, on the rear, in little cabinets. This one guy broke out, ran over there, got that telephone, and coordinated the attack. Then the tank wiped out the Japanese.

He did a real good job.

Dean Ladd, 101, Second Marine Division: My luck ran out when I was wounded on top of Mount Tapochau. That was an awful close call. We had three of our own 155mm Long Toms accidentally get called in on top of us. They didn't think we could possibly be that far out. But we were. One round hit the tree I was under. Had it not hit the tree, I would have been pulverized. One of the other rounds landed near the unit that I'd been in as an enlisted man. The only reason I recognized one of the dead Marines was by his glasses. Only reason I knew who it was. I recognized his glasses.

I was in the aid station for about two days. But a big Japanese counterattack hit us, and all walking wounded were released. We had to go back up because there were about four thousand Japanese killed in the fighting. We had to bury all the bodies—*four thousand*. They were all chewed up by artillery fire. Someone dug a big trench, then we dragged them all in. It took the better part of a day. Can you imagine the stinking mess that was? Flies everywhere, *maggots*. The same day we were doing that, I went back to get my arm dressed and walked through an area that had three Japanese hiding in a bush. I looked back—and they were alive. I killed them all. That night forty more were killed from that same area. I'd walked through a whole group! They were going to let me go through so they could attack that night.

On July 7, 1944, the Japanese launched the largest banzai charge of the war and lost more than four thousand men in under forty-eight hours. After the battle, Marines and soldiers advanced north, destroying additional pockets of resistance, and extracting civilians from the battlefield. Incited by propaganda that suggested US troops were rapists and murderers, a small portion of the population—primarily Japanese immigrants relocated to Saipan prior to the war—fled toward the island's tip at Marpi Point.

Dean Ladd, 101, Second Marine Division: Right after that battle, we did a mop-up, and each company probably killed fifty to one hundred—*just in the mop-up*. They were still hiding away all over. They weren't going to surrender.

Roy Earle, 98, Fourth Marine Division: They did not surrender, nor did we take prisoners. The Fourth was noted for that fact. Think about this for a minute: You're moving out and you run into the enemy. You have a firefight, and some of the Japs want to give up. Where are you going to put them? They wanted to die for the Emperor, and we wanted to help.

Harold Rediske, 94, Fourth Marine Division: There were some, when we were up on the line, that *would* take prisoners. But it would take a guide to get them back, out of the way. The guides would get over a hill or out of sight, then they'd come back pretty quick. They'd say, "Them buggers tried to get away from us, so we shot 'em." Rather than walk all the way to headquarters, then come back again, they'd just get out of sight and shoot them! I couldn't stand that.

Burt Withee, 95, Second Marine Division: Some guys would see a dead Jap, go over, get a pair of pliers, smack them across the face to loosen the teeth, then start pulling out the gold. I never could stomach that. But guys did it. They kept jars and socks full of gold teeth. In combat, there was a certain class of guy that just let everything go. Nothing was too bad; nothing was too violent, ugly, dirty, or nasty to do. Combat gave you the excuse to do whatever you wanted to do, and some guys took that liberty. But most of the guys wanted to get in there, get it done, get it over with, and get out.

Keith Tucker, 100, Second Marine Division: I did see that. They'd take an entrenching tool, stick it in their mouth, then flip them over on their back, hit them a few times; knock their teeth out. I wouldn't have done that if there were thousand-dollar bills coming out of their mouth. But some of those guys were that way.

Melvin Gribble, 95, Fifth Amphibious Reconnaissance Battalion: I didn't want any part in crap like that. It wasn't the right thing to do.

Marvin Strombo, 95, Second Marine Division: I could never do that.

Wallace "Wally" Hamlin, 99, Second Marine Division: I think they went overboard. Of course, the Japanese weren't any better; they were just as bad to the American troops.

Dean Ladd, 101, Second Marine Division: One of the lieutenants in our battalion had been an ambulance driver with the Eighth Army in North Africa. One day the Japanese came out with a white flag. Like a fool, he stood up, went out there, and was going to receive them. His men kept yelling, "Don't do that! Don't do that!" He got killed by a sniper.

Harold Rediske, 94, Fourth Marine Division: I was standing there once, and I happened to look down. Out of the corner of my eye, I saw a Jap move his eyes. He was playing dead. I told Selby, "That guy's alive!" Selby said, "The heck! Yes, he is!" He took a carbine, stuck it right down on the guy's head, and pulled the trigger.

Dean Ladd, 101, Second Marine Division: Then the bodies would start swelling in the hot weather. Within a short time, you'd have maggots in there.

Keith Tucker, 100, Second Marine Division: It was their diet or something. They rotted three times quicker than anybody else. They turned yellow and bloated up. But that wasn't any worse than when we went back to some of our cemeteries.

Harold Rediske, 94, Fourth Marine Division: I've seen a lot of people pull bodies out and sit on them and eat their lunch. That was pretty common. They were laying all over.

Keith Tucker, 100, Second Marine Division: Usually we'd see civilians after the artillery worked over a mountainside. When everything cleared, whoever didn't get killed came pouring out of the caves; civilians, carrying kids. God, they were thirsty. We tried to give them water. The women crouched in mudholes and washed the kids off—*terrible.*

Clyde Lacquement, 95, Second Marine Division: I looked into a cave and there was a teenager inside. He wasn't dressed as a soldier and didn't have a weapon. I said, "Come on." By the time I got down to the valley, my guys had all moved out. I knew the direction they were going, and I started after them. Pretty soon, here comes my corporal looking for me. He didn't treat the prisoner as nice as I did. The guy acted like he was really weak, but my corporal jammed a gun in his ribs, and he livened up.

Harold Rediske, 94, Fourth Marine Division: We came to one cave—and it was full of young girls. They were all wounded or hurt really bad. This one girl had her leg blown off; just had a stump for a leg. We were still about half a mile from a medical center, so we picked all the girls up and carried them down. They fixed them up there.

Keith Tucker, 100, Second Marine Division: The civilians were coming down by the hundreds. We were helping them get into the trucks to haul them back. This Marine I knew spotted a pretty decent ring on a woman's hand. He grabbed ahold of her and said, "Wait just a minute." He wanted that ring. But I could see tears coming down the woman's face, so I said, "Joe, for God's sake, don't even think about it." After taking a second to think, he told the woman, "Go ahead, get on the truck." He thanked me for it later. He said, "I don't know what I was thinking."

Harold Rediske, 94, Fourth Marine Division: We had men clear across the island, in a steady stream, moving ahead together. The island comes to a point and there's a sheer cliff at the end. There were a lot of families there—*and women*—but they were told all kinds of junk about what would happen if they were picked up or surrendered to the Americans. We had a loudspeaker on a jeep, talking in their native tongue, telling them that we'd take care of them. Some civilians bought it;

some of them surrendered. But there were a lot more that didn't. Women would throw their babies over the cliff, then they would jump in after them. They had the babies wrapped in these beautiful white little dresses. It looked like birds, fluttering down. They wouldn't stop; we were begging them to stop. There were Japanese soldiers in among the families, but we didn't dare shoot at them. We just had to take it. There was a path down to the waterline and a bunch of civilians took ahold of each other's hands and walked right out into the ocean and disappeared. The undertow was so strong that when the waves went back in, you couldn't swim against it. So, they just got carried on out to sea. I'll never forget it.

Roy Earle, 98, Fourth Marine Division: You know what the Japs told the civilians? That the Marine Corps was the meanest fighting force in the world; that we were so tough that we had to kill our father and mother to get in. Can you imagine? The women certainly weren't going to fall prey to that kind of vicious character, so they jumped off the cliffs and killed themselves. And if they had children, they threw their children over and killed them, too. We had guys that spoke Japanese on a loudspeaker, talking to them; telling them we'd take care of them. Nope, they decided to go off.

Burt Withee, 95, Second Marine Division: That was—that was bad. That was a bad scene. You'd see native women: they'd throw their babies over the cliff, and they'd jump in after them. Oh, that was terrible! That was horrible! Oh, God! At one end of the island, we had compounds where we were feeding them. They were getting excellent care, and we were giving them medical treatment, clothing, and food. At the other end, they were jumping off the cliffs and killing themselves. The Japs had told them that we were going to do bad things to the women. God, that broke my heart. I watched a woman throw a baby over—oh, God!

Roughly eight hundred civilians jumped to their deaths or drowned at Marpi Point in the final days of the battle. More than three thousand Americans and roughly twenty-seven thousand Japanese were killed in combat. With the island declared secure, the Marines descended toward the beach and prepared to invade a small, ten-and-a-half-mile-long island southwest of Saipan called Tinian.

Roy Earle, 98, Fourth Marine Division: We had to walk fourteen miles back to the beach, after fighting all that time. We didn't march back, we walked, with a group on each side of the road. When we got to the bottom, we thought maybe we were going back to a rest base in Hawaii—*wrong!* The officers said that Tinian was only three miles across the water, so might as well take it too. The "powers that be" decided that the Fourth Division would go in first and the rest would come in as a supporting force.

Around that time, someone came by and said they needed somebody to volunteer for kitchen duty. We'd been living on K rations (which are for the birds), so I shoved my hand up and said, "Yeah, I'll help." I was on juice duty, pouring orange juice. I would pour a couple of glasses—then I'd pour a glass for myself. A couple more glasses for the officers—then one for me. I don't know how many glasses I drank, but I hadn't had anything like that since we'd left our rest base in Hawaii. They had powdered eggs, too. Every time I put food on an officer's plate, I put some on for me. Boy, I stuffed myself! I finally went back to my unit, and we got ready to go.

We boarded an LVT, but they put so many people on that the thing was riding really low in the water. All the exhaust fumes started flowing down onto the deck, around where we were standing. It didn't take much of that before I was sick as a dog. Oh my God! They'd given us all three hand grenades, packed in round six-inch-high tubes. I took the grenades out, hung them on my belt, and puked into the tube.

When I filled it up, I put the top back on and threw it over the side. But I was still sick, so I got a second one out—filled it. Got the third one out—filled it. The guys around me saw what was happening and volunteered their tubes. Obviously, when we got to the beach, I was as weak as could be. We went over the sides of the boat, and I was able to make it ashore. A sergeant said to me, "Come on, grab that drum of wire." The wire's eighty-five pounds, with a rod jammed through the middle for carrying. He had one end, and I had the other. But I only made it two or three steps before I fell. I got up, made another two or three steps, then fell again. He said, "What's the matter with you?" I said, "I was on mess duty last night and I hadn't eaten since we left the rest base and I stuffed myself. It all came up on the boat." He said, "Oh, my God! No wonder!" Then he said, "Look back to our left, there's a small pillbox. We just cleared that out. There's a downstairs: If you go in, down the steps, there's nothing in there. Go and sleep it off and we'll take care of this. As soon as you get up, get back here, and join us. You're no good to us as you are right now." So, I went over there, went down the steps, and found a big wide room inside. I went into the corner, took my helmet and pack off, and fell asleep right away. I must have slept for the entire night.

By the time I woke up, I was just about better. I put all my stuff on again, went back up, and tried to find my guys. But I didn't know where they were—there was nobody from my unit around. I finally found them and one of the guys said, "Where have you been?" I said, "In there," and pointed back towards the pillbox. He said, "Oh, you missed all the fun!"

I said, "What was that?" He said, "The Japs attacked us last night in a banzai." Apparently, in the middle of the night, the Japanese came roaring down in a banzai charge—but we were ready, and we slaughtered them. The fella said they counted some 790 bodies, just in front of our outfit. But I missed the whole thing!

Roughly 1,241 Japanese bodies were recovered the following day, strung over barbed wire, mutilated by shrapnel and small arms fire. The engagement cost fewer than one hundred Marine casualties. Joined by the Second Marine Division, infantry units continued across the island to eradicate the final vestiges of Japanese resistance.

Dean Ladd, 101, Second Marine Division: When we moved out the next day, there was an open field covered with shell holes. The Japanese occupied the position and could have shot us. But they didn't. We'd get twenty yards away and they'd just blow themselves up with a hand grenade; rather than shoot, they'd blow themselves up. Hundreds did that. We formed a skirmish line on the way up—*WHAM! WHAM! WHAM!*—and had very few casualties. We couldn't believe that they'd do that. But they weren't about to be captured.

I was a company commander then and we had orders to take a ridge. That was a scary situation. As we approached, one Japanese blew himself up. His body went sailing seventy-five feet in the air. Boy, he went sky high! But it was a rough night on the ridge. The Japanese got through our lines and came in all around us. It was a scary night. My radioman was killed. He got called back to help lay telephone line. He said, "I'll meet you down at the CP, if I don't get my head shot off." Well, he did—he died.

Charles Pase, 99, Second Marine Division: There were caves on the south end of the island; a sad, sad thing. Women and children and old men—civilians—occupied those caves, alongside the Japanese Army. Somehow the civilians learned that they would be allowed to live if they came peacefully back to our lines. I don't know how many, perhaps one hundred or more, women and children, tried to join us. But the Japanese killed *every* one that tried to reach our lines. Women and children! And a few old men! When that happened, there was no mercy shown to the Japs in those caves. I think we killed every damn one of them.

Dean Ladd, 101, Second Marine Division: We were on a cliff overlooking the Japanese and delivered an ultimatum: By a certain hour, if they didn't surrender, we were going to let them have it. They wouldn't budge. We fired mortars and machine guns at them, and they all jumped off. It was an entirely different situation. At that time, we considered them nothing more than just an animal, I guess. Odd, isn't it?

Harold Rediske, 94, Fourth Marine Division: We classified them as animals; animals that you'd trap or something. There was a place on Tinian where the ocean kept beating against the cliff and created a cave, way back inside. At low tide, there was a path that went down into the cave. I and another guy were laying there watching the path when, all of a sudden, seven Japs came up like ducks in a row. We started shooting—they fell dead or just jumped off, down into the ocean. We had target practice with them! That was the only time where I actually knew I was shooting someone. After that, we decided that we'd better get out of there because we could hear—*Fweeet! Fweeet! Fweeet!*—bullets going through the leaves.

Burt Withee, 95, Second Marine Division: The day after the island was declared secured, we were encamped on a plateau, when about one or two hundred Japs hit us that morning. It was a bad scene, a lot of guys got hurt.

Larry Pressley, 96, Fourth Marine Division: When it was over, we went down to the coast. Someone said that all the ships in the harbor were for the Fourth Division to go back to their home base in Hawaii. I'd just come from there as a replacement. But they transferred all the new guys to the Second Division instead. That's where I got my break: if I'd stayed in the Fourth Division, my next battle would have been Iwo Jima. Instead, the Second went to Saipan and built a camp there. That was our home for the rest of the war.

Due to extended Japanese resistance on Saipan and the beginning of the Battle of the Philippine Sea offshore, the invasion of Guam was rescheduled for July 21, 1944. The largest island in the Marianas group, Guam stretched thirty miles in length and possessed a series of airfields, harbors, and facilities vital to the planned air offensives against the Japanese homeland. The Third Marine Division and the First Provisional Marine Brigade would land on separate beaches flanking the Orote Peninsula, while the Army's Seventy-Seventh Infantry Division waited in reserve. The day of invasion dawned beautiful and sunny, but soon clouded over with a gray din from the preinvasion bombardment. The landings began at 0808.

Frank Wright, 96, Third Marine Division: When the Raiders broke up, I was transferred into the Third Division as a squad leader with the Twenty-First Marines. That was my first big landing with a large group. We started out in LSTs, but as we got closer to Guam, there was a coral reef. We had to transfer over to an amtrac and landed in an open area with coconut trees all around. There weren't too many Japanese because we landed near the edge of a rice field. We were fired at when we passed through the open. I remember a water buffalo standing in the middle of the field, just chewing away, with mortars landing all around it.

Louis Bourgault, 97, Third Marine Division: I hated to be under mortar fire or artillery fire. We got pinned down by knee mortars when we first went ashore, down on the beach. For twenty minutes, I just hugged the damned ground, trying to make myself melt into the dirt. They were pounding the hell out of us with mortars. But artillery—*Jesus, God!*—that scared the hell out of me.

Jack Rasmussen, 94, Third Marine Division: On the way in, three guys in my unit were killed: the lieutenant, the company commander, and the platoon commander. All three were dead right off the bat, which was heartbreaking.

Donn Thompson, 95, First Provisional Marine Brigade: The only reason I'm still here today is because the amtrac driver saw what was happening on the landing beach and decided to go one hundred yards south, so we could go in where it was protected.

John Marx, 97, Third Marine Division: We had to go up this hill and it was completely covered in brush. You could hardly climb up it. The Japanese were rolling hand grenades down, and a guy named Clayton Kubu from Jersey got his foot blown off. As he went down the hill, he yelled, "I'm going home!" I couldn't get up there with my machine gun, so I crawled back down. I told two other guys, "I'm gonna find a way up this hill."

I saw a little trail and said, "You guys want to follow me?" They said, "Yes." I went up and opened fire. The Japanese scattered—or what was left of them. There was an article in the *Chico Record* that said I had killed nineteen Japanese. But I don't know who would have gone out and counted them. I think that's mostly baloney. You don't go out counting the enemy and I'm sure they don't count you.

Frank Wright, 96, Third Marine Division: That night, we set up camp above the rice paddies. We had our first banzai attack. They came in between our company and P Company. We lost quite a few guys—and I learned how to fight with my bayonet.

Jack Rasmussen, 94, Third Marine Division: It's better when everyone's firing because you don't necessarily feel like you killed anybody. Some guys take all the credit, but that isn't the way it is.

Chuck Meacham, 96, First Provisional Marine Brigade: You don't even think about killing. How would you like someone running at you with a bayonet? It was just instinct.

Donn Thompson, 95, First Provisional Marine Brigade: You're trained to do your job, and that's what you do.

Louis Bourgault, 97, Third Marine Division: I was back at the Battalion CP when we were overrun. They were all around us. Some were coming up this little draw behind us and we killed three or four of them. One was an officer. This kid saw his saber and jumped up to grab the souvenir—*crack!* He got a bullet right through the mouth.

John Marx, 97, Third Marine Division: They came down a valley that night and I could hear them, but I couldn't see them. They would have seen my silhouette if I raised my gun up, so I took two hand grenades and threw them. Neither one of them went off. Somebody said, "You didn't pull the pins!" I said, "Here's the pins! They just didn't go off!"

Chuck Meacham, 96, First Provisional Marine Brigade: In the early morning, it got really bad. We took a full battalion straight at us. The next morning, I think the official count was four-hundred-and-some dead. We had eighty Japanese laying around us. We lost so many people that we had to fix up the company. It was really decimated. Anyhow, we stopped them. The commander, Colonel Shapley, said if we hadn't held Hill 40, they would have kicked our ass off the beach.

Frank Wright, 96, Third Marine Division: Around the fourth night, we had another banzai attack. I shot two clips of ammunition, but I couldn't load fast enough so I started fighting with my bayonet. I got stuck in the stomach by a Jap, and I fell backwards into my foxhole. A nearby Marine shot the Jap, but he fell down on top of me. I stuck my knife up through his throat and killed him. He laid on top of me all night—and bled on me. I guess everybody thought I was dead.

The banzai attack went through our company lines and down to the beach. All the wounded were carried down the hill the next morning. I was still walking, but there was a hole in my stomach from the bayonet. A corpsman came up, patched the hole, and put sulfur on the wound. There weren't too many of us left, so I decided to stay with my squad. We went over to Agat and ran into a lot of pillboxes. A friend of mine, Lieutenant Leonard, found a pillbox and cleaned it out all by himself with hand grenades and a carbine. Lieutenant Leonard got killed—but I think he received the Silver Star for his actions.

My wound was bleeding quite profusely. One of the guys saw it and hollered, "Corpsman!" A corpsman came up, cleaned it out, took some heavy tape, and taped it together. That's what the first guy should have done—tape the hole together. But he didn't. The corpsman's name was Gleeson. He was a former Raider. He took care of—*God!*—I don't know how many people up there. Doc Gleason died not too long ago, a good man.

Jesse Arney, 100, Third Tank Battalion: Not long into the battle, we got hit in the front sprocket three times while we were crossing a little dirt road. It was a camouflaged Japanese tank shooting—*Bam! Bam! Bam!* But he didn't kill us. As soon as I found out where he was, I disabled him with a shell. My tank commander said, "You shot that tank all to pieces!" That was the only enemy tank we saw, as far as I remember. I always wanted to get into a running fight with one, but we never did find another.

It was hot and a lot of the time I slept under the tank. But one night, two guys from the infantry asked if they could sleep under the tank. I said, "Okay, yeah. I'll sleep inside the tank." So, they slept underneath—and there was a banzai charge that night and the next morning they were dead.

Jack Rasmussen, 94, Third Marine Division: When we moved towards Agat Bay, one of my buddies stepped on a mine designed for tractors. It blew both his legs off; stripped all the meat off the bones. We tried to comfort him and tell him it was going to be okay, but we knew he was a goner.

John Marx, 97, Third Marine Division: We had a guy from Boston who was supposed to go over a ridge. But a friend was killed right in front of him, and he cracked up. From then on, all he did was take care of the seabags.

Melvin Ogg, 100, Third Marine Division: We had six sergeants sitting around a foxhole near my position. A mortar hit right in the center—killed three outright and just about blew the faces off the other three. They had to be transferred out to a hospital ship in the bay. If I'd been standing up, I probably wouldn't be here today.

Tom Shields, 93, First Provisional Marine Brigade: The lieutenant in my platoon was killed on Guam. We were out by the old Marine barracks and a piece of shrapnel caught him in the groin and severed his artery. When it did, he bled to death. I held his head in my lap when he died. That had a profound effect on me, it really did. I loved that man. You could count on him—all those guys, you had to count on. Your life was in their hands. We took care of one another. You don't have that kind of comradery unless you're one of us; you just don't have it. And you don't get over it either: That stays with you the rest of your life. But I remember those guys just like they were my own brothers. We were all kids, we were all kids.

Art Perez, 96, Third Marine Division: We saw a Jap coming down a tree one day and our corpsman, who was very athletic, said, "Don't shoot him, let me get him!" He had a carbine, even though corpsmen weren't supposed to carry weapons (Red Cross and all that baloney). He shot seven times and hit seven times, but the Jap kept running. Our corpsman took that rifle and said, "They give me something like this to protect myself?" He smashed it against a coconut tree. That Jap had to be dead, but we weren't going to follow him.

Chuck Meacham, 96, First Provisional Marine Brigade: The spooky part was you didn't know which one was dead and which one was waiting to take you out. That was kind of a messy operation.

Jack Rasmussen, 94, Third Marine Division: I remember, as we attacked one day, we saw about twelve or thirteen native dead. Some of them had their heads cut off.

Tom Shields, 93, First Provisional Marine Brigade: The Guamanians were really good people, but the Japs treated them like shit. The Japs were a terrible bunch of people back then. They were as close as you could get to an animal, and I never had any pangs of remorse about killing them. And I still don't have any. It was "good riddance." They acted inhuman. The things they did to our people is unbelievable. They'd mutilate them. But I don't have any animosity toward them today. I think things have drastically changed, and I respect a lot of the things they've been able to accomplish. But at that time, they were going to die if I got around them.

After fighting up the Orote Peninsula, and north across the capital city of Agana, Guam was finally declared secure on August 10, 1944. More than eighteen thousand Japanese defenders were killed, while American casualties numbered north of seven thousand. In two years of occupation and three weeks of combat, nearly 10 percent of the Chamorro population was killed. Some ten to fifteen thousand natives, subjected to forced labor and prostitution during Japan's reign, were living in concentration camps in the central and southern portions of the island upon liberation. For the Americans, seizing Guam, Saipan, and Tinian was a major strategic victory: the Army Air Forces could now employ the new B-29 "Superfortress" bomber on raids over mainland Japan.

12 ★ ★ ★ ★ ★ ★

PELELIU

With the Mariana Islands secured, American forces prepared to seize Peleliu and Angaur in the Palau Islands. It was believed that the capture of Palau—in association with landings on Yap and Morotai—would clear Japanese opposition in the western Pacific and open a direct path back to the Philippines. Shaped like a lobster's claw, Peleliu possessed a complex terrain of mangrove swamps, white coral beaches, and an imposing system of ridges known as Umurbrogol Mountain. The First Marine Division would land across five zones, seize the southern half of the island, capture the airfield, then drive north into the hills. Marine infantrymen were told that it would be a brief four-day operation—"rough but fast," in the words of the division commander, William Rupertus. At the same time, the Army's Eighty-First Division would capture Angaur to the south, before moving to support the Marines on Peleliu. D-Day was scheduled for September 15, 1944.

Bob Ehrlich, 94, First Marine Division: I was in a replacement battalion when the First Marine Division came down and made maneuvers offshore of Guadalcanal. I knew a guy with the First Division, so three of us took our rifles and went "over the hill" to get in with them. We all got summary court-martials later. But I didn't care—just as long as I got into combat. I was really gung ho then.

We were in an amtrac on D-Day, and the thing got hit. A lot of guys didn't get out, but I did. I waded to shore and got back with the outfit. The island looked like a hellhole. The big battleships were still shelling, and it was bad. Things didn't look too good. I thought combat would be neat. But guess what? It isn't.

Carl Sampson, 98, First Marine Division: The amphibious tanks were on the zero wave. Not the first wave, but the zero wave. We went in first to take the bulk of Japanese fire so the Higgins boats and other amphibious tractors could get ashore without getting shot up. We drove up on the beach, then went inland to fight on the front lines. But our vehicle got stuck in a tank trap and couldn't go any farther. We were fighting for our lives out there.

Robert Evans, 97, First Marine Division: Going ashore on D-Day, we were hit twice by a 40mm cannon. It shot right through the amphibious tractor, killed the kid in front of me, and knocked my front teeth loose. One guy's leg was gone, and a long string was hanging out. I remember that. I wondered what that string was. Well, it was the tendon, pulled right out of his knee. Of course, you're not allowed to stop and help him.

William Darling, 98, First Marine Division: We landed on Beach White One on the far-left flank of the division and we were taking gunfire from a 40mm in a pillbox that was hidden on a point of land about twenty-five yards up the coast. It was firing parallel to the beach and hitting almost every amphib tractor coming in. Ours got hit and it jammed the latch on the ramp, so when the tractor stopped, the lieutenant said, "Everybody out over the side!" I went out over the side, behind another tank that was dead, and saw my best buddy floating face down in the surf. That hit me bad. I remember we were supposed to get ourselves off the beach as soon as possible.

Don Bishop, 98, First Marine Division: We hit the reef, and the tank went up in the air, then slammed down. No sooner had we hit the ground when a shell landed on the left side of the tractor, and it turned the engine around inside the vehicle and disabled it. Everybody had to go over the side. A friend of mine said, "Catch my gun!" He tossed it, then came barreling over. He said, "Where's the gun?" I said, "Right down there where you threw it!" He said, "Jump under and get it!" I said, "You jump under and get it! I have sandwiches that the Navy gave us in my pack!" We finally got some guys to poke around and pull the gun up. Then we all started in, staying low in the water. They were shooting at us, but very sporadically. We got in and passed by the end of a tank trap. There was a tank stuck in that damned thing; couldn't get out because of the soft sand. We went around the end of it and—*boy!*—there were Japanese all over the place.

Carl Scott, 98, First Marine Division: The first thing I saw on the beach was a Marine with no head. There were all kinds of awful things to look at: Marines that had been killed in the waves ahead of us. Some officer came along and said, "Get off the beach!" I started walking to my right and someone said, "Don't step there!" I glanced down and there was a land mine right next to my foot. I looked over to thank the person, but there was nobody there. My sister says that was my guardian angel. It made a believer out of me.

While the Fifth Marine Regiment and the Seventh Marine Regiment swept inland, the First Marine Regiment pivoted toward Umurbrogol and met a rocky mass known as "the Point," extending into the water on the extreme left flank of the landing zone. Securing "the Point" fell to K Company of the Third Battalion commanded by Captain George Hunt. Hunt's men would have to seize and hold the position to prevent a Japanese counterattack from piercing the American perimeter and sweeping across the beachhead.

William Darling, 98, First Marine Division: We had been told that capturing the Point was going to be critical. Our mission was to take a left turn, go up the island, and kill off that position. But I got pinned down in a tank trap near the beach and couldn't get out all morning. When I finally escaped, I didn't know what to do because there was nobody around; everybody I saw was dead. Finally, I noticed a guy wandering back, trying to find an aid station. I took him down and spent the rest of the day helping other walking wounded back. It was around then that we ran out of water. We each had two canteens, but most of us had already gone through both during the morning. I think the temperature was about 115 degrees. We tried to get more water from the ships, but it was contaminated; whoever filled the storage cans forgot to scrub all the oil and gasoline out. Everybody was retching from it. I went back and found a shell hole with a dead Japanese soldier inside. But there was water in the bottom. I just closed my eyes, filled my canteens, then put a whole bunch of salt tablets in. I drank it because I was so thirsty. A lot of guys did that.

The second morning, I was still sitting near the beach when a corpsman came by. I asked where he was going. He said, "I'm going to the Point." I said, "I'll go with you." The skipper was up there with two platoons from the company. We didn't see many Japs on the way up, but I did kill one. Other than that, we didn't see very many of them. It turned out that the skipper's two platoons had formed a defensive perimeter on the Point and the Japanese had attacked all night long; they were desperately trying to take the Point back.

When I got there, they were still holding—they hadn't backed up any. I reported to the captain. He said, "Where's the Second Platoon?" I said, "I don't know, I haven't seen them." He said, "Well, fall in on the line here." So, I fell in with—I think it was the First Platoon. We had a firefight, then things kind of settled down a little bit. The second night, they *really* hit us. They were screaming and coming towards us. But we were getting them killed—*fast*. They were starting to pile up, body upon body.

The next morning, I think there were several hundred dead Japs laying around. After that, they finally gave up and withdrew. When we moved into their staging area, the Japanese already had a brand-new 40mm gun ready to replace the one we had destroyed at the beach.

By the time fighting ended at the Point, roughly five hundred Japanese soldiers had been killed. Captain Hunt's command was crippled in the engagement, reporting just 78 survivors from the original 235-man company. It was clear, after days of intense fighting, that the battle for Peleliu was not going to be a "rough but fast" operation like intelligence reports had suggested.

More than ten thousand Japanese troops had transformed the island into a coral fortress pitted with caves, tunnels, and seemingly impenetrable fighting positions. The Japanese had also elected not to expend manpower defending the beaches, instead withdrawing to positions inland that were designed to kill and maim American assault troops. On the right flank of the First

Marine Regiment, the Fifth and Seventh Marines were meeting equally intense Japanese resistance as they advanced toward the airfield on D-Day.

Russel Nelson, 98, First Marine Division: As we went across the island, we'd see dirt-covered hatches pop up; there were Japanese soldiers down in the ground. They'd raise a piece of steel or plywood and machine gun us. We had one young fella who realized that, so he went up and stood beside a hole. When the Jap raised the hatch, the Marine pulled a pin on a hand grenade and tossed it in the opening. Poor little guy, he didn't shoot anymore.

Gordon Black, 94, First Marine Division: We were moving inland and got pinned down behind a 6x6 GI truck. That was my first experience under fire. You could hear the bullets singing. We finally used a flamethrower and got that machine gunner settled.

Carl Sampson, 98, First Marine Division: The flamethrowers would go up to the caves and fire napalm gas inside and they'd come out screaming and on fire—and we'd shoot them.

Richard Nelson, 98, First Marine Division: You'd see so many dead bodies, just piles of dead bodies all over. It was quite an experience, I would say.

Russel Nelson, 98, First Marine Division: I shot a Japanese out of a tree. He was up pretty high, but I hit him with the first shot. When he was killed, he fell forward, down to the ground, and we just went on. I talked to a junior high class in Eugene, Oregon, a few years ago, but I didn't dare tell them about that.

Ernie Ferguson, 98, First Marine Division: I was in the first wave on Peleliu, and my objective was the airport. I've spent seventy-five years trying to forget about it. Somehow, I was one of the first to get to the field, but I don't know how I got there or what I went through getting there. I was drawing sniper fire from a pillbox off to my left when a tank came up and shot it with a flamethrower. A Jap came running out, burning from head to foot. I think every rifleman in the area zeroed in on him. He didn't make it more than one or two steps.

In the late afternoon, somebody hollered out, "Here they come!" I looked down the airstrip and five Japanese tanks were heading in our direction at about thirty miles per hour. Most of the flamethrowers and bazookas assigned to our battalion didn't make it to shore, so we were stuck with small arms fire. They moved up a 37mm artillery piece and the first shot knocked the conning tower off one of the tanks. It reared up like it was going over backwards. But I didn't watch for very long because the other tank came crashing through our lines. He went back into the beach area and ran over one of our boys. Then an airplane came over, shooting at the Japanese tanks. The empty cartridges were landing like hail on our helmets.

Russel Nelson, 98, First Marine Division: I called an American tank commander on the radio, and he reported back, "Three minutes away." It felt like a long time before he got there, but he wiped out three Japanese tanks. Another tank was taken out by a flamethrower guy. That was pretty scary, to stand up and see a tank about fifteen feet from you. The Japanese soldiers came out from the top. Of course, they got shot. One of the guys ran alongside the tank and tossed a grenade into the hole and, as soon as it exploded, the tank stopped.

George Bradbury, 98, First Marine Division: The first night, the Japanese knew where we were and kept firing at us. If we raised up our antenna for the radio, they'd try and shoot the antenna down. Bullets were just zinging over our heads. I said, "We need to dig down deeper." We all had a little shovel-pick, so I started to dig. But I stuck the thing right into a dead Jap. I don't know whether they buried him or whether a shell explosion covered him up. But he was down about six inches, and my pick went right through him. He was so bloated that he literally spewed up on us.

Carl Scott, 98, First Marine Division: After we dug in, the Japanese attacked us again. One of the Marines was killed by a Jap officer with a saber. We beat them back and only lost a couple of men. The next day we moved forward, next to a causeway. There was a pillbox right in the middle and some of the Marines had to knock it out. A sergeant was killed and one of my best friends got hit. It messed up the stock of his rifle and he got shrapnel in his private parts and legs. He came back to where I was. I said, "Where are you going, Art?" He said, "I'm getting the hell out of here!" He survived, but he was never able to have babies after the war.

The next day we got past the causeway and had to take another position. One of the guys came up to me and said, "You stay back here with the company CP, and I'll go up with the platoon." He went up and they took the area. But when they came back, I asked where he was. They said, "He was killed." If I had gone, I don't know what would have happened to me. He took my place. We weren't good friends or anything, so why he volunteered to switch places with me, I'll never know. After we secured the area, we had to go across the airfield to higher ground. That's where the Japs were dug in.

Ernie Ferguson, 98, First Marine Division: I threw my pack on, then headed down the middle of the airstrip. I got one or two hundred yards across, then looked to my right and left, and realized that I was the only one there. I didn't bother to look back. I was drawing sniper fire and I saw a projectile coming down on my right, about a hundred yards in the air. It was tumbling. I'd never seen anything like that. I couldn't stop until I got to the other end of the airport. The Japanese had laid down some coral rock as a parking area for their planes. I dug it up and made an edge around my position. You didn't dig foxholes on that island—it was all coral.

I put down a few hand grenades and six or seven clips of ammunition. I carried a BAR—that's Browning Automatic Rifle—and sat and waited. It was ten or fifteen minutes before more American troops started coming in. I felt kind of lonesome out there, all by myself, because the Japs were on each side of me, within a hundred yards. I still don't understand why they didn't come after me. At that time, there wasn't anything to fire at because the Japs were hidden in caves and bunkers. I think it reached 115 degrees that day, but when it bounced off the coral, it felt like 130. We had accidentally put our drinking water inside gas drums. Boy, that was some putrid tasting water!

Bob Ehrlich, 94, First Marine Division: It tasted like gasoline more than water. I can remember that—that was terrible.

Harmon Hunter, 101, First Marine Division: That was bad, that was the worst. That whole place was one big firecracker. It would top out at 110 degrees, and we had no fresh water. What I missed most was water. Even today I drink a lot. But man, we were running around the jungle looking for puddles. You'd lay down on your belly, but you had to make sure you don't sip too hard, or you'd suck up some mud.

In the days to follow, additional men and material flooded ashore and infantry units turned north to face well-entrenched Japanese defenders in Umurbrogol Mountain.

Grant Duncan, 100, Provisional Force Signal Battalion: I landed on D+1. We lost three guys killed on the beach, and ten or eleven others were wounded. I was the only one that didn't get hit by the incoming shell. Joe Prete was my best friend. I stayed there with him, with his head in my lap, waiting for the corpsman to come, when he died. It was a bad scene.

Ernie Ferguson, 98, First Marine Division: We secured the airport and the swamp area around the field. That night, around day three, they put me on an outpost and brought up a Doberman pinscher. Him and I stood at the outpost that night. When it got good and dark, a Jap stuck his head out of a bunker and hollered, "Marines, you die!" I kept waiting for him to come out, all night, but he never did come back.

Bob Ehrlich, 94, First Marine Division: One night, we had a Marine crack up and start yelling and screaming. They damn near shot him, until some guy went up and knocked him out. Then they took him away. He must have been on Guadalcanal or one of those earlier islands. We had a lot of guys that cracked up—but I never got close to it. I sometimes wondered if they really were cracking up, or if they just wanted to get out of there. But you can't fault anybody; you can't read their mind.

Harmon Hunter, 101, First Marine Division: I've seen guys go into a frenzy. It's the tough guys that lose it. They're always acting tough—bullshitting, this and that. But when *it* hits the fan, they fold. Most of the guys could take it, but it was always the guys with a lot of bullshit who folded.

Ernie Ferguson, 98, First Marine Division: The naval bombardment had turned the island into a moonscape; there were tree stumps sticking up everywhere. Every night the Japs would come out: We could hear them in the shrubbery. We'd just keep shooting until they wouldn't return fire anymore. That was about every night. It was pitch dark and we just fired at whatever we saw—*mostly rifle flames*. The next morning we'd collect souvenirs and gold teeth. To me it was just a souvenir. I had a pretty good sack of gold teeth in a little bag.

James Rosenmiller, 99, First Marine Division: We had one guy—he had a helmet half full of gold teeth. He'd go around and pry them out with his Ka-Bar knife. Yeah, that's true. There are no falsehoods there. I've actually seen it.

Richard Nelson, 98, First Marine Division: I tried to knock a lot of gold teeth out, but I don't know what I did with them.

George Bradbury, 98, First Marine Division: I was guilty of it myself. I remember this sergeant took a Japanese, reached in his mouth, got ahold of a gold tooth, and swung his whole body around before he finally got it out. Dog tags and gold teeth were good souvenirs. After the fighting was over, they would let the Marines go out and visit the Navy ships and trade souvenirs for food and water.

USMC PHOTOGRAPH BY KARL SOULE

A patrol from the Fifth Marine Regiment crossing the Lunga River in September of 1942 on Guadalcanal.

USMC PHOTOGRAPH

A cheval-de-frise covering a jeep trail in the Coffin Corner area on Guadalcanal. George Mason, interviewed for this book, is pictured on the far left.

COURTESY OF THE AUTHOR

Dean Ladd, 101, in a World War II helmet in 2022. Ladd served with the Second Marine Division on Guadalcanal, Tarawa, Saipan, and Tinian.

COURTESY OF THE AUTHOR

Dean Ladd (center, seated) in Quantico, Virginia, after returning from the Pacific in 1945. In four years, Ladd rose from the rank of private to captain.

USMC PHOTOGRAPH

A column of Marines advances on Bougainville in late 1943.

COURTESY OF THE AUTHOR

Milton "Red" Cronk, 98, served with the Third Raider Battalion on Bougainville. His platoon leader, Mike Strank, later became famous for raising the flag over Iwo Jima.

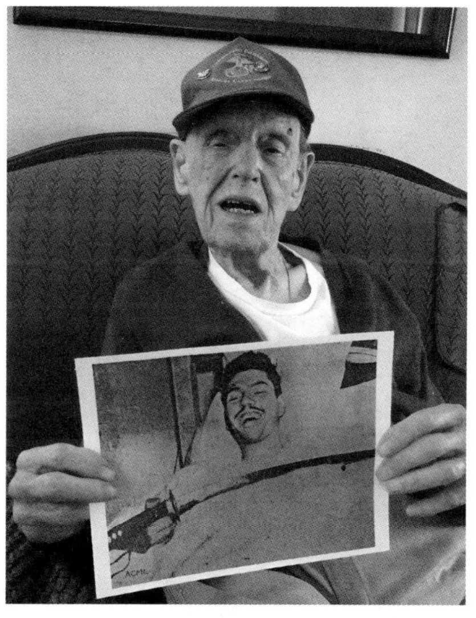
COURTESY OF THE AUTHOR

John L'Abbe, 97, holds a wartime photo depicting L'Abbe in a hospital bed with a captured Japanese sword after being wounded on Tarawa.

USMC PHOTOGRAPH

Marine riflemen push inland during the Battle of Tarawa in November of 1943.

COURTESY OF THE AUTHOR

Robert Evans, 97, holding memorabilia from his service in the Marine Corps. Evans fought on Guadalcanal, New Britain, and Peleliu with the First Marine Division.

COURTESY OF ROBERT EVANS

Robert Evans (right) and friend display war trophies in 1944.

COURTESY OF ROBERT EVANS

Robert Evans being pinned with a Purple Heart for wounds received at Cape Gloucester, New Britain.

USMC PHOTOGRAPH BY SERGEANT ROBERT R. BRENNER

Marines from B Company, First Battalion, Seventh Marines on New Britain in February of 1944. Carl Scott, interviewed for this book, is in the center (facing camera, with helmet).

USMC PHOTOGRAPH

Faris Tuohy (left), 96 when interviewed for this book, drinking a cup of coffee aboard ship after fighting in the Marshall Islands in February of 1944. According to Tuohy, the man on the right with no shirt, Stephen Garboski, was later killed on Guam.

USMC PHOTOGRAPH BY SERGEANT BOB COOKE

Harold Rediske (right) on the beach of Namur in the Marshall Islands in February of 1944. Rediske would earn a Silver Star for evacuating wounded during the battle.

COURTESY OF THE AUTHOR

Wallis "Wally" Hamlin, 100, served as an artilleryman with the Second Marine Division.

USMC PHOTOGRAPH

The first waves of Marines land on Saipan, June 15, 1944.

Chuck Meacham, 96, displays a flag removed from a dead Japanese soldier after the fighting on Hill 40 on Guam. Meacham served with the Third Raider Battalion on Bougainville before joining the Fourth Marine Regiment for landings on Guam and Okinawa.

COURTESY OF THE AUTHOR

Chuck Meacham in uniform while serving with K Company, Third Raider Battalion.

COURTESY OF CHUCK MEACHAM

COURTESY OF THE AUTHOR

Howard Frye, 95, with a Third Marine Division patch in 2020.

Howard Frye (left) with his artillery piece.

COURTESY OF HOWARD FRYE

USMC PHOTOGRAPH

A Navy corpsman tends to a wounded Marine on Peleliu in September of 1944.

COURTESY OF THE AUTHOR

Richard Nelson, 98, holding a First Marine Division unit history book in 2021.

COURTESY OF THE AUTHOR

Genevieve Lashaw, 95, in her apartment in 2019.

Genevieve Lashaw in uniform. Lashaw was among the first women to serve in the Marine Corps.

COURTESY OF GENEVIEVE LASHAW

USMC PHOTOGRAPH

Marines disembark on Iwo Jima under heavy Japanese fire in February of 1945.

USMC PHOTOGRAPH BY EUGENE JONES

A corpsman guides a wounded Marine, identified as Bert Rutan, to the beach on Iwo Jima.

COURTESY OF THE AUTHOR

Bert Rutan, age 95, holds the photo in his apartment in 2019.

COURTESY OF THE AUTHOR

Kenneth Brown, 95, poses with a Japanese rifle and flag captured on Iwo Jima. The flag is signed by friends in the Fifth Marine Division.

COURTESY OF KENNETH BROWN

Kenneth Brown in his dress blue uniform.

COURTESY OF THE AUTHOR

Donald Brown, 95, at his home in Boise, Idaho, in the spring of 2023.

COURTESY OF THE AUTHOR

Donald Brown in uniform before shipping out for the Battle of Iwo Jima.

COURTESY OF THE AUTHOR

Donald Brown (center, below the Marine with the sword) and friends pose with souvenirs captured on Iwo Jima.

COURTESY OF THE AUTHOR

Frank Wright, 96, displays a "Gung Ho" knife similar to the blade he carried as a member of the Fourth Raider Battalion.

USMC PHOTOGRAPH

A flamethrower tank burns out Japanese caves on Okinawa.

COURTESY OF THE AUTHOR

Tom Charlton, 95, on his porch in Montana in 2021. Tom served with the First Marine Division on Okinawa.

COURTESY OF TOM CHARLTON

Tom Charlton in China on occupation duty circa 1946.

COURTESY OF THE AUTHOR

Francis Stanger, 92, the last known World War II veteran from the Flathead Indian Reservation.

COURTESY OF THE AUTHOR

Luther Hendricks poses with a Seventh War Loan poster featuring the flag raising on Iwo Jima.

Bob Ehrlich, 94, First Marine Division: I got some. I used to use a pair of pliers to pull them out of their mouth. I had a friend by the name of Kimble. *Oh God!* That guy must have collected hundreds of them. That's all he did, was pull teeth out. I have about three, I think. That's all I ever took. It kind of irked me. It wasn't a good thing to do. Did I see guys collect skulls? If I had, I probably would have shot the guy. A head? *Yuck!* Some guys got crazy. I heard about it, but I never saw it. Probably depends on the person. Some guys got crazier than a loon, they'd do anything.

Carl Sampson, 98, First Marine Division: The Japanese would find a Marine that had a tattoo on them, and they'd cut the tattoo off. So, it went back and forth. Some guys even cut ears off and pickled them in a jar.

Gordon Black, 94, First Marine Division: I remember seeing the cook vomiting out behind his tent. I said, "What's the trouble there, Mac?" He pointed—there was a dead Japanese soldier on the ground. He was pretty ripe, and the flies had taken over. That was my first experience with a dead Japanese.

Ernie Ferguson, 98, First Marine Division: On New Britain it was mosquitoes, on Peleliu it was blowflies.

George Bradbury, 98, First Marine Division: When the infantry got into where the pillboxes were, they came in from behind and knocked the doors off. When the Japanese started running out, the flamethrower took care of them. The stench was terrible because so many Japanese had already been killed before we got there, during bombings and strafings. They were just covered with flies and bloated. It was a terrible thing. If I had been older, I couldn't have withstood it.

Bob Ehrlich, 94, First Marine Division: I saw quite a few living Japanese, but I saw even more dead ones. It got to stinkin' after the first day. Oh my God! You'd go by one and it'd make you puke. Their bodies were really starting to bloat. But the more dead ones I saw, the safer I was.

Don Bishop, 98, First Marine Division: We used to find their pillboxes, get up on top of it, move the grass around, find the ventilator, and drop a phosphorous grenade in there. They would run out through the door, burning. Boy, that's a bad way to go.

Richard Nelson, 98, First Marine Division: It didn't bother me to see dead Japs. They'd be laying in the road—and trucks would be rolling over them. One dead Jap I found had a bloody flag. I took it, brought it home, and finally gave it to my son. Our guys were always laying around, too. That bothered me, in a way. But you get used to it. It's just one of those things: I was only, at that time, twenty years old.

William Darling, 98, First Marine Division: Pretty soon, we went down in front of Bloody Nose Ridge. We were getting some heavy fire and one guy got shot in the gut while I was beside him. To this day, I don't know who he was. But I went over and his guts were coming out. I was trying to push them back in. I got a battle bandage, put it on the wound, and soaked it with blood. I told him, "Keep that on there or you're going to die!" Two guys came up with a stretcher. I picked up the back end, and the other guys grabbed the front. We were going along, but I couldn't see where my feet were landing, so I stumbled and fell. As I was getting ready to stand, I looked over—up on the ridge, I saw a cameraman. He waved at me, but I don't remember waving back. Maybe I did. Then I went back to the aid station. I had been shot in the knee while I was working on the beach on D-Day, and I was trying to ignore it. But it became horribly infected. A doctor said, "We're going to evacuate you," and they put me on a hospital ship.

Russel Nelson, 98, First Marine Division: My buddy caught shrapnel right in his stomach, and I had to pull him out of his foxhole. I had dreams about that for quite a few years—of his guts and everything. But you just have to go on.

Ernie Ferguson, 98, First Marine Division: I got on top of a ridge, then looked up and saw a mortar round coming down. There was no cover, so I just flattened myself as best I could. I was waiting for the mortar to explode. But it didn't go off. The round was just laying there, only about ten feet away from me. When the next mortar came down, I knew it would probably explode, so I rolled off the ridge and joined up with two other Marines. The three of us went around the base of the hill and—*suddenly*—were looking down the barrel of a 75mm artillery piece, a machine gun, and men from a Japanese artillery unit. The Marine beside me emptied his rifle, then stepped back behind some cover to reload. I emptied my BAR, then I stepped back to reload. The third guy didn't even get a chance to use his rifle—a machine gun bullet caught him. I sat there and watched him change colors. That's how I learned that you turn a little yellow when you die.

Bob Ehrlich, 94, First Marine Division: That was a bad situation. Some of the hills were straight up and down. We got on top of one and it was probably twenty feet off the ground. The stupid Japs had a machine gun up there and we all had to jump down because he was really putting it to us. I didn't get injured or anything, but that was quite a jump.

Gordon Black, 94, First Marine Division: It was just a big rock mound. They had caves in the mountains, where the Japs were hidden. They used our 155mm guns to seal the caves. It was pretty effective. In fact, when they pulled the lanyard string, you had to duck down because some of the rocks would come back at you.

James Rosenmiller, 99, First Marine Division: The Japs didn't stay and fight like a "Jarhead" would. They'd take off and go find a cave to crawl into. That was the name of the game with the Japs, they were constantly retreating into caves. The only way you could deal with that was with flamethrower equipment. But to see a guy burn up is no pleasure, it's no pleasure at all.

Ernie Ferguson, 98, First Marine Division: We were expecting the Japs to attack one night; to try and kick us off the mountain. But they didn't do it. Instead, they infiltrated our positions. When you're in the service, you usually don't make close friends because it hurts too much when they get killed. But I made two friends. One of them, Louis, was standing guard that night. His rifle jammed almost immediately, so he had to use it like a baseball bat. When a Jap would stick his head over the ridge, he'd knock them off the path, down into a hundred-foot drop.

On September 28, the Third Battalion, Fifth Marine Regiment executed an amphibious landing on the nearby islet of Ngesebus; a small coral scab located just six hundred yards north of Peleliu. Supported by aircraft from VMF-114 (newly arrived on Peleliu's airfield), the Marines quickly overwhelmed the beachhead and progressed inland toward several ridges and Japanese-occupied pillboxes. Pfc. James Rosenmiller, from Morris, Illinois, landed with I Company and distinguished himself during the action.

James Rosenmiller, 99, First Marine Division: Our platoon was assigned to protect a tank as it moved through a valley. When we got out there, the Japs threw a cannon barrage at us. One of the shells hit the turret of the tank and put a gouge in it as big as your fist. The tank made a circle and came back to our front lines. But one of our boys was hit by shrapnel during the shelling, and he was dropped out there. I took off, out into the field of fire, and called for a corpsman to follow me. One did. We picked up our buddy and brought him back to the safety of our lines. But he was already dead. That was part of my "Silver Star event."

The other part: the best I remember, we came into contact with this five-inch coastal gun. There were five Japanese soldiers manning it, and we wiped them out. But, after we took the pillbox, this one Jap I shot with a tommy gun started to get up again. I had called for a BAR-man to come up with me, but he didn't hear me evidently because he wasn't there. Fortunately, another guy, one of my buddies, came up alongside of me. He had a carbine—and I heard it go off. He nailed the Jap—and that was the end of that. That was a close call. If my buddy hadn't come up, I wouldn't be talking to you now. That Jap would have had me.*

For attacking the coastal gun and recovering the deceased Marine, Pfc. Rosenmiller would later be awarded a Silver Star. On September 29, 1944, after suffering just thirty-eight casualties on Ngesebus, the islet was declared secure. Back on Peleliu, elements of the Fifth Marines and the Seventh Marines advanced deeper into

* Citation in appendix.

Umurbrogol, battling over pinnacles and depressions christened Bloody Nose Ridge, Pope's Ridge, and the Pocket.

Ernie Ferguson, 98, First Marine Division: I get my dates mixed up, but sometime around day sixteen we got pulled off the line. We ended up in a beach area and rested there for a day. A group of us took turns wading out into the ocean to wash our clothes; we hadn't had our clothes off since we boarded LSTs on Pavuvu and headed for Peleliu. After our baths, we sat in a ditch beside a road and relaxed. We had already run out of salt tablets. You generally take a couple of salt tablets for every canteen of water. But through the heat and humidity, we had been taking six or seven per canteen.

Anyway, one of the ships sent more salt tablets in, with a few cases of fruit juice. We had a guy in our outfit, we called him "Rebel Lee." He saved his can of juice until he could find some homebrew, then he ended up getting a little tipsy. A lieutenant came by, saw him, and decided to chew him out for being drunk. But you just *don't* chew out someone who's been on the front lines for seventeen days—especially when he's high on moonshine. "Rebel Lee" picked up his bayonet and chased the lieutenant around a tent a couple of times, then the lieutenant broke off and headed for the RCT (Regimental Combat Team) headquarters. I never did see him again. After that, we went back to the swamp area and started hitting the ridges again until we got sent off the island. We were there for thirty days.

On November 27, 1944, Peleliu was finally declared secure. The final cost for the First Marine Division was devastating: nearly seven thousand killed or wounded. The Army's Eighty-First Division, who joined the battle piecemeal throughout September and October, fared little better with more than three thousand casualties. The Japanese garrison, like on previous islands, had been destroyed. Only three hundred defenders (mostly Korean slaves) surrendered to Marine and Army forces. The necessity of the operation remains controversial.

Just before the First Marine Division landed on September 15, 1944, a carrier raid on the Philippines revealed that Japanese airpower was drastically diminished in the region; Yap, Morotai, and the Palau Islands could likely have been bypassed. But by the time the report was received, orders had already been issued for Peleliu and thousands died for an island that would see little use for the remainder of the war.

Bob Ehrlich, 94, First Marine Division: It made you think about your life. I found my Savior then, I really did. And I've known him ever since.

Ernie Ferguson, 98, First Marine Division: It pays to be young and dumb. I had enough sense to be careful, but I don't remember ever being scared.

Harmon Hunter, 101, First Marine Division: Peleliu was a real doozy.

Richard Nelson, 98, First Marine Division: Peleliu was a bitch.

Carl Scott, 98, First Marine Division: There were two hundred Marines in my company. When we left Peleliu, there were only twelve of us left. I consider myself pretty lucky.

Bob Ehrlich, 94, First Marine Division: I wasn't as gung ho as I was before. As they used to say: "It went out your ass."

Ernie Ferguson, 98, First Marine Division: When we got aboard ship, we looked back at Peleliu. I couldn't understand how I'd made it across the airstrip without getting hit. I'd looked death in the face more times than most average people will in six or seven lifetimes. There were four or five USO girls waiting on the beach at Pavuvu with fruit juice when we came off the ship. We thanked them for the fruit juice, but all they meant to us was that we couldn't go swimming in our birthday suits.

13 ★★★★★★

THE PHILIPPINES

By the fall of 1944, the Japanese had been swept from key bases across the southwest and central Pacific, opening a passage back to the Philippines. The archipelago was selected for assault to secure positions within reach of mainland Japan and to sever supply lines to the Dutch East Indies. Leyte, a 110-mile-long island of diverse, tropical terrain, would act as a launch point for further operations in the Philippines, particularly against the principal island of Luzon. Four US Army divisions landed across the eastern shores on October 20, 1944. Originally designed to be an "all-Army" operation, a logistical anomaly deposited fifteen hundred Marines of the Eleventh 155mm Gun Battalion, the Fifth 155mm Howitzer Battalion, and the Corps Artillery Headquarters Battalion on the invasion beaches.

Burt Reynolds, 97, Eleventh 155mm Gun Battalion: I was a telephone man—or a wireman, as they called us. There were three of us picked out of the whole group in Hawaii. We went into this outfit because they needed communications men. We just happened to be the ones—I think it was because we scored high on a test.

We landed on D+1, which was the twenty-first of October, at 10:44. We set up camp, they brought the guns off the ship, and we started firing. We supported four Army divisions during the battle. I almost got shot a few times and we had lots of bombs go off, but that's about it. We basically didn't have a whole lot to do.

The landings were lightly contested, and 130,000 American troops quickly advanced inland. In response, the Japanese enacted a multipronged naval assault aimed at destroying the American invasion force. A small contingent of United States Marines, known as seagoing Marines, would witness the battle from aboard ship. Specially selected after boot camp for their physical stature and mental aptitude, each man endured a rigorous eight-week course before receiving assignment to a cruiser, battleship, or aircraft carrier. Although their primary function was to operate a secondary gun position, they were also trained to fight fires, perform shipboard ceremonies and sentry duty, and act as a raiding party if necessary. Most seagoing Marines, like Robert Schultz of the USS *California*, were already veterans of several campaigns by late 1944.

Robert Schultz, 102, USS *California*: My first engagement was in the Mariana Islands: Saipan, Tinian, and Guam. Our primary function was antiaircraft, and our primary enemy was the Japanese suicide planes. We had several attacks there, took some fire, but never really got hurt. After Saipan, Tinian, and Guam we went back to Hawaii for a while to recuperate.

Our ship ended up in the Philippines for the Philippine engagement. We did our usual bombarding: four turrets, three apiece, with fourteen-inch guns. We did a lot of that, which left nothing for us Marines to do; there weren't a lot of Japanese planes around at the time. The big thing that happened there:

On one particular night, the Japanese came into Leyte Gulf through a body of water called the Surigao Strait. We were in a tactical position that the Navy guys thought was wonderful because they could "Cross the T." That meant we could fire all our big guns, and they could only fire forward. We had a very distinct advantage. But the Marines had nothing to do with that, we just sat back and listened. Noisy as hell! It went on for several hours. Anyways, in the morning they said our target had disappeared, which evidently meant that we had sunk the ship we were shooting at. So, that's the "big story" of the Navy at Surigao Strait.

Fought between October 23 and 26, 1944, the Battle of Leyte Gulf was the largest naval battle in modern history, consisting of four major engagements: the Battle of Sibuyan Sea, the Battle of Surigao Strait, the Battle off Cape Engano, and the Battle off Samar. The Japanese Navy was effectively destroyed during the fight, losing four aircraft carriers and twenty-two other vessels.

Following the victory, Task Force 38 retired to Ulithi for a brief ten-day rest before returning to the Philippines to provide additional air support for the invasion. On December 18, after days of high-tempo combat operations, an unexpected typhoon swallowed TF-38 while it attempted to refuel three hundred miles offshore of Luzon. The Task Force—consisting of seven fleet carriers, six light carriers, eight battleships, fifteen cruisers, and about fifty destroyers—was thrashed by seventy-knot winds and waves reaching up to ninety feet.

David Mertell, 98, USS *Monterey*: Our ship done a roll over to the port side, and a sailor fell out of a forward antiaircraft gun position. When the ship rolled back starboard, it left a big void in the water. The sailor was up on top of the wave, over on the other side! And when the ship rolled back in, he started swimming. His buddies were waving at him—and they got him aboard when the wave crashed across the deck. We called that the Miracle of the *Monterey*.

But during that last roll, an airplane on the hangar deck broke loose. The prop hit the side of another plane, made a spark, and ignited aircraft fuel on the hangar deck. It didn't explode, but the air pressure from that igniting almost blew us out of our gun position, it was so hard. When they found out we were on fire, the Flag (Admiral "Bull" Halsey) asked our captain to abandon ship. Admiral Halsey got a return call that said no, we were going to work it out.

After the storm moved out a little bit and the fires were extinguished, we tied onto a tug because the engines were all dead on our ship. They started towing us back to Pearl Harbor. But the engine crew, commonly called the "black gang," got one of the engines started and we managed to get to Pearl Harbor on our own. We sat at Pearl Harbor for a few days, then they got the other engine started, so we headed back to Bremerton Naval Yard to get the ship rebuilt. They split the twelve-hundred-man crew into three pieces and turned a third of them loose to go home for a week. I took the third leave in order for my girlfriend to turn eighteen, and we got married on February 20, 1945. After I got back to the ship from five days at home, they got us refitted with all the modern hardware and we went back overseas.

The tropical storm, known as Typhoon Cobra or "Halsey's Typhoon," damaged thirty-one ships, sank three destroyers, and killed nearly eight hundred sailors and Marines. The USS *Monterey* lost eighteen aircraft and sustained severe damage to her hangar deck. It was one of the greatest disasters in US Naval history. The USS *California*, under repair in the Admiralty Islands, escaped the calamity and returned to the Philippines in January of 1945, and steamed to western Luzon in preparation for the Lingayen Gulf landings.

Robert Schultz, 102, USS *California*: The war was coming to an end, and the Japanese were getting desperate. The kamikazes—these guys were just killing themselves in their airplanes. We had a few encounters; near misses. We had one, I remember, where a plane came in behind us. Evidently, he veered off and crashed about a hundred yards ahead of us and thirty yards to the side. When he hit the water, his plane exploded, and it blew him up in the air about a hundred feet. He was obviously dead, but somehow his parachute opened. It was real strange: Here we were, sailing ahead, and there's this Japanese guy floating down beside us. That was really weird.

Another time this kamikaze got a bead on us. We were doing our thing: firing 20mm, 40mm, and five-inch guns. But he came through it like he was an angel. And he was coming straight at me! *Straight at me!* I was thinking, *Oh, shit! I can't run! And I can't dig a foxhole!* At the last second, he veered off to the left and he hit our ship, only about thirty feet away from me. I felt the heat. I wasn't hurt, but he did some serious damage to the ship and he killed a bunch of guys.

One of the worst things about injuries on a ship—it's not like you get a shrapnel wound and they take it out. You get hurt bad. The worst injuries were burns. When they hit a ship, the plane explodes, and the bomb explodes and there's a flash of fire. If you're within twenty feet, you get burned. We had a lot of guys with severe burns on their faces. That was our worst engagement: Several Marines were injured, and we had a lieutenant that was killed; Lieutenant Breeden. He was in a little turret, all enclosed. A plane hit that thing directly and destroyed it—and the two guys in it. That sent us back to the States.

When you're on a ship and you have casualties, you can't bury them; you can't dig into a steel deck. So, we had dead guys and nowhere to put them. A smell I'll never forget was all those guys rotting. The South Pacific is hot no matter where you are, and we had no air conditioning. We laid those guys out in an area that we called the "barber shop" because that's where we cut hair. We couldn't do anything while we were in action. But once we got some free time, we did a burial. The appearance—*and the thought*—of those guys being buried at sea sticks with me until this day.

The dead were sewn into canvas bags, with a five-inch projectile by their feet, so they'd sink. Then there'd be an apparatus on the side of the ship for the body. They'd lay the guy on it, the chaplain would say a few words, then—*clunk!* They'd slide off. For a long time, I had visions—*dreams*—of these guys down there, moving in the tide. All dead. Friends! That bothered me for a while.

Between October of 1944 and January of 1945, it's estimated that 1,400 Japanese aircraft launched kamikaze attacks, scoring 121 hits, and killing thousands of sailors and Marines in the waters off the Philippines. On the USS *California* alone, 44 Americans were killed and another 155 were injured. The crew serviced the damage, finished the bombardment of Lingayen Gulf, and completed a patrol in the South China Sea before departing to the United States for permanent repair and modification.

Although the Philippines Campaign would stretch deep into the summer of 1945, the invasion of the island nation succeeded in liberating thousands of American prisoners of war and Filipinos from Japanese oppression. But the toll in human life was tremendous: two hundred thousand Allied casualties and four hundred thousand Japanese. The Filipinos suffered the deepest wounds, losing more than one million people.

14 ★ ★ ★ ★ ★ ★

GARRISON AND HOME FRONT

To meet increasing manpower needs in the Pacific, the Marine Corps began recruiting women for war-essential, non-frontline duties in early 1943. The program, known as the Marine Corps Women's Reserve, would accept twenty thousand recruits between 1943 and 1945. Trained primarily at Camp Lejeune, North Carolina, the WRs were directed by Ruth Cheney Streeter, a Marine colonel with a prewar résumé that included service as the president of the Welfare Board in Morris County, New Jersey, and time with the New Jersey State Relief Council. Similar in concept to the Navy's WAVES (Women Accepted for Volunteer Emergency Service) or the Army's WAACs (Women's Army Auxiliary Corps), the program successfully released thousands of men for combat duty in the latter half of the war.

Gladys Stevens, 97, Women's Reserve: When the war came along, I moved to San Diego; that's where I joined. They sent me to Camp Lejeune, North Carolina, and I took some general tests for intelligence. If you got a good score, you were sent to a school. At that time, there were only two schools open for women: it was Cooking or Pay Office. There were six of us that passed and went to work at the pay office.

That's when Camp Pendleton opened for girls. Three of us were told we were going to Pendleton. I didn't really want to go home to California; that was only about thirty-five miles from where my parents lived. I wanted an adventure. But it turned out okay.

The pay office girls always knew when a large group of troops was shipping out: they'd get a special paycheck before they left. But back then, we never knew how many of those boys were getting their last check.

Hattie Kelley, 98, Women's Reserve: I was a recruiter. I travelled around the country and enlisted Marines. We'd set up in a post office and do a little spot announcement or a blurb in the paper, letting them know we were coming. You didn't have to sell anyone because they were already sold. The Marines had a reputation—and the fact that they were taking women was a miracle; that's the way everybody felt.

Genevieve Lashaw, 95, Women's Reserve: I met my husband at a football game at Camp Lejeune. It was a Sunday afternoon, and a few of us were out shooting the breeze. One of the gals from a different clique—we called groups "cliques"—came by and said, "Anybody want to go to a football game?" I said, "I'll go with you." I grabbed my hat and coat and off we went. I swear, when we got to the field, there were twenty thousand men there. We walked from one goalpost to another before we found a place where we could sit together. A voice inside me said: *Root for the Navy, root for the Navy.*

I was sitting alongside this Marine sergeant, and when the Navy got the ball, I started rooting for them. Every time I did, he bumped me with his elbow. All through the game—every time I cheered—he'd bump me.

The game ended and the Navy sunk the Marines good. I got

down to the field, and this Marine sergeant found a spot on my left. He said, "What's your nationality?" I said, "I'm French." He said, "That makes two of us." He said, "What's your religion?" I thought, *Uh, oh. This is the end of that guy.* I said, "I'm Catholic." Much to my surprise, he said, "That makes two of us." We started chatting and worked our way back to the barracks. He asked me for a date. I said, "Okay." He wanted to know what time to pick me up. I told him, "There's supposed to be a pretty good movie tonight—eight thirty would be fine." He said, "Who do I ask for?" I told him my name, then wrote it out. To this day, I don't know why I did that, because I never did it for any other guy. We went to the movie, and he asked me for another date on Wednesday night. Then, on Wednesday night, he asked for a date on Friday.

On Friday afternoon, he got orders to take a group of men down to the beach, and he was going to be gone for quite a few days. He called the barracks and left a message for me—and said he'd look me up when he came back. In January, he came into the PX, where I was. I didn't see him come in because I had my back to the door. I heard someone say, "Are you free tonight?" And that was it, we started going out. We began dating in January and it was only three months before he proposed.

By late 1943, as American forces advanced across the Pacific, the Marine Corps needed to field additional divisions to prosecute the culminating years of war. On January 21, 1944, after establishing three new regiments, the Fifth Marine Division was officially activated at Camp Pendleton, California. Placed under the command of Major General Keller E. Rockey, the division began absorbing Marines from duty stations across the country; a process that developed a unique cadre of combat veterans and untested men fresh from boot camp.

Bill Gropp, 97, Fifth Marine Division: The Raider Battalions had been broken up and the paratroopers were broken up, too. We had a lot of veterans of the South Pacific in our division. We had one guy, John Basilone, who was a Medal of Honor recipient. He was in the Twenty-Seventh Regiment. I started off in the Twenty-Seventh Regiment, in Headquarters Company, but I was transferred into Signal Company. That's where I was during my only combat experience.

Ken Brown, 95, Fifth Marine Division: Our Fifth Division was made up of new recruits, but they also brought in some of the best fighting men to work with us. We had some experienced Marines who had fought all the way from Guadalcanal. Unfortunately, a lot of those men didn't survive; didn't make it through the battle for Iwo Jima.

Mike Ladich, 96, Fifth Marine Division: I was in a Raider Battalion when, all of a sudden, me and another guy got pulled out. Those guys went overseas, and they kept us in the States. Later on, I found out that the sergeant was saving my ass by putting me in a guard battalion. That lasted about four months or so, then we were in the Fifth Division.

Bill Gropp, 97, Fifth Marine Division: There was a lot of marching and training out in the boondocks. I can't remember anything that was especially exciting. We did offshore rubber raft training, but mainly marching.

Ralph Simoneau, 97, Fifth Marine Division: Just before we left for overseas, we had a ten-day liberty. Somebody said that you could go to the airport and catch a ride on a military plane; it wouldn't cost you anything. But I couldn't get a ride and ended up wasting a day of leave. Ultimately, I got on a train. But the trip from San Diego to Milwaukee was three days there and three back. That's six days of my ten-day liberty. Of course, that wasn't enough for me, so I took thirty-three days. When I got back to San Diego, I was arrested and placed in the brig. When we went overseas, I was in handcuffs.

Howard Rieckers, 100, Second Armored Amphibian Battalion: Every time I got aboard ship, I'd go down to the galley and get a job. The cooks would hand us crackers—and if you ate them, it kept you from getting seasick. Afterwards, we would steal a loaf of bread on the way back to our bunks. Then our buddies from the tank would sit together and—*man!*—they'd devour that loaf of bread. You couldn't hardly get it out from under your jacket!

Bill Gropp, 97, Fifth Marine Division: We landed in Hilo, Hawaii, on the Big Island and ate a bunch of green coconuts and got dysentery. They had a narrow-gage railroad that went up to Hāmākua that was used for hauling cane. We rode in open-sided cars over the canyon; it was pretty exciting. Then we took trucks into Camp Tarawa. It was just rows and rows of tents. We did more training in the hills and out in the bush.

The Fourth Marine Division arrived on Maui during the rainy season of 1944 to rest and refit after a brutal contest in the Mariana Islands. Billeted near Ha'ikū on the slopes of Haleakalā, the "Fighting Fourth" was already accustomed to life in the islands. The division had logged several months on Maui after a successful campaign on Roi-Namur, developing a robust encampment that included a USO club, an amphitheater, a chapel, parade grounds, and substantial athletic facilities. The relationship between locals and the Fourth was so strong that men in the division were often referred to as "Maui Marines."

Harold Rediske, 94, Fourth Marine Division: On Maui there were five men to a tent. In the summertime, it got so hot that we'd just roll the sides up and make them wide open. Then we'd put mosquito netting over our beds. My sister-in-law was really nice: She wrote me one time and asked if there was anything I'd like to have. I said that I'd sure like to have a radio. How she ever got it through, I'll never know. But here came this little radio in a package.

We had a forty-watt light bulb in every tent, so we scraped the wires and ran that into our radio. There was a big dance pavilion on Honolulu, and it was close enough that we could pick it up. At night, we'd just roll up the tent flaps and people would holler, "Turn that up louder! We can't hear!" About the fifth or sixth day, a runner came up to our tent and said, "Rediske, the captain wants to see you right now." I went down and there were a bunch of officers in the tent. I thought, *Oh, what the heck did I do now?* But I couldn't think of anything. The captain said, "Rediske, have you got a radio in your tent?" I said, "Yes, sir." He said, "What are you doing with it?" I said, "Well, we're listening to it, sir." Then I told him that we wanted to tune in on a band in Honolulu. Long story short, they ended up taking it away from me.

Another thing that happened: On Maui, one of the big industries was sugarcane. Way out in the middle of the damned fields, you'd always see smoke coming up. I asked someone once, "What the heck's out there?" He said, "Oh, they're making 'Five Island gin.'" I said, "That's some name." He said, "Yeah, they figure if you take one drink of it, you can see all five islands at once." But the rest of the time, I was busy driving senior officers.

On the west end of the island, there's a big whaling community, and we had a lieutenant that was dating some teacher there. I always took him to his girlfriend's house—

then I'd wait for him all day. He'd usually come out at about five o'clock and say, "Come and get me in the morning, I'm staying the night." Then I'd show back up at nine in the morning and get him. I was like a nursemaid or something. But it was better than what the rest of the men were doing—*marching.*

For American troops passing through the Hawaiian Islands, the capital city of Honolulu was the most desirable port in the Pacific because of a diverse selection of bars, tattoo parlors, brothels, and beaches.

Robert Hall, 95, Marine Administrative Command: Downtown Honolulu was just full of servicemen: Army, Navy, Marines.

Jack Becker, 99, Marine Barracks, Pearl Harbor: I spent a lot of good liberty in Honolulu. We got drunk. What else would we do? Then we tried to pick up women. In those days whorehouses were wide open, wide open! You'd see a big line snaking out, going up the street.

Ray Garland, 96, USS *Tennessee*: I only made two liberties in Pearl Harbor because it was just a wave of sailors; thousands of men. I usually just stayed aboard ship. It didn't appeal to me to fight a crowd like that.

Keith Tucker, 100, Second Marine Division: One time we went out and maneuvered for about a week, then pulled into Honolulu. We got liberty, but we didn't have the proper khaki uniform or anything like that. I remember there was a kid from Kankakee, Illinois, who had a brother in the Third Marine Division on Oahu. He went ashore and told his brother about the situation. His brother got about eight uniforms and brought them back to the ship. It was the damnedest looking group, with all kinds of mismatched clothes.

The war in the Pacific, in many ways, was a war of logistics. The complexity of supplying a massive military force as it traversed the world's largest body of water was a monumental task. The landing on Saipan alone entailed moving 535 vessels, carrying 127,000 men, more than four thousand miles without delay or obstruction. To meet the military's herculean demands, thousands of men were assigned to permanent stations in Hawaii and across the United States to perform vital structural support to the Marine Corps.

Robert Hall, 95, Marine Administrative Command: I spent two years at Pearl Harbor during World War II, working at Marine Corps headquarters. What we did, mainly, was keep records. A group of us would sit around a big table, receiving information sent from different outfits throughout the Pacific, then store the information on cards. Originally, I may have wanted to go into combat. But when I got to Hawaii, I decided maybe I was better off where I was. I left it up to fate. I wasn't volunteering for anything. I always felt guilty because some of my friends went into the Pacific—and a few got killed or wounded. They were taking my place, more or less. But I think I redeemed myself in the Korean War, even though I was a little reluctant to go there too.

Jack Becker, 99, Marine Barracks, Pearl Harbor: I had no desire to see combat. I don't know. It never dawned on me. People would've said, "Are you frickin' nuts? You have a nice job, and you want to go into combat? Are you crazy?"

Bill Town, 95, Guard Battalion, MCB, San Diego: I don't know why, but I stayed in the United States the whole time.

I told them I wanted to go overseas, but my commanding officer said, "Well, we can't do it right now." Four years later, I was still here. It kind of disappointed me.

Numerous islands throughout the Pacific were retrofitted and developed into training grounds and rehabilitation centers for forward operating combat units. Due to Guadalcanal's size and location, hundreds of thousands of Americans passed through the island between 1943 and 1945, including four Marine divisions, three parachute battalions, four raider battalions, various Army divisions, and untold sailors, Coast Guardsmen, and airmen.

Early inhabitants—notably the Third Marine Division, which stayed on the island from June to October of 1943—were often subjected to Japanese bombardment and sporadic sniper fire from holdouts hidden among the hills. In September of 1944, the Sixth Marine Division, the only Marine division activated overseas, was formed on Guadalcanal in preparation for the landings on Okinawa. The "Striking Sixth" consisted of four regiments: the battle tested Twenty-Second Marine Regiment, the largely untested Twenty-Ninth Marine Regiment (only the First Battalion had seen combat, on Saipan), the Fifteenth Marine Regiment, and the Fourth Marine Regiment; a storied outfit destroyed in the Philippines in 1942 but reestablished by veterans of the elite Marine Raider Battalions in 1944.

Jack Rasmussen, 94, Third Marine Division: One of the first nights I was there, a Jap bomber came in and dropped its load on us. We scrambled for cover, but all we could find was the latrine. We didn't want to get hit, so we all dove in. Early the next morning, we were all working on foxholes, not wanting a repeat of the night before!

We met locals who had worked with the First Marine Division when they landed in '42. They bragged about killing three or four Japanese earlier in the week. We said, "Bullshit, there were no Japs still on the island." The native insisted there were. One of the guys said, "Okay then, prove it. Bring us some ears or something." The native agreed and walked off.

The guy came back the next day, carrying a bag with him. When he emptied it, two Jap heads rolled out. We asked how he did it. The native said that he would go over to the Japanese and tell them that the water was bad, so they needed to drink from coconuts. Then he would say, "Look up at the top, that's where the best coconuts are." When the Jap looked up, he'd hit them in the neck with his machete.

Frank Wright, 96, Third Marine Division: We were having a problem locating the Japanese in the boondocks, so I went out alone and tried to find some. I was just hunting for Japs. I came across several—and disposed of them. They were looking for a place to cook their food and grow their vegetables. They'd been on the island for a long time. I usually followed my nose. I could smell meat cooking and I'd sneak around behind them. But sometimes I'd be heard, and they'd be gone. They called me "Frank Boondocks." They'd say, "He's going out to boondock again" or "Here comes a boondocker." They kind of tagged me. It was fun being out there alone, but it was a crazy thing to do.

Eldon Cedergreen, 96, Sixth Tank Battalion: We joined the Sixth Marine Division that was just being formed on Guadalcanal. It was a combination of recruits and veterans. We continued training there, but we weren't expecting jungle warfare. We used Henderson Field for running our tanks. It was all grown over with jungle grass, five or six feet. One time, a tank took off through the grass, not paying much attention to anything, and ran smack into a fifty-gallon drum of aviation gas.

Suddenly his tracks were on fire. Fortunately, it just burned out and he was okay. But there were a few moments of thrill during our training period.

Donn Thompson, 95, Sixth Marine Division: Tokyo Rose would talk to us and tell us how many people we had and what division we were in. How she got all that information, I don't know. She'd always come on and say, "How do you think your wife is? Where do you think she's going with other men? There won't be enough of you left to put you in an LCI to go home when we get through with you." We would laugh and have fun with it. She would play "White Christmas" and all the popular songs from those days.

In late 1944, the First Marine Division arrived back on Pavuvu in the Russell Islands after a prolonged campaign on Peleliu. Located just sixty miles north of Guadalcanal, Pavuvu was an abandoned coconut plantation, overrun with land crabs, mosquitoes, and rats. No more than ten miles long, the island was so small that regimental maneuvers often required the Marines to skirmish around tents and along company streets. Beyond a few lush swimming areas, the island was unanimously hated by its inhabitants.

Carl Scott, 98, First Marine Division: We were hoping to go back to Australia, but no such luck. We ended up at Pavuvu, which was a terrible place to train. It was a coconut plantation, untended for a long time, with rotten coconuts all around. We cleaned up the whole place, built roads, and set up our tents between the trees.

David Fusinato, 97, First Marine Division: Oh God! That was a hellhole! Why in the hell they ever chose that for a camp—with rotten coconuts on the ground, raining every other day, and land crabs. They'd crawl in your shoes if you didn't pick them up off the floor. It was all one big tent camp, too. It was a lousy, lousy place.

Eugene Thomas, 92, First Marine Division: I was on Pavuvu when the remnants of the division arrived from Peleliu. While they were coming in, we were asking about souvenirs they'd picked up. One guy said, "Here's your souvenir," and grabbed his hind end.

William Darling, 98, First Marine Division: I went back and rejoined the division after being wounded on Peleliu. A bunch of guys who had been over there since the beginning at Guadalcanal had been rotated home. There were a bunch of new guys on Pavuvu. It had all changed. They had moved Red Cross ladies in—and put up a fence around them. The roads were better, the food was better. We had electricity and showers. Then we started training for Okinawa.

Ernie Ferguson, 98, First Marine Division: We were in training all the time: We'd be out marching, crawling for half a mile; sometimes it was under live ammunition. And we did an awful lot of shooting coconuts.

Bob Ehrlich, 94, First Marine Division: Shitty, hot, steamy—Pavuvu wasn't a good place. The food wasn't too bad, I kind of enjoyed some of the food. A lot of the time you'd go out on maneuvers, go up in the hills; stuff like that. There were horses there, too. This guy from Texas, George Cheryl, talked me and another guy into going out and getting on a horse. I got on one, but he didn't want to be ridden. He kept bucking toward the coconut trees. As we got close, I finally went off. George Cheryl said, "Now you get back on that horse and ride him! You're gonna get afraid and you won't ride him again!" Boy, I sure told him what I *thought* about riding another horse!

Richard Nelson, 98, First Marine Division: You had a lot of good buddies there and a lot of guys you hated. Some guys were really untrustworthy. That's the reason you stenciled your name on your clothes. If you didn't do that, somebody would steal them. Hang it up—ten minutes later it would be gone.

Ernie Ferguson, 98, First Marine Division: One of the boys went out of his mind on Peleliu and some of the guys had to take him down from Bloody Nose Ridge and tie him up. That poor man: When we were getting ready to go to Okinawa, he committed suicide. He didn't want to face another beach landing.

James Rosenmiller, 99, First Marine Division: I'll tell you—you see some awful weird things. And you don't want to remember them. I've seen a guy batter his head against the butt of a rifle. I've seen guys shoot themselves in the leg, just to get out of the war. That was a common thing, that was a common thing. It wasn't unusual for a GI—one that was physically weak and couldn't handle the stress and strain of war—to shoot himself. At nighttime, you'd hear a shot every once in a while; somebody'd shot himself. That's true.

Tom Charlton, 95, First Marine Division: On Pavuvu, there was a guy that would sneak into your tent at night and look at you. One night, I woke up and he was standing there. I came up after him and got wrapped in my mosquito netting! Guarrda was in the bunk next to me. He said, "What's going on here!" The guy ran out and smashed into our hanging mess gear; rattling, banging, and everything else. They finally caught him: He was down on the beach, playing with crabs—nuttier than a fruitcake.

Richard Nelson, 98, First Marine Division: At noon, when it was time to eat, they'd throw pills in your mouth so you wouldn't get malaria.

Bob Ehrlich, 94, First Marine Division: You took Atabrine. But then you'd start turning yellow. Some guys really got bad—and a lot of guys *still* got malaria. My best friend got malaria, and I didn't see him again until Korea.

Ernie Ferguson, 98, First Marine Division: Pavuvu was a rest island—or supposedly a rest island. I guess they tried to make it so rough that you'd be glad to get back into combat, where you could take out your frustrations on something.

After the Marianas were secured in mid-1944, the principal islands—Saipan, Tinian, and Guam—underwent drastic development in support of the planned bombing campaign on mainland Japan. Five substantial airfields would eventually be constructed, supporting hundreds of B-29 Superfortress bombers from the Twentieth Air Force. Meanwhile, patrols from the Second Marine Division (garrisoned on Saipan) and the Third Marine Division (garrisoned on Guam) would continue to engage Japanese holdouts scattered in the hills.

Larry Pressley, 96, Second Marine Division: I was almost killed on Saipan. Whenever they sighted some Japanese up on the high ground, the Marines were sent out to take care of them. It was like a rabbit hunt—except these rabbits shot back. On my eighteenth birthday, I was assigned to work as the point man. I always hated that duty, but it was divided fairly. The sniper's first shot glanced off the outside of my helmet. Of course, I hit the deck. I was new to the war, but I remembered that I was supposed to spot the enemy so we could return fire. I eased my head up—and there was another shot. This time, he shot the heel off my right shoe. The sergeant said, "Pressley, keep your head down!" They finally spotted where the shots were coming from. They flanked him, fired about forty rounds, and killed that group.

Art Perez, 96, Third Marine Division: Guam was secured around August and our battalion ended up on the north end, which was all jungle. We patrolled that area until December. The regiment or division used to put out a little note every day that kept track of how many Japs we killed. When it got over a certain number, they called the division back and formed a skirmish line and swept north to try and completely clean the area out before they moved on. As soon as that operation was over, we moved the division to the central part of Guam to get ready for the next operation.

Don Pilcher, 95, Third Marine Division: Although everything was over, there was a Japanese soldier that flew a small plane. We called him "Washing Machine Charlie." He would fly over and fling a bomb. I remember the first time we had an attack: I got in a foxhole, and it was really the first time I felt vulnerable.

Don Browning, 95, Flag Allowance: We had quite a time on Guam. They told us the island was secured, yet there were still Japanese in the jungle. We used to go out and investigate caves. One of the most awful things I saw: We went back into a cave, and I stepped on something. It gave way under my foot. I didn't have a flashlight, so another guy shined a light on me. My foot had sunk into a dead Japanese.

Donald Harr, 100, Marine Night Fighting Squadron 534: There were, indeed, Japanese still on Guam. When we started unloading our equipment, some Japanese sniper took a shot at us and—fortunately for me—the bullet went six inches over my head. At that point, the master sergeant in charge decided that we should do the remainder of the unloading at a safer spot.

I don't know his reason for making the choice, but he said, "Harr, you stay here and guard what's already been unloaded. I'll send two guards down to take over for you later." Somehow or another, he became sufficiently involved with other things, and he never sent the guards down. So, I spent the night "enjoying" guard duty. It was a long night, believe me.

At some point in the evening, I heard someone walking around in the distance. When he got about twenty yards away from this little fort I'd built in the equipment, I started firing. Whoever was making the footsteps took off running in the other direction. But the next morning, there were no dead bodies around.

Conrad Gillette, 100, Ninth Defense Battalion: In my unit, we had to sign up to go out on patrol. Naturally, everyone wanted to go shoot somebody, so I put my name on the list. The patrols always lasted twenty-four hours: you went in at noon and you came out at noon. Our patrol leader knew the island pretty well—and he had probably killed quite a few Japanese on other patrols. Well, we were moving along in the jungle when—*all of a sudden*—we smelled smoke. We found a group of Japanese, snuck up, and killed all six of them. We all fired, so I wouldn't say I killed anybody. All I can say is that I shot.

It was getting dark around then, and our patrol leader decided to prop the dead Japanese up near the fire and set an ambush. He knew there was too much food in the pot; there had to be more Japanese in the area. At around midnight, I heard a gun going off. We saw our patrol leader blow a guy about ten feet backwards with his tommy gun. About that time, the Japanese started throwing hand grenades down on us. They didn't know exactly where we were—and they were hitting all over the place. When a bullet or shrapnel hits coral, it makes a lot of sparks. We started crawling out of there, just to keep from getting hit.

The next morning, we ran into another Japanese group that was cooking breakfast. We crawled up on them and shot all five. In total, we killed eleven on that patrol. I don't know if I'm supposed to tell you this, but the rule within the Marines was: "Don't take a prisoner." And we didn't. But we were told that the Japanese would never give you a chance; they'd fight back. If we said, "Surrender!" they'd just throw a hand grenade at you. It was a way to save your own life, by shooting first.

Luther Hendricks, 96, Fifty-Second Defense Battalion: The Japanese are smart people. They hid in caves, hid in the mountainsides, dug in any way they could. Some would give up, then pull out a machine gun hidden behind their back, just to shoot us when we were close enough. Some would hide hand grenades under their arms or between their legs. As long as they could kill one or two Marines, they were happy.

It got to where we wouldn't take any prisoners. They'd come to us with their hands up, but we wouldn't believe it—just shot them down. Most of the time we were right. The carnage and devastation you see is enough to make a person go out of their mind: People with legs blown off, stomach blown out, heads gone. *Better you than me*, that's the way I felt. You had no "off days," you had no "sunny days," you had no "stormy days." All days were the same—*survival.*

One time, I came really close to a Japanese. I guess he must have wandered off from his group or something. I saw him, I chased him, I killed him. You might think I'm barbaric, but I drug him back into a clearing, poured gasoline on him, and set him on fire. That's the training, though: They train you to kill. I just went overboard with it. They did have gold in their mouth and gold was worth a lot of money then. It still is. I saw some teeth-pulling being done, but I never did it. I had no desire to take anything from them, just wanted to get home.

The final Japanese holdout on Guam, Sergeant Shoichi Yokoi, would not surrender until 1972. By the winter of 1945, a new invasion force was gathering in the Pacific, consisting of three Marine divisions. The objective was simply known as "Island X."

James Shriver, 98, Fifth Marine Division: We moved from the Big Island over to Oahu, and we were in Oahu for about two or three days. They let us go out on liberty. When I came back, I was going up the gangway to the transport. Down comes two MPs holding the elbows of my BAR-man (I was an assistant BAR-man). I said, "Harris, where the hell are you going?" And one of the MPs said to me, "He's only fifteen years old," so they were taking him off. That made me *the* BAR-man. I don't know whether that was a promotion or a demotion.

Clayton Narveson, 99, Second Marine Division: My squad had loaded aboard an LST for Saipan and Tinian. But we were only there for a day when it blew up in the West Loch Disaster. I was injured—got some metal in my back, and my stomach ruptured. They put me in the hospital, and I missed the Saipan invasion. When the Second and Fourth came back to Hawaii after, they put me in the Fourth Division. I was gunner on an 81mm mortar. In January of 1945, we loaded the ships again, but I didn't know where we were going.

Art Perez, 96, Third Marine Division: Tokyo Rose came on the air and said, "All you men in the Third Division aren't going to need those field jackets you're putting in your bag. We're going to make it hot enough for you where you're going next." And they did. The next operation was Iwo Jima.

Billy Byrd, 98, Fifth Marine Division: About halfway there, they called each platoon down into a little room to look at a model of the island. They said, "Well, this is what we've been training for, folks."

Les Anderson, 97, First Provisional Field Artillery Group: Before daylight, we were coming towards Iwo Jima, and you could see all the fireworks up ahead: naval bombardment.

W. Lee Robinson, 97, Fifth Marine Division: Whenever you go into a battle area, you're bound to feel some excitement.

Mike Ladich, 96, Rifleman, Fifth Marine Division: A lot of us were half-crazy. We were looking forward to it, believe it or not. I wanted to test myself.

James Shriver, 98, Fifth Marine Division: At seventeen, you're immortal, so I wasn't worried about it.

Donald Brown, 95, Fifth Marine Division: We wanted to kill Japs. The war was coming to an end, and we wanted to get into it.

Elburn Cooper, 95, Fifth Marine Division: I had a lot of anxiety, not knowing if I was going to make it or if I wasn't.

James Freel, 99, Fifth Marine Division: They told us, in the briefing, that it would be a maximum four-day mopping-up operation; that most of the Japanese we'd find would be dazed because they'd been bombing it for seventy-two days and shelling it for hours. But it didn't work out that way.

15 ★ ★ ★ ★ ★ ★

IWO JIMA

On the morning of February 19, 1945, more than 450 vessels blanketed the horizon surrounding the small volcanic island of Iwo Jima. Shaped like a pork chop, Iwo measured only five miles in length and was commanded by a dormant volcano at the northern tip, known as Mount Suribachi. Seizure of the island would provide emergency airfields for damaged bombers returning to the Mariana Islands and serve as a launching point for further air operations over mainland Japan. For the initial assault, the Fifth Marine Division was assigned to secure Mount Suribachi, while the Fourth advanced on the underlying airfields. The Third Marine Division, nearly twenty-one thousand men strong, would remain in floating reserve. The first wave landed at 0900.

W. Lee Robinson, 97 Years Old, Fifth Marine Division: D-Day was February nineteenth on Iwo Jima. H-Hour was 0900. I remember H-Hour because it found me coming down a rope ladder from a troopship into a landing craft.

Bill Gropp, 97, Fifth Marine Division: All the units were circling around, getting ready to go ashore.

James Shriver, 98, Fifth Marine Division: We finally turned and started in towards the beach. You could see a lot of artillery exploding on Mount Suribachi, but there was no indication of return fire from the Japanese at that time.

Ralph Simoneau, 97, Fifth Marine Division: Everybody was doing a lot of talking. It was a new experience for virtually all of us except for our sergeant, who was a combat veteran. There was a lot of talking and pointing, watching the planes pass by, and so on. But the closer we got to Iwo Jima, the less talking there was, until—*finally*—it was almost completely silent.

Don Brown, 95, Fifth Marine Division: The Japs didn't shoot much at first and we thought it was going to be a cakewalk. They let us fill the beaches with Marines. Then they opened up. They had easy targets and shot the hell out of us.

Walter O'Malley, 98, Fifth Marine Division: They expected us to go inland about two hundred yards with the amtracs. But because of the soft volcanic ash, there was no traction. They just couldn't do it. We got out two yards up the beach, mostly on our bellies. There wasn't too much upright walking.

James Freel, 99, Fifth Marine Division: I wasn't there very long before I got hit. We landed almost unopposed, until we got ashore. That's when the Japanese opened up from the mountains and caves. Mount Suribachi: it was tunneled. There were trenches all over the place that we didn't know about.

Mike Ladich, 96, Fifth Marine Division: Mount Suribachi was up there pouring artillery down. One round hit the left side of our tank. I happened to be on the right side, but about six guys got it right there. *Boom!* The goddamned tank went up in the air about a foot or two. I can still see it being lifted up by that artillery shot.

Burt Rutan, 95, Fifth Marine Division: As soon as I landed, the guy with me was killed. He fell right at my feet and his back was broken open. I could see his lungs. It was a terrible thing, but I couldn't just stay there with him. I called for a corpsman. When one showed up, I started running towards where I thought my outfit was.

James Shriver, 98, Fifth Marine Division: It's unforgettable. The opening two seconds on that beach will be something I'll never forget as long as I live.

Eugene Jones, 94, Fourth Marine Division: When my assault boat landed, we had already taken air bursts two hundred feet out. There were two Indian scouts at the bow and both of them had been killed. When the ramp went down, we had to kick their bodies and trample them as we ran out. I was a human bomb. I was carrying the rear end of what was called a Bangalore torpedo, which is a pipe, four inches wide, filled with explosives. My job was to rush up to a big pillbox thirty feet inland from the water and destroy it. But about half of my boatload, mostly flamethrowers and demolition-men, were shot dead immediately.

Joshua Clark, 100, Fifth Marine Division: They opened the bow doors, dropped the ramp, and me and a buddy ran out. There were bullets kicking up sand in between us as we hit the beach.

Bill Morgenroth, 100, Fifth Marine Division: There were bodies floating everywhere in the ocean, all around the Higgins boats.

Donald Raasch, 100, Fifth Marine Division: We came in on a Higgins boat, but the front gate didn't go down like it was supposed to. We had to jump over, into the water. The beach was long, uphill, and coarse. And there were a lot of dead Marines on there. The first thing I saw was a head. Nothing but a *head*.

James Shriver, 98, Fifth Marine Division: There were dead Marines all over the place.

Eugene Jones, 94, Fourth Marine Division: The first thing I saw was a huge sixteen-inch dud shell from a battleship, like a giant bullet lying on the beach, with yellow powder falling out. Next to it was a shell hole with two Marines laying inside. All I could see were their heads and arms, raised up near the lip. I ran like a madman, jumped in beside them. Then I realized both were headless. A single shard of shrapnel had decapitated both. At that moment, a wonderful young guy—we called him "Billy Joe," after some singer or something—jumped into the hole. He saw the headless men and went absolutely crazy, throwing up his hands, screaming, crying, throwing himself down against the sand. It was unbelievable.

Harold Rediske, 94, Fourth Marine Division: Wally Waddell was shot in the wrist. He yelled, "Ah, they broke my arm! They broke my arm!" I said, "Let's look at it." He zipped his jacket down and started peeling it off. He said, "God, my arm isn't broken 'cause I'm using it!" Then he realized that he was going home. He threw off his radio, threw his carbine away, and took off running down the beach. He was the luckiest guy in the world. I bet he didn't spend fifteen minutes on Iwo Jima. As he was running down the hill, we could hear him yelling, "I'm going home. I'm going home!"

Roy Earle, 98, Fourth Marine Division: When I landed, I found all these dead guys laying around. I yelled to a nearby Marine, "Hey! Where's your wire team?" He pointed and said, "You're looking at them." I said, "What?" He said, "They were running up the beach and a shell landed right in the middle of them—killed them all."

Howard Rieckers, 100, Second Armored Amphibian Battalion: We were all hit pretty hard there. We lost sixty percent of our tanks. The first day, we were kind of running around, not knowing what to do because the officers were gone. Whenever the Japs cut in on us, we'd crawl under the tank. I saw a lot of things you don't forget. The first wounded that I saw—a corpsman working on him. But the top of his head was blown off.

Mike Ladich, 96, Fifth Marine Division: You had to go over those two big embankments and that was holy hell. They had a crossfire from each end.

Ralph Simoneau, 97, Fifth Marine Division: There were several large terraces on the beach, probably in the neighborhood of eight to ten feet high. Each one was very, very difficult to move on. The black sand wasn't really sand. It was volcanic ash, beat to hell by all the waves. It didn't support any weight: The more you moved, the deeper you sank. It was extremely difficult to get off the beach. That put a little bit of fear into me. The longer we were on the beach, the more equipment and material piled up. Other landing craft were coming in. It was getting pretty busy.

James Shriver, 98, Fifth Marine Division: After a few seconds on the beach, one of my tent companions, by the name of Don Rogers, said, "Come on Shriver, let's get the hell outta here!" so we started up.

Donald Raasch, 100, Fifth Marine Division: While we were advancing, we came up against a Japanese foxhole. I looked for cover and jumped down into a shell hole. I carried a grenade on my belt with tape wrapped around the handle, so it wouldn't accidentally come off and explode. I took that grenade off and threw it into the Japanese position. Nothing happened. I had forgotten to remove the tape. A second later, I looked up and realized the Japanese had thrown the grenade back. It landed right in front of my hole. I leaned over and picked it up, took the tape off the handle, and threw it back again. It lit in their hole. I think it killed the Japanese because I saw a cap fly out of the foxhole—and I imagine part of his head was with it.

Walter O'Malley, 98, Fifth Marine Division: The first Jap I saw on the island was dead. He was a big sonofabitch, had to be six four. I said, "I thought these guys were supposed to be little?" Then we ran into an antiaircraft trench and that's where I saw my first live Jap. He was out, looking to see where we were. I got into a hand grenade fight with him. But his grenades were falling short. Thank God! Ours hit the mark because we had pretty good ballplayers. Then a bazooka team came up and wiped the rest of them out.

Mike Ladich, 96, Fifth Marine Division: When the Japs went into their shelters, this one poor bastard got stuck outside. He was in a foxhole, groggy—just knocked silly. I didn't want to kill him and neither did Ted Johnson. We were laying there, alongside each other. Ted kept kicking me and saying, "Shoot him! Shoot him!" I said, "You shoot him!" I didn't want to kill the poor bastard with my rifle, so I threw—*Jesus Christ*—I threw a hand grenade in his hole and blew him up. Poor little bastard. I'm sorry to say that I didn't tie him up or something. But we killed him, and that was that.

Ken Brown, 95, Fifth Marine Division (Chaplain's Assistant): We had a doctor and a little sick bay on our troopship. They were bringing some of the wounded aboard. That was the first time I'd seen injured men. Some of them were dying. We brought them aboard on stretchers, up the side of the ship. They were in terrible pain because the morphine had worn off. The chaplain and I went down and helped. Some of the men were giving their last words; they knew they were going to die. I took down notes of what they wanted to say, something to send back to their parents. That was my first experience with how hellish war is.

Elburn Cooper, 95, Fifth Marine Division: Prior to landing, I and another guy were sent to a hospital ship. I don't know what the other guy did, but I was put to work with the corpsmen; trying to keep guys alive until they could get them into the surgical section. That was a really scary time. There were guys in there with holes the size of baseballs in their chests and they could hardly breathe. That was a scary time.

Ken Brown, 95, Fifth Marine Division (Chaplain's Assistant): When we finally got sent ashore, one of the landing craft next to ours got hit and tipped over. All the Marines aboard floundered in the water because they had heavy backpacks on. We tried to get our coxswain to stop and let us help them but—*no*. His orders were to get us ashore, without trouble. He ignored them, and those men were left out there to die. The shore was littered with dead and wounded. As soon as we hit the beach, a corpsman saw me holding medical bags and thought I was one of them. He yelled, "Come and help!" The chaplain and I went over, and for the first day or two, we assisted with the wounded; trying to get them down to the shoreline, then evacuated back to a hospital ship. It was a terrible endeavor, kind of a futile one.

Bill Gropp, 97, Fifth Marine Division: There were lots of bodies by the time I got there. It was pretty bad, bodies and pieces of bodies. That's something you'll never forget. I can remember crawling through the sand. It seemed like you'd take one step forward and slide back two. I finally made it up and got on top of the bank. You dug in as much as you could. Or you just got into a shell hole for protection because the Japanese were hitting us from Suribachi on our left. Up on the other end of the island, we were getting artillery and mortars. It was pretty nasty. We lost a lot of people at that time. It's a wonder anyone got through, the air was so thick with mortars and artillery.

Eugene Jones, 94, Fourth Marine Division: By then, the Nips were on us *every* goddamn minute with mortars and artillery. It was just unceasing. All around us—and I swear I'm not embellishing—were dead Marines, in the most horrible, convulsive positions; some cut in two.

Mike Ladich, 96, Fifth Marine Division: I was laying on my goddamned stomach and the bullets were going through my pack. I was digging sand out from under me, just so I'd sink. In our training, we were told that the Japanese machine guns didn't have any vertical action; it was all horizontal. If you were under their line of fire, you were pretty safe. I realized that. But, for a little insurance, I was digging sand out from under me just hoping I'd sink deeper into the ground. My pack got all shot up. *That's true!* I can still hear gear and food rattling around from bullets hitting my pack.

James Shriver, 98, Fifth Marine Division: By the time we got off of the beach, up on solid ground, it was getting to be late afternoon. I started looking for a hole that I could get in for the night.

Walter O'Malley, 98, Fifth Marine Division: I'm digging—and now there's shells coming over, from our ships, whistling. My assistant, he was about five six, came from New Orleans, yelled, "Let me dig! Let me dig!" I yelled, "It's our own shells! It's our own fuckin' shells!" But he jumped in and dug the entire hole. I couldn't convince him it wasn't the enemy.

Mike Ladich, 96, Fifth Marine Division: We took turns standing watch. We had about four guys to a foxhole, and we'd take two-hour shifts, watching what was going on.

Elburn Cooper, 95, Fifth Marine Division: The nights were long: They went on and on and on.

Harold Rediske, 94, Fourth Marine Division: Iwo Jima was kind of cold, it was so far north. We'd been in a tropical climate for two years.

Billy Byrd, 98, Fifth Marine Division: They sent flares up at dark. It was flares, all night long.

Robert Brutinel, 100, Fifth Marine Division: The first night, our commanding officer, the exec, and his runner were in the same hole when a shell hit; killed all of them.

Donald Brown, 95, Fifth Marine Division: Someone passed word to fix bayonets and prepare for a banzai charge. That meant hand-to-hand fighting. The Japs would run at our lines and kill as many Marines as they could. They were very successful with their banzai charges.

Billy Byrd, 98, Fifth Marine Division: I was in a foxhole with two other guys, trying to sleep, when a couple of Japs got in our hole. There was a big battle. One of them hit me under the left eye with the butt of his rifle. Some Marines from another foxhole next to us came over and helped. They got rid of the Japs real quick. Then they dragged me back to sick bay and they put eight stitches under my eye. Within a few hours, I went back to my company.

Dennis Meyer, 98, Fifth Marine Division: At night, you better make damned sure somebody's awake. The Japs wandered around at night. If they found your foxhole, they'd stick you with a bayonet. If you fell asleep, you're a dead man. Two men from my unit got bayoneted to death. The soil there was mountain ash, and it would jam your rifle. When we looked things over the next morning, trying to figure out what the hell happened, we discovered that one of the guys had tried to fire his rifle. But it didn't go off because it was jammed with ash.

Eugene Jones, 94, Fourth Marine Division: One of our assistant flamethrowers was killed right beside my foxhole. Dead people frequently talk to themselves—they fart, they gasp, a hand rigidly raises in the air, a neck twists. These convulsions are motivated by gas releasing from the stomach. At about midnight, he started talking to himself, farting, pissing, and making noises. Then I heard a voice from the rear of my hole. Somebody whispered loudly, "Any friendly dead there?" I croaked, "Yes." And he said, "Is he near you?" I said, "Right outside my hole, laying on his back." He said, "We'll throw you a rope, so we can drag him back and take him down." They threw the rope in. I reached up, tied it around his wrist, and they pulled him out. I lay back in the hole, but they had to pull him across me. And, in so doing, the body disintegrated. I was covered with his intestines, feces, and so forth. Almost as if someone had thrown buckets of it on me.

By the morning of February 20, a beachhead had been secured and roughly thirty thousand Marines were ashore on Iwo Jima. But twenty-five hundred Americans were already dead or wounded. The Third Battalion, Twenty-Fifth Marine Regiment, suffered the loss of twenty-two officers and five hundred men while attempting to neutralize the "Rock Quarry" on the extreme right flank of the beachhead. The Twenty-Eighth Marine Regiment, despite heavy losses during the landing, had successfully cut across the island and isolated Mount Suribachi. They now faced the task of uprooting two thousand Japanese defenders from more than 120 blockhouses along the base of the peak. Dennis Meyer, a nineteen-year-old from Wisconsin, was a fire team leader serving with George Company during the assault on D+1.

Dennis Meyer, 98, Fifth Marine Division: Suribachi was looking right at us, just full of snipers. If you stuck your head up, you were dead. Two of my men called me and said, "Denny, come over here!" So I went over. They were all getting ready to open up on this group of men below us, maybe a hundred feet away.

There were eight or nine people down there. I said, "My God, them are Marines!" Everything was moving so fast that they had mistaken Americans for Japanese and were getting ready to shoot them; to kill them all. If I hadn't said something and stopped them, they would have killed Americans! Those eight or nine Marines never knew I saved their lives.

I ordered Roberts to go back and make contact with our outfit, and to tell them we needed some kind of support. Well, he got out of my sight, then came back a while later. He said, "I couldn't make it back." I said, "That's okay." I moved to where the rest of the guys were and said, "Roberts said he couldn't get back, so I don't know what we're going to do right now." But one of the guys piped up and told me, "He never even tried to get back. He just came up here and laid by us." I jumped Roberts and threatened to shoot the sonofabitch for lying to me!

Just then, a Japanese soldier popped up and caught my attention. I started shooting. When I got done, I told one of the other guys, Bougey was his name: "Come on Bougey!" We took off and tried to run back to the beach, but I hit the wrong trail. I said, "That's the wrong way! Back up and we'll go the other way!"

Now we were running out in the open. All of a sudden—*whack!* I got shot right through the center of my thigh. It took part of the bone out, and the nerves. I told Bougey to keep on going, make contact with the main force, then send a corpsman out. He did. A corpsman eventually came back and bandaged me up.

We all carried a bottle of brandy. You carried a bottle of brandy just in case you got shot, to ward off the shock. I drank my bottle of brandy and started to crawl back further when one of the guys said, "You don't look very good. You better have another drink." I said, "You better hang on to it yourself.

You might need it." He said, "I'll get another one." So he gave me his bottle, and I drank it. Then they threw me into an amphibious tank. My platoon sergeant was laying in there. He'd also been wounded. He was an ex-Raider; had the Silver Star, the third highest rated medal you can get. I told him, "Sarge, now you've got a Purple Heart, too!"

The Japanese were trying to shell our tank. If you ever lay in a barrel and let someone hit it with a sledgehammer, you'd know what it sounded like when the shells went off. The concussion—it was banging on the tank *hard*. But they didn't hit us, and they hauled us back to the beach where they had a hospital set up.

While the Twenty-Eighth Marines assaulted Suribachi, the Twenty-First Marine Regiment of the Third Marine Division was released from corps reserve and joined the Fourth and Fifth Divisions assaulting the airfields.

Frank Wright, 96, Third Marine Division: On the morning of the twentieth, we got off the *President Jackson*, and into our Higgins boats. We were reconnoitering, getting ready to go to shore. But the beach master waved us off. They couldn't take any more people on the beach—too many dead Marines and too many destroyed amphibious tractors and LSTs. The Twenty-First Marines kept circling around the ship, waiting for clearance so we could get back aboard. We ferried around the USS *President Jackson* for six hours in the waves and the rain.

Finally, we were ordered back onto the ship, and they gave us sandwiches. We went back into our Higgins boats the next morning, on the twenty-first. I transferred with my squad onto an amtrac because our landing area wasn't clear. We were near—I think it was Yellow Beach. There was a rockpile full of Japs and they started firing at us. We rolled up on the beach twenty feet inland and jumped off. I lost two men from my squad.

John Marx, 97, Third Marine Division: There were legs and arms and torsos laying all over the place. There were sharks in the shallow water eating bodies—big hammerheads and tiger sharks. If you stayed on the beach, you were going to be killed. Sooner or later, you're going to be killed. Even the artillery guys were getting shot. It was like the O.K. Corral.

Art Perez, 96, Third Marine Division: Where we landed, it wasn't level, and there was a big embankment ahead. I didn't think we'd ever get to the top of that damned bank. You had to keep low, dig in, and push yourself up. But we finally got to the top and started moving towards the position that we wanted. My captain lost his leg on the way, a guy on the right was killed, and I don't know how many more. Then we got caught between two artillery barrages on a little plain beneath this ridgeline. I thought, *Well, this is it. This is what you came to get in.* At that moment, I didn't know whether I was going to be hamburger or not. I don't know how, but by nightfall, we had a skirmish line up on the ridge. We made it, someway.

Kenneth Luttrell, 99, Fourth Marine Division: We got up early on the third day, and I got hit at about seven o'clock in the morning. I had a five-man team. But the explosion pretty much wiped them out. We were erecting a TBX antenna, and I guess the antennas were prime targets. The Japanese had that island graphed and I'm sure they could take out any spot they wanted to. I took a fragment through my face: It went into the left side and came out of the right side. It took out my palate, sinuses, and teeth. Also scratched my eyeballs; it was kind of severe. Fortunately, we were still close to the water, and they got me to a hospital ship very rapidly.

Jesse Arney, 100, Third Tank Battalion: We had three or four tanks disabled on the airstrip because of bombs buried under the ground. We ran into one and it blew the front left side of our tank out; killed the driver. The assistant driver and I were left in the tank for dead. The other two guys got out. I was knocked unconscious with a gash on my chin. But it wasn't long before I came to and slipped out.

James Shriver, 98, Fifth Marine Division: I came across a revetment: It was a big round circle, dug into the ground with sandbags around it. In the middle of the circle was a Japanese antiaircraft gun. But the gun was all bent-up. On the other side, laying up against the wall, was my closest friend, Bob Livingston. His chest was wide open. I could see big yellow bubbles coming out. He was still breathing—but he was on his way out.

Billy Byrd, 98, Fifth Marine Division: I ran back after some ammunition, and I came across the body of my best friend, Walter Kaufman of St. Louis. He had half of his head off. I stopped for a minute, then I kept on running.

Paul Frederick, 98, Third Marine Division: We hadn't been on Iwo for more than two or three days when the Japs threw in a few shells and killed my lieutenant and two or three of the top sergeants; a bunch of the rest were wounded. We were really shorthanded.

W. Lee Robinson, 97, Fifth Marine Division: Our platoon accidentally moved ahead of the skirmish line and one of our own tanks thought we were the enemy. He opened fire on us and DeLoyd Sargent got hit. He said, "Somebody help me! I've messed my pants! Help me take my pants down!" Nobody moved to help him—because it was obviously not a bowel movement. His blood and guts were rolling out into his dungarees. I think that was the first really close encounter I had, where somebody died right by my side. Sargent only lasted a couple of minutes, then he was gone. He blamed the lieutenant. Had we maintained our flank, that wouldn't have happened. Sargent said, "Tell my sister the goddamn lieutenant killed me." I don't know if anyone ever did or not—*probably not.*

Ben Carson, 96, Fifth Marine Division: I only lasted four days on the island. It was my birthday, February 23, 1945. I was proud I'd made it. I think I was twenty-two years old then. We took some bombardment, and I was wounded in my upper left arm. I was unconscious for about an hour, laying on the battlefield. In fact, I'd been passed up by several stretcher-bearers. I had a bad concussion. Finally, someone said, "Hell, we oughta pick this guy up, he's still alive." I opened my eyes, looked around, and said, "What the hell is going on?" They said, "Shut up, we're gonna get outta here."

Frank Wright, 96, Third Marine Division: On the morning of the twenty-third, at about ten o'clock, we heard all kinds of commotion out in the harbor; horns blowing and everything. God, we couldn't figure out what was going on. The flag had been raised on Mount Suribachi. I got my binoculars from the scout. I could see something up there, but I couldn't tell exactly what it was. But someone said it was a flag, so I said, "Great!" We went on and continued fighting. A little while later, a bigger flag went up. I got the binoculars again and I could see the big flag clearly.

A patrol from Easy Company, Second Battalion, Twenty-Eighth Marines summited Mount Suribachi on February 23, 1945. Using a derelict pipe found among the rubble, a small American flag was secured, and raised above the island. Not long after, another much larger flag was erected in place of the original. The second raising was captured by Associated Press photographer Joe Rosenthal, and would become the most iconic image of the battle.

Ken Brown, 95, Fifth Marine Division: I was down at the bottom of Mount Suribachi. I did a lot of crawling on Iwo Jima. I was crawling from one safe place to another when I picked up an old pair of broken Japanese binoculars with just one lens. When the first flag went up, a cheer went across the island. I looked and could see the little flag through the binoculars.

Elburn Cooper, 95, Fifth Marine Division: That was a big deal, guys were firing their rifles in the air.

Howard Rieckers, 100, Second Armored Amphibian Battalion: When that happened, they started blowing sirens all over the island. Right away, I looked up and saw the flag.

Roy Mays, 99, USS *Idaho*: I could see it very clearly. Our battleship was that close.

Don Pilcher, 95, Third Marine Division: I was down in the bunker, and we got a message: "Old Glory is flying on the 'hot top.'" I went up and there it was. That was great.

Ken Brown, 95, Fifth Marine Division: Up to that time, I thought we were going to lose the battle. Seemed like everybody was getting killed. I couldn't imagine us getting through it. But when that flag went up, we knew we'd taken their high ground, and the battle would surely end in our favor.

Howard Rieckers, 100, Second Armored Amphibian Battalion: We thought it was over with.

Jack Rasmussen, 94, Third Marine Division: Boy, we felt good. We thought raising the flag meant things were about over. That was a big lie.

Les Anderson, 97, First Provisional Field Artillery Group: When they put up the flag, that was the signal for the artillery to go to shore. We went over the side, down a cargo net, and into a Higgins boat. Our artillery was set up right at the foot of Suribachi. We had to wait until the hill was secured.

W. Lee Robinson, 97, Fifth Marine Division: That flag flying on Mount Suribachi was a godsend for us because we could now face north without any danger of Japanese troops firing at us from behind.

On February 24, 1945, the remainder of the Third Marine Division (minus the Third Marine Regiment) landed on Iwo Jima. General Harry Schmidt, the commander of the Fifth Amphibious Corps, ordered all three Marine divisions to attack north into General Kuribayashi's main defensive belt. The Fifth Marine Division, sweeping along the island's west bank, crashed into Nishi Ridge, Hill 362-A, and Hill 362-B, before being swallowed by a maze of boulders known as "the Gorge." After securing the Rock Quarry along the eastern beachhead, the Fourth Division entered a horrendous area later known as "the Meat Grinder." Meanwhile, the Third Marine Division battled across two adjoining hills nicknamed Peter and 199-Oboe, before assaulting Hill 362-C and entering a stone jungle called "Cushman's Pocket." The weeks to follow would be among the bloodiest in Marine Corps history.

Mike Ladich, 96, Fifth Marine Division: The Japs were crazy sonsabitches. They'd chop your fucking head off with a samurai sword if they captured you. That's the way they were. I can tell you a "funny" story about them: We had about thirteen trapped in a pillbox. I still remember the phrase: "Fuku o nugi nasai, sore kara mizu o ageru yo," which means, "Take off your clothes and we'll give you water." They couldn't get water in their pillboxes. You know what they replied? "Babe Ruth, eat shit!" I'll never forget that. They were baseball fans. They played baseball over there and they liked it. And they thought we hero-worshipped our baseball players, so they said, "Babe Ruth, eat shit!" That's the honest-to-God truth.

We had a crazy guy with a flamethrower. He said, "Buddies, you speak English? You're going to find out who eats shit in about two minutes if you don't come out of there with your hands up." Every other guy that had a flamethrower had thrown it away because the snipers usually got you. But this nut kept his. And he burned them up—about thirteen of them. I can still see him turning that goddamned flamethrower on that pillbox and the Japs running out on fire.

Robert Brutinel, 100, Fifth Marine Division: I'd use the flamethrower, then we'd make a bunch of C2 plastic explosives, and we'd drop them in to seal these caves off. We learned the hard way—if we *didn't* close the cave up, they'd come back at night, behind you. And those caves were everywhere!

Les Anderson, 97, First Provisional Field Artillery Group: It didn't make any difference whether you rolled in the sand or not: The napalm either killed you or suffocated you. The heat and the flames would suck the air out of the tunnels. Then our bulldozers would come up and push sand over the entrances. That stuff's why I've never talked about the war before.

Howard Rieckers, 100, Second Armored Amphibian Battalion: The flamethrowers were the worst thing. You'd go by where they'd killed a bunch of Japs and they'd be burning. The oil just sheared them. The smell from that . . .

Ray Kempf, 90, Fourth Marine Division: The smell of death is indescribable. You can explain your sight and you can explain what you hear. But you can't explain smell.

Harold Rediske, 94, Fourth Marine Division: There was an awful stink to that island.

Jack Rasmussen, 94, Third Marine Division: Our lieutenant said, "Jack, get your mortar section up on the airport." I said, "You've got to be crazy!" He was a new lieutenant. He said, "No, we've got orders to get up there." Hell, I wasn't up there for more than ten minutes when—*bango!*—I got hit in the hand and lost my rifle. I dropped down into a defilade. The corpsmen came up and said, "Do you want a shot to kill the pain?" I said, "Hell no! I want to get outta here!" He said, "We gotta take your rifle." I said, "I don't know where it is." He said, "It's right up there." We went up and got it. By golly, it had the gas chamber shot off. My hand was hit, the chamber was hit, and the butt of the rifle was hit; there were three bullet holes.

Walter O'Malley, 98, Fifth Marine Division: I got hit on the sixth day. We were on an offensive to take this ridge that was heavily protected. In that assault, seven of us in the squad of thirteen were wounded. We were being held down by machine gun fire and we couldn't move. Then they started laying in mortars. I had the BAR stock right beside my head, underneath my helmet. After I got hit, McNair says, "Look at the rifle." The stock was gone; it was just about obliterated where it got hit by shrapnel.

W. Lee Robinson, 97, Fifth Marine Division: It must have been the seventh or eighth day after we landed when the Japanese fired a barrage of artillery shells. "The Rabbit," "Little Smitty," and I made a dive for a shell hole. It lasted ten or fifteen minutes. The shells were close enough that they were blowing dirt on our backs; really giving us hell. It finally stopped and the Rabbit and I got up. But Little Smitty didn't. A piece of shrapnel caught him right in the small of the back. It crushed his spine. He was immediately unconscious. We said, "Smitty, are you okay?" He said nothing. "Smitty?" Then we realized . . .

Donald Raasch, 100, Fifth Marine Division: One thing about a mortar: you can hear it when it's coming down close to you; the *swish, swish* of the tail fins. One day we were moving behind a high cliff, looking for cover because the Japanese were shelling us with mortars. I heard the *swish, swish*, and I hit the ground. The mortar shell exploded behind me, very, very close. The concussion was so great that it knocked me unconscious. I don't know how long I was unconscious, but what woke me up was the sound of one of our men calling for a corpsman. The corpsman came, but it was too late. The guy that was hollering fell over dead. He only had one leg. I didn't *really* realize I had four holes in me until the corpsman came to fix me up. I had two holes in the arm, two holes in the leg.

Some guy told me to find a Marine to help me back to the first aid station. I did, and we made it there.

Art Perez, 96, Third Marine Division: When I got hit, I was laying down covering fire for a patrol moving across an open road. There was a Japanese tank up there, half buried, that could still fire its gun. I thought I was pretty safe, sitting up against a tree trunk, pushed into a corner. I leaned over to put out my cigarette when—*suddenly*—a chunk of my leg was gone. I looked over at our corporal and asked if he was okay. He said, "Yeah!" I said, "Your face looks like hamburger." He wiped his face, and I almost passed out. There was a chunk of my leg splattered on him.

Mike Ladich, 96, Fifth Marine Division: Adolph Fang had a real sense of humor. He got hit by five goddamn bullets across the chest—and lived. I picked him up, carried him down, and put him on a tank. He was bleeding like hell. I leaned him up against the turret and told the tanker to get down to the battalion aid station or he was going to bleed to death. Fang said, "Do you think I'll get the Purple Heart?" He was always funny to the goddamn end. I said, "Yeah, I think you're going to get it. Maybe you deserve five of them."

Harold Rediske, 94, Fourth Marine Division: Dwyer Duncan crawled out of our foxhole, and a shell landed nearby. A piece of shrapnel hit him near the brow. Everything fell out of the side of his head. I reached up and took his wrist, but I couldn't feel a pulse. I figured that he was dead. We'd been aboard ship for about fifty days, and he happened to have quite a bit of money from gambling. I reached into his pocket and pulled his wallet out; I knew the burial party wouldn't turn the money in. After the battle, I sent it to his mom with a note that said, "I'm sorry about Dwyer." I got a letter back from her that said, "Dwyer can distinguish between daylight and dark." He was blind, but alive.

Don Brown, 95, Fifth Marine Division: Dan Howard was my BAR-man. He got killed somewhere around two weeks after we landed. I was standing right next him. He got hit right in the throat and fell into my arms.

W. Lee Robinson, 97, Fifth Marine Division: A little boy from Texas named Strasburger was our runner. Our platoon was held up behind a big ledge. It was maybe four or six feet high. The platoon leader asked Strasburger to take a message to the company commander. He stood up and—*bang!*—just like that, caught one in the back, and he fell right at my feet. A neat kid, he was probably around eighteen.

Howard Rieckers, 100, Second Armored Amphibian Battalion: I will always remember one guy in our outfit: He came from Oregon, up in the timber region. His family sent him logger boots. He had them on when the Japanese blew him up. Everybody thought, *There goes those boots*. He was always bragging about those boots.

Robert Riechman, 98, Fifth Marine Division: One of my best friends stepped on a land mine—blew his arms and his legs off. We had to use our belts as a tourniquet. We wrapped whatever part of the limb that was still connected to the body to stop the bleeding. That was a gory thing; one of the things that I still think about.

Mike Ladich, 96, Fifth Marine Division: Sergeant Maeder jumped the goddamned ship and came back with his arm in a sling. I said, "What the fuck? Are you nuts? For Christ's sake! You were on a hospital ship! You were outta here!" He said, "I can't leave my boys behind." He was killed later. I saw him when they were burying him. Oh Jesus Christ—*horrible!* A lot of my buddies were killed there. War's no fun.

Ken Brown, 95, Fifth Marine Division: Being on Iwo Jima, under all that fire, was like trying to go through a rainstorm without getting wet.

Donald Brown, 95, Fifth Marine Division: I got hit in the leg with a piece of shrapnel. The corpsman bandaged it up and sent me back to my outfit.

W. Lee Robinson, 97, Fifth Marine Division: A Jap sniper shot our platoon leader through the face. It went through his jaw, took out a lot of his teeth, then went right into the head of another guy. Of course, the other guy was gone.

John Marx, 94, Third Marine Division: They were all underground. You'd walk by a hole and all of a sudden somebody would drop dead.

Jack Rasmussen, 94, Third Marine Division: I never saw a Jap there. They were all underground.

Ralph Simoneau, 97, Fifth Marine Division: I only saw four or five Japanese soldiers there. Most of the time, you were shooting at a movement, a shadow, or a noise. And thank God for that. I had very mixed feelings on killing. I'm a Christian, and I believe very strongly in the Ten Commandments. One of the Ten Commandments says, "Thou shall not kill." There's not a comma after that. I felt very strongly that killing is not right. It was difficult for me to deal with. Not that I would hesitate in combat. But nonetheless, it was very difficult, having someone in your sights, then shooting and killing them.

Burt Rutan, 95, Fifth Marine Division: I grew up in a strong Christian church and we really believed that you were in the hands of God. You could take risks: I believed that as a young Christian. It didn't bother me to say yes, when others would say no. I felt I was in God's hands, and whatever would happen, would happen.

A week into the battle, a tank came along, and they wanted someone to spot targets for it. I found out—*later*—that everybody else in my squad had refused to go. I was stupid enough to say, "I'll do it." I went out in front of the tank, and I was pointing my rifle at possible targets when I got knocked down by an explosion. Shrapnel hit my jawbone, went in sideways through my throat, and lodged in the back of my neck. It knocked me out, and I was sent to a hospital ship.*

Frank Wright, 96, Third Marine Division: I got hit in the head by a piece of shrapnel on Iwo and was knocked out. My squad moved on without me because they thought I was dead. I found them later, over by the sulfur pits, on the other side of Airfield Number Two. But there were only three of them left by then—"Pig" McCoy, Navaro, and myself. We couldn't find our company, so we stayed there overnight.

The next day, a general came by to pick up the remnants of the Fourth Division. One of the general's aides asked what unit we were with. We said, "Twenty-First Marines, Third Division." He said, "Where's your force?" I said, "We don't know." He said, "Well, you're going to help us out, then." So

* Burt Rutan was awarded a Silver Star for his actions. Citation in appendix.

we became part of the Fourth Division. We moved out from there, down in the sulfur pits, over to Motoyama Village, the radio station, and finally up to Hill 362. We wiped the Japs out and took that hill—but we sure went through hell. That hill was *really* bad. At the end of February, we took off for Hill 382. We tried to go over the top but got beat back by hand grenades and fire from two pillboxes armed with machine guns. We lost a lot of men on that attack. We tried again on March 1 and 2, but still got beat back. Finally, we tried using artillery from the big ships offshore, but they couldn't take out the pillboxes either.

On March 3, we went up again, this time with two of my guys in the lead. They went up the hill, over the top, then kept going, right around to the backside—and didn't get shot. There was absolutely no machine fire from the two pillboxes. Then my BAR-man took off and went over the hill. That's when they opened up. He went down on his belly and crawled into an area where they couldn't hit him. As I went over the top, the Japs trained the machine gun on me, and I got sprayed. I got shot in the chest, arm, and one round cracked my clavicle. I went down hard. A corpsman came up and pulled me back down, into one of the protected shell holes on the attack side. The two machine gunners on 382 were really doing their job—the wounded came pouring back down. The corpsman started putting sulfur on my wounds. Around that time, my BAR-man snuck out of his hiding place, moved up, then riddled the machine gunner and his partner. Someone else shot the Jap on the other side. The hill was now clear.

My BAR-man, a guy named McCoy, came walking down, jumped into my shell hole, and sat down. He had hundreds of bleeding holes in his back from a hand grenade that had gone off right behind him. His green blouse was just painted with spots of blood. The Japs had our range and started throwing mortars at our position. McCoy said, "Can you walk, Wright?" I said, "Yeah, let's get the hell outta here." He and I scooted backwards, got down behind some cover, and headed for the field hospitals set up on the beach. He was bleeding and so was I. My blouse was getting quite bloody.

We walked past Airfield Number Two and, just about that time, a B-29 came in and flew over, looking for a spot to land. God, those things are big. We made it to the field hospital and talked and visited as they redressed my wounds. Then they called for all the walking wounded to get aboard the LSTs. We said our goodbyes, had our last cigarette—and McCoy took off. The last time I saw him, he was walking up the ramp on that LST. That was on March 3, 1945. They took me out aboard a Higgins boat, then laid me on the deck of a hospital ship by crane. I laid there for a while, until the doctors could get to me.

Finally, I got into the operating room, and they dressed my chest and stitched me up. I heard one of the doctors say something with my arm. He said, "It looks like the muscle's gone. Raise your hand, Wright." I tried raising my hand, but I couldn't raise it; I couldn't manipulate my left arm at all. He said, "We'll have to take it off. You can operate a prosthetic. You can't use that arm anymore; it'll just hang there." That got my attention. I replied, "No, I don't want that." He said, "We're going to have to. Don't you agree, doctor?" The other doctor looked at my arm and said, "Well, he doesn't seem to think so, but it will be a lot better for him if we do." About that time, I raised up and swung. I hit the surgeon just above the shoulder with my good arm, and I knocked him across the room. He fell backwards and upset the surgical tray and the IV. Oh boy, then the shit really hit the fan! They called the orderly in and held me down while they straightened up the place. Then they put a patch over my arm and put a tag on my collar that read: "Combat Fatigue." That's all they put.

I arrived in Saipan a few days later. They took me off the ship, looked at the tag, and put me in the combat fatigue ward. I was still bleeding, had a big pad on my chest. But nobody was looking at my wounds. Finally, the ward doctor came in and he checked me out with a stethoscope. He said, "We're going to have to perform a tap. We'll do that in the morning." It didn't make any difference to me what they did. I was just glad I still had my arm. After the doctor left, I asked someone, "What's this tap stuff they're talking about?" The guys said, "It's a procedure. You're bleeding inside—the inside of your chest is full of blood. They'll stick a long needle in your back that goes up into your chest and it'll siphon the blood out." I said, "Holy mackerel! I've got that to look forward to tomorrow."

That night, I was pretty restless. I felt something wet, and I thought, *Oh God! I peed my pants!* I called the night nurse. She came over and turned the bed light on and gasped, "Ach!" Then she turned off the bed light and rushed away. I said, "What the heck is going on?" I thought she was probably going to get some more linen, but she came back with a doctor and a couple of nurses. As it turned out, I was laying in a pool of blood. Sometime in the night, I'd turned over on my left side—and all the blood that was in my chest emptied onto the bed. And here I was, laying there thinking I'd peed my pants! The doctor came over, looked at that, and said, "I guess we won't perform a tap in the morning."

After that, they put me on a PBY-3, and we flew to Hawaii. We landed on Johnston Island, taxied over to the dock, and two corpsmen came over and sprayed us with disinfectant. We'd been deep in the Pacific, and they didn't want any new bugs in Pearl Harbor, I guess. We left Johnston Island, got up to Pearl, and taxied up to the landing ramp. Then they unloaded us and took us to our respective wards. They looked at my tag and I got put in the combat fatigue ward. I had no one to change my bandages for a while. Finally, they took me over to the surgical area with an armed guard. Evidently, word got around that I was a little combative. They changed my bandages and put me back in the ward. I left Pearl and went to San Diego on the USS *Hope*. I got into a San Diego hospital and was put in the nut ward again. I found a nurse that agreed to take me over to get my bandages changed periodically. I stayed in the San Diego hospital for quite a while.

Back on Iwo Jima, the Third Division was driving toward the northern coastline, while the Fifth Marine Division battered a pocket of resistance in the west. The Fourth Division, bloodied by heavy combat at Turkey Knob, assaulted another pocket to the east. Appeals for surrender, broadcast over loudspeakers in Japanese, were largely ignored by the starving and dehydrated defenders.

James Shriver, 98, Fifth Marine Division: On the twelfth of March, we went down a road, turned left, and got into a canyon; it's always reminded me of a miniature version of the Grand Canyon. It was very steep-sided, but the top was only twelve or fifteen feet above the bottom. And we really got into a helluva firefight in that canyon. As the day wore on and we started to secure in for the night, word came out that we were going to change tactics. We weren't going to wait in our holes until dawn—we were going out at dark, early the next morning. At the same time, they brought up replacements. One of the replacements joined me in the foxhole. There were only two men out of my platoon—*that I knew*—that were still with us. One was a sergeant, myself, and a guy by the name of JJ Martin, from Phoenix, Arizona.

At dawn, someone came in and began to shake our shoulders and get us going. Orders were: "Keep contact with the man on your right." But as we backed out of the canyon, back onto the road, I lost contact with the guy on my right. I started walking down the road—and I kept looking for him, but nobody was there. I recognized that first light was just beginning to come over the horizon. Then I saw an opening along the side of the road; looked like a turnaround for a vehicle. I walked myself into that opening and—*my God!*—it looked like the Fourth of July. The whole side of the canyon started firing. The next thing I knew, there was a hell of an explosion, and I went flying up in the air.

When I came down, I was laying on the ground. But I could hear someone speaking Japanese. I thought, *Where the hell's this goddamned Japanese at?* I turned over—and watched as a cover lifted up and a Japanese head popped out of a hole. He saw me and I saw him. He must have been as surprised as I was! When he disappeared, my adrenaline was flowing. I was very alert. I *knew* what was going to happen; I *knew* he was going to throw a hand grenade at me. Sure enough, I heard—*thump! thump!*—and out came a grenade. Fortunately, he threw it directly into my right hand. I just caught it and threw it back into the hole.

At that time, I thought, *I'd better get the hell outta here!* I got up and started down the road, but I was losing a lot of blood. When I got partway up, off to my left was JJ Martin. He was yelling something to me, but I couldn't hear. As I lay in the road, I realized that the Japanese were using me as bait. Anytime someone got near me, they opened up on him. Then I looked up. At the top of the road, I saw an American amtrac. It started down towards me. I was kind of apprehensive: I was afraid that he was going to run me over—but he ran *over top of me*, opened up a hatch underneath, and took me inside. Then they took me to an aid station.

Bill Byrd, 98, Fifth Marine Division: Up north, when we almost had the island under control, one of our guys was laying out in the open. We couldn't get to him because the Japanese would shoot us. We finally came up with a scheme to throw grenades in their direction, then move. We counted to three, threw our grenades, then one of the guys ran out and dragged him in. There were things like that going on all the time. They had a lot of caves in there, and it was bad.

Bill Morgenroth, 100, Fifth Marine Division: The Japanese had what they called embrasures; little slots they could stick their rifles through. They could hold back a whole company of Marines with only two or three men and do a lot of damage. I was part of a little group assigned to get rid of those pillboxes.

One day, they sent us up to put one of those things out of business. Three of us ran up near it and jumped into a tremendously big hole. We got out our demolitions equipment and started getting ready to blow it. A friend of mine—his name was Enders, from Chicago—crawled up the side of the hole and tried to find a nice spot to stick the dynamite. There was a shot and—*boy!*—he came rolling down the hill. He landed in the sand, down where I was. I got ahold of his foot and pulled him down deeper.

I pulled his pants off to see the wound—and there were three holes. Enders thought he had lost his family jewels! But he hadn't. He was hit in the leg, near the crotch, and the blood was coming out like Jell-O. I'm no doctor, but I knew a tourniquet would be the best thing. I told the third guy in our group—a kid from New York; nice kid—to watch him. I was going to see if I could get a stretcher and a couple more Marines. I thought—*maybe*—if we got six guys on a stretcher, we could run and get him out of there.

I knew the Japanese had a bead on the hole, so whoever shot Enders was going to try to shoot me. I was afraid to get out of the hole! I looked up a couple of times, to see if I could find another place to take cover. I noticed a nearby hole and thought, *Well, I don't know. That one looks like it leads back to our lines*, and that's where I wanted to go. So I made up my mind: I was going to hit the open, as fast as I could, and run. That was probably the only chance I had.

I got up and ran like crazy and jumped into the next hole. But as I was sliding down, I looked around: there were about three or four Japanese sitting there, with their backs against the wall. And they all had rifles! I thought, *Jesus! Did I ever pick a bad hole! I got to get outta here!* I turned around to run—but I noticed one Japanese soldier fall over. They were all dead! They had already been killed by a shell burst.

I got out of that hole, as fast as I could, and ran towards our lines. And that's when I got hit; I got shrapnel from a shell burst. It blew me down onto the sand. I was unconscious when a corpsman found me. He gave me a shot, and I didn't feel much anymore. When I came to, he told me that our lines had already passed, and someone had found Enders and took him back. They put me on a stretcher, loaded me into a truck, and brought us over to a field hospital.

Robert Brutinel, 100, Fifth Marine Division: We got held up by a Japanese pillbox, and I just went up and hit it with a flamethrower. I used up all the fluid, so I came back—there was a guy that had one that was full, and he let me have it. I went back, and I finished it. Then, to make sure there wasn't anyone inside anymore, I threw a satchel of C2 in there.*

* Robert Brutinel was awarded a Silver Star for his actions in disabling the pillbox. His citation is listed in the appendix.

Eugene Jones, 94, Fourth Marine Division: On the twenty-sixth day, I was throwing explosive charges into a cave with a number of other Marines. We were really thin on the ground—and by that, I mean there just weren't very many of us left. Most of the time you're fighting with total strangers—*replacements*.

I was trembling when I got to the cave entrance, more from fatigue than from fear. There were two Marines with rifles on the other side of the cave. The entrance was only four feet wide and eight feet high and it sloped down into flat ground at the bottom. I threw the charge in—and there was a dead silence. I had cut the fuse wrong.

We knew there were a lot of Japs inside, so we kept waiting for something to happen. After about two minutes, the explosive charge came sailing back out. The Japs had reset it. By sheer coincidence, it exploded right between me and the two other guys. They were obliterated. I was thrown back, all the way down to the flat ground at the bottom. My wounds were minor: I was, what they call, drenched in shrapnel.

As I lay there I heard, not a scream, but a howl. I looked up at the cave entrance and a huge naked guy jumped out of the cave entrance. This guy—he couldn't have been, God, about eighteen—was screaming the old bullshit phrase: "Banzai!"

There were about five or six "scraggly-ass Marines" down the slope, only about fifteen or twenty feet away. They immediately shot the shit out of him. His body, with the momentum, whirled around and landed right beside me. He was still alive, vomiting and gurgling. His elbow was touching mine. I leaned over and saw that he was wearing a thousand-stitch belt; that's a jockstrap made out of beads. Japanese families, when a son or a husband went to the war, would get every friend, relative, or person they knew in the community, to contribute a bead. Those beads, usually vivid colors like yellow, red, green, and blue, were then sewn onto a tiny jockstrap. Then they would wear that in combat.

Just as I noticed his jockstrap, all the other Marines ran over, one of them screaming, "See that jockstrap? It's mine!" He and another guy dropped to their knees and started physically slapping at each other's hands to get the jockstrap. A third Marine came over, sat down on top of the Jap's chest, calmly pulled out a pair of pliers, and with the man still gurgling, pulled out his gold teeth.

Bill Gropp, 97, Fifth Marine Division: We had one fella in our company that went after teeth. But that was a little disturbing to me, I wasn't that type of person.

John Marx, 97, Third Marine Division: I didn't like it. We had a guy who was a mortuary man, and he did all kinds of terrible things like that. I thought it was wrong. He cut body parts off, too. Who would want to take something like that home? I sure wouldn't.

Ken Brown, 95, Fifth Marine Division: I didn't see any of that, but I understand that some of that was done. The Marines had a great hatred. They'd seen the Japanese kill their best buddies and they didn't hesitate to do things they should not have done. That was not part of the Marine Corps code or method—*at all*.

Robert Brutinel, 100, Fifth Marine Division: That was a big deal in the Marine Corps—*souvenirs*. The joke was: When they shot a Nip, before he hit the ground, they had him stripped.

Ralph Simoneau, 97, Fifth Marine Division: The Marines have always been known as good souvenir pickers. And the

Japanese took advantage of that. In many cases, the bodies were booby-trapped. If you rolled a guy over, a grenade might explode and kill you. I kept away from the dead.

Stew Lahey, 97, Second Separate Engineer Battalion: There was a guy in our platoon, he was about twenty-eight, and had a daughter. At the bottom of Mount Suribachi, there were crates of Japanese parachute flares. He mentioned, in passing, that those parachutes were made of silk: "I want to get one for my daughter!" I started to say, "Ted, don't go! Ted! Ted! No! Stop!" But he was about ten feet ahead of me. I couldn't stop him. He opened up the crate—and it was booby-trapped. He blew both hands off. He died right in front of me, just keeled over.

Mike Ladich, 96, Fifth Marine Division: There were two sailors that jumped ship and came down looking for souvenirs. A sniper got one of them. The other one came running over to us, crying his fucking eyes out, saying his buddy had been shot. We looked at him and said, "Half our fuckin' platoon's been shot! Why the hell should we worry about your buddy, for Christ's sake? What the hell are you doing here in the first place? Go on back to your ship and do your goddamn crying over there."

Bill Byrd, 98, Fifth Marine Division: A Marine was killed up there, and his close friend was crying like a baby. I remember that.

Bill Gropp, 97, Fifth Marine Division: I remember one fella—I won't say his name—that went a little berserk. We didn't know what to do with him. When you're pinned down by mortars, it's pretty rough. Instead of getting in a foxhole, he started running, and waving his arms. Someone took him down. He was all right after that, but it was pretty shocking to a lot of us, though.

Les Anderson, 97, First Provisional Field Artillery Group: I laid on top of a young kid—who I think he was a year or two younger than I was—because he was eager to get out of the hole to run during a bombardment. That's the worst thing you could do, so I laid on top of him.

Ken Brown, 95, Fifth Marine Division: I saw a major in our company come back completely crazy. They tied him down and tried to evacuate him.

Mike Ladich, 96, Fifth Marine Division: Bobby Hunt and Martin were Okies; kind of backward types. There was a little rise in the ground near where we dug in one evening. I dug in *behind* the rise, but those nitwits stayed up high. I yelled at them, "A fucking sniper can get you from there!" "Oh, we'll be okay, we'll keep our heads down." Well, Martin got his fucking head blown off by a sniper and Hunt cracked up. He cried, and cried—cradled the guy all night, crying. Then they took him away.

Robert Riechman, 98, Fifth Marine Division: When bad things happened to me, it was no big deal. It didn't bother me to the point where I lost control of myself. *It is what it is*, I thought. *Accept it. Accept the goriness of it.* It never did bother me. Like when I lost my friend John. He got killed by the same shell that exploded and hit my knee—he got his head blown off.

Robert Brutinel, 100, Fifth Marine Division: Word came in that a corpsman had been hit; he was crippled or dead. The guy in charge was a first sergeant because all the officers were dead. He said to me, "You know where that company is?" I said, "Yeah, I do." He said, "You go and take this new corpsman down to them." I said, "Okay," and off I went.

Not far away, there was this great big indentation in the ground. I thought, *If I go down that end and come up the other side, I won't be in the line of fire.* But just as I went down, this Nip stood up and fired. I saw the bullet! No one can say I didn't, because I did! I saw this bullet coming in—and it hit me in the face. I just stood there until the corpsman pulled me down. I was bleeding pretty heavy; I could feel hot blood coming down my arms. I thought I was dead! The corpsman took me back—and the first sergeant saw me and said, "Well, you didn't make it very far, did you?"

Mike Ladich, 96, Fifth Marine Division: About the last goddamn day we were there, a Jap came out from a cave, nearly naked, and charged me with nothing; he was committing suicide. All he had was a little patch over his testicles—*that's all.* The rest of him was naked as hell. But I figured he had a grenade hidden under his loincloth, otherwise I would have just knocked him on his ass because he was so small. There'd been nothing to it. But I figured he had a grenade, so I shot him. I hit him in the stomach and knocked him down. But he kept crawling towards me, and I kept stepping back. Finally, I realized he didn't have a grenade. He crawled up to me and looked me right in the eyes. Almost as if to say, "I know how to die!" Boy, if you think that isn't touching—even if it was the enemy. Then his face hit my shoe, and he died.

Ken Brown, 95, Fifth Marine Division: They were really a rugged people.

Blair Hyde, 103, Third Marine Division: We had a new regimental commander who was a really nice guy. I liked him a lot. But he came up, threw his arm around me, and said, "Blair, I'm going to do you a favor. I'm going to give you K Company, make you a company commander up there. You've got to get it on your record that you've held this particular job; it will help you with your future in the Marine Corps." I said, "Colonel, when this is over, I'm getting out of the Marine Corps. I'm not staying around; it's not part of my life plan." He didn't like that. But I went up there and took over the company. We only had one attack, and then it was over. We were on the northern end of Iwo.

Billy Byrd, 98, Fifth Marine Division: We spent one more night in the north, before we headed back south. We thought everything was over, but about five or six Japanese came out of their holes and invaded our platoon. A couple of them had swords, one had just his shorts on, and the other I saw had a gun. Of course, they cut him down real quick. We got rid of them—and that was their last stand. In the morning, our lieutenant, Armstrong, came up. The whole battalion got in a double file going south. It was about four miles down to where we first started. God, we were shocked to see a cemetery had been built while we were fighting on the north side. We were just shocked to see that cemetery—with little white crosses lined up perfect. We walked among them to see some of our friends. There were so many of them.

At dawn on March 26, 1945, roughly three hundred Japanese soldiers launched a final banzai charge, striking American positions west of the second airfield. In the melee, forty-four airmen were killed in action, some slashed with sabers or stabbed by bayonets while they slept. The Fifth Pioneer Battalion, accompanied by scattered Seabees, antiaircraft operators, and elements of the Twenty-Eighth Marines, beat off the attack and eradicated the Japanese by first light. After thirty-six days of carnage, Iwo Jima was finally declared secure. American forces had suffered 25,851 killed and wounded in the battle. Only 216 Japanese soldiers from the original 21,000-man garrison surrendered.

Ken Brown, 95, Fifth Marine Division: When we got to Iwo, I went ashore with the chaplain. I was with him for about four or five days. Then all replacements were called to the front line because they had so many casualties. I was sent up to the Twenty-Sixth Marines. They knew I was a machine gunner, so I was assigned to a machine gun platoon. I was on the line for about eight days with the unit and went through the worst of the battle. One day, the captain called us down and said, "We're going to take the hill tomorrow morning. If you need to write letters home, now's the time to do it." We sat around writing letters and telling our families everything was fine. A runner came up from the rear area and said, "Do you have a chaplain's assistant up here named Brown?" Someone said, "Yeah." The runner said, "He's needed back at the cemetery. They've secured a piece of land at the bottom of Mount Suribachi and they're beginning burials for the dead. He's needed back there for his duties. Here's his replacement."

I went back to the cemetery and spent the rest of my time assisting with burial of the dead. The bulldozer would come along and dig a trench about twenty feet long. Then they dug a grave for each man. After they got everyone in a grave, the chaplain would give a prayer, and they'd cover them up. They did a very efficient job.

Les Anderson, 97, First Provisional Field Artillery Group: I remember truckload, after truckload, after truckload of bodies being brought in. Our artillery was set up right next to the burial area.

Elburn Cooper, 95, Fifth Marine Division: Our job was to pick up artillery shells that hadn't blown up. We were picking them up and putting them in the back of our half-ton truck. They'd bounce around like crazy as we hauled them to the dump. Then our group went from there over to burial duty. That was a sad time. We were picking up the guys that had been killed in body bags that were really nothing more than mattress covers. Our job was to lift them from the place that they had been deposited alongside the rows, down into the graves. We did that—seemed like forever. But I think it was only three or four days.

Ken Brown, 95, Fifth Marine Division: They had a mimeograph machine on the island that mimeographed the casualties each day. A copy of that was given to the chaplain, so he would know who was coming in. On about the tenth day, I was looking at the list and I saw my friend's name on it. When they brought his body in, I waited, then I helped personally bury him on Iwo Jima.

Elburn Cooper, 95, Fifth Marine Division: When it was all over, I felt blessed.

Mike Ladich, 96, Fifth Marine Division: It's almost like it was a nightmare, none of it was reality.

Howard Frye, 95, Third Marine Division: You're numb.

W. Lee Robinson, 97, Fifth Marine Division: Of the eleven men in my squad, two of us were uninjured, six were dead, and three were wounded. Sixty-eight hundred Marines died on Iwo Jima. It was the bloodiest battle in Marine Corps history.

Donald Brown, 95, Fifth Marine Division: In our platoon, we went in with just over sixty men. We came back with seven.

Mike Ladich, 96, Fifth Marine Division: Going in on the troopship, every bunk was taken; full-up. Coming back, two-thirds of the bunks were empty.

Howard Rieckers, 100, Second Armored Amphibian Battalion: I lucked out, I lucked out. I think the good Lord was with me.

Herman Kulla, 100, Third Marine Division: I was just so lucky. Boy, I had enemy bullets hit the tripod legs on my machine gun. How it missed me—beats the hell outta me. I don't know, I was just lucky. Lots of times I was lucky.

Les Anderson, 97, First Provisional Field Artillery Group: Even to this day, I couldn't tell you whether it was worth all those dead bodies to take that island. But I know we saved a lot of airmen.

Don Pilcher, 95, Third Marine Division: I had a good friend who was in the Air Corps. He would always tell me how grateful they were that we'd taken Iwo Jima.

Robert Riechman, 98, Fifth Marine Division: Somebody once said, "Boy, you're a hero!" I'm not a fuckin' hero. I was eighteen years old, and I had to go. I wasn't a hero.

Harold Rediske, 95, Third Marine Division: The only heroes are the guys under the white crosses.

Ken Brown, 95, Fifth Marine Division: The heroes are all dead. They're the ones that died. Nearly seven thousand of them died. In my opinion, they're in the graves over there. Those of us who survived—we were just lucky.

Bert Rutan, 95, Fifth Marine Division: A real hero, to me, is a person who knows danger and faces it. That can happen in a variety of ways. I didn't realize what I did was dangerous. Some guys did. They volunteered for tough missions. Just like the guys who took the top of Mount Suribachi. They knew they were going to be exposed, but they did it anyway.

Bill Gropp, 97, Fifth Marine Division: We had some good people doing their job—*that was it.*

16 ★ ★ ★ ★ ★ ★

OKINAWA

After the fall of Iwo Jima in March, American forces amassed the largest invasion force of the Pacific War to capture an island south of Kyushu in the Ryukyu Islands. Okinawa was a sixty-seven-mile-long patchwork of farm fields, ancient cities, and rolling hills capable of providing a launch point for American bombers and naval vessels for the eventual invasion of mainland Japan. Intelligence reports estimated that more than one hundred thousand Japanese soldiers inhabited Okinawa, alongside hundreds of thousands of Okinawan civilians (a group historically considered racially inferior by the Japanese, despite their proximity to Japan). The Army's Seventy-Seventh Division would vanguard the assault by striking the Kerama Retto island group, just fifteen miles west of the island, on March 26, 1945. The main invasion would land troops along Okinawa's western coastline on April 1, 1945, at 0830.

Eldon Cedergreen, 96, Sixth Tank Battalion: We were all lined up in Higgins boats, racing towards the shore, wondering if we were going to make it or if we were going to drown out there. The young fella who was running our boat did a good job: I don't think we walked through three feet of water.

Everything was pretty calm for a landing, and everybody was totally surprised.

Donn Thompson, 95, Sixth Marine Division: It was April Fool's Day when we landed—and we didn't hear a shot. We kept advancing, figuring all hell's going to break loose before we know it. Never did. We got up to Yontan Airstrip, our first day's objective, in a matter of hours. We dug in and it was getting dark when a Japanese Zero—a fighter plane—circled the field and landed. As the pilot got out and looked around, some dummy in our outfit shot him. He had come all the way from China and didn't know the Americans had landed. We could have used him for information, but some nut had to shoot him.

Ernie Ferguson, 98, First Marine Division: We spent two days crossing the island and didn't fire a rifle.

George Bradbury, 98, First Marine Division: My only excitement on that little trip was when I helped deliver a baby. An Okinawan woman was hollering, and a corpsman went over to see what was going on. She was starting to have her baby, so I helped them with that. But we crossed the island, went almost ten miles, and never fired a shot.

Chuck Meacham, 96, Sixth Marine Division: I don't remember any enemy contact. We climbed up and around mountains and moved along pretty fast. We even got kind of careless. You could look across the valley, see our guys, and give them hand signals.

Carl Scott, 98, First Marine Division: We ran into a cave—and about four Japs ran out and disappeared into a hut down below. We fired at them and set the place on fire. But the Japs never came out. That was the only action we saw. One day I was out on patrol, and I found a pony. I decided to ride him back to camp—and I did. But some officer saw me and said, "What are you doing? That's somebody's pony! Get off of there!"

Eugene Thomas, 92, First Marine Division: We patrolled the mountainous area around Nago and found no Japanese there. While on one of these patrols, I jumped off a wall of rocks while carrying my twenty-one-pound rifle and twenty-one pounds of ammo and sprained my ankle. I hobbled back about two miles to camp while the patrol went on. They came down with trucks and took us back to Kadena, in the Army sector.

It was there, in a flat area, that Navy planes dove in and shelled us with rockets by accident. I looked around, seeing these feet in shoes and leggings—but the rest of the body wasn't there. In a bush, over by the feet, hanging in the branches, there was his genitals and pieces of stomach skin.

On April 6, 1945, as American forces progressed rapidly across northern Okinawa, the Japanese launched their final naval offensive of the war. Comprised of various air and sea elements, Operation Ten-Go was a desperate attempt to drive American forces away from Okinawa through a decisive multipronged strike. Mimicking tactics first employed during the Battle of Leyte Gulf in the Philippines, the Japanese would utilize kamikaze attacks; a suicidal form of warfare in which teams of aircraft intentionally crashed into American vessels.

Gordon Black, 94, First Marine Division: That was my first experience seeing a kamikaze operation. I'll never forget it.

We landed in the first part of April and there was a big white hospital ship out in the water. This Japanese Zero circled above, then peeled off, and went right down the stack. I was glad I wasn't on a ship.

Roy Mays, 99, USS *Idaho*: I saw one kamikaze come in as close as me to you, just off the gun mount. I could see the Japanese pilot's face looking up at me. A few minutes later, there was a guy taking his ear around. That's all they could find of the pilot.

Robert Beale, 97, USS *Bennington*: We were constantly under attack, at general quarters twenty-four hours a day. We even had C rations delivered to our battle stations because there was no time to go to the mess hall. There were a lot of close calls. The *Bennington* was one of the few carriers that wasn't hit—we were very lucky. Our job was to defend against attacking planes, but I never actually saw any of the planes that we hit because I was constantly grabbing 40mm shells from the loader and dropping them into the breach. Then I'd go get another and drop it in the breach again. If I were looking up in the sky to see if we were hitting our target, I wouldn't have been doing my job. So I didn't see the war—even though I was right there, if you know what I mean.

We had several kamikazes miss just off our fantail and splash into the ocean, very close calls. We had one: A Jap plane made a dive on the carrier at the bow and went the entire length of the *Bennington,* only two hundred feet above the deck, before pulling up into the sky again. It's speculated that he probably couldn't engage his bombs and, for whatever reason, gave up. That was the closest we came to a real hit. But there's no fear, there's no fear. You're concentrating on the job. You get the shells from the loader, you drop them in the breach, you get the shells from the loader, you drop them in the breach. We learned this at school in Norfolk.

After our shakedown cruise, going to San Diego, we practiced every day. Then again from San Diego to Pearl Harbor. We practiced every day, every day, every day. We were like a well-oiled machine, eleven guys working together; we were a team. You do it by memory—it becomes part of you.

Although Operation Ten-Go ultimately failed, kamikazes were able to sink 36 ships, damage another 368, and inflict more than ten thousand casualties. On land, the period of relative peace ended abruptly when the US Army met stiff Japanese resistance in the south. Likewise, in the north, men from the Sixth Marine Division were uncovering heavily defended positions in and around the Motobu Peninsula.

Eldon Cedergreen, 96, Sixth Tank Battalion: There were a lot of pine trees on the north end of Okinawa and the tanks couldn't do much while the infantry hunted the Japanese. We had a week or two off and didn't do anything. But it didn't last. I darn near lost my life up there: I was out on guard duty in the middle of the night and the Japanese gave us a little surprise. We were bivouacked on level ground in a small pasture, gathered in a circle like covered wagons. We were being kind of careless since we hadn't seen any resistance. That night, I had the first call on guard duty. There was a small amount of moonlight, just enough so you could see. All at once, the guard on the tank next to me yelled, "They're out there—and my Thompson submachine gun's jammed!" About that time, a little Japanese patrol, covered by the pine trees, fired a Nambu machine gun. I yelled to the guys in the tent, "Get out of there! We've got company!"

I looked down the trail and there was an enemy soldier,

staring up at me. I pulled my pistol out and took a shot—but I didn't hit him. He disappeared, so I turned my attention back to the group, over in the trees. Luckily somebody had taken the bow gun out of my tank and set it up. I took a belt of ammunition, put it in, hit the trigger, and away it went. Boy, I was tickled! Now I had something to fire back with. My first concentration went towards the group hiding in the trees. I couldn't see them, so I threw a bunch of lead up there. They didn't like my machine gun fire and took off. One Marine from another tank came running by. He pointed at something in front of me and said, "There's one!" then he kept running. I thought, *Why don't you stop and do something about it?* I couldn't see anything, so I sprayed and scorched the earth. I was really throwing lead! Then everything went quiet and there was no more movement.

Our lieutenant came up behind me and said, "What do you see, Cedergreen?" I waited a minute, then I said, "I'm seeing nothing." My shift was over and pretty soon things quieted down. The next morning, I was pretty slow to get up. But the first thing I did was go out to see if I'd hit anything. I saw the Nambu cartridges and some shoes; they'd just kicked off their shoes. I thought, *What in the world?* Maybe they were cranked up on sake or something. I heard voices down below and I ran across the trail—and there was our first kill of the war. He was hit by my machine gun fire, laying out in the field. That gave me a funny feeling. Taking a man's life is an emotional thing. One bullet went through his helmet—out of all that machine gun fire. I was on the crew that buried him. Then I put it out of my mind: *That's it, that's war.* Somebody asked, "Who got him?" They said, "Cedergreen did!" I was a hero for a couple of days. They were talking it up around our company.

I brought the Japanese guy's helmet home. For me, it had two meanings: I'd taken the life of a young fella, but at the same time, it was a trophy. I'd done a piece of good work. But at home, my brother said that it really upset my mom seeing that helmet, so I tossed it.

Chuck Meacham, 96, Sixth Marine Division: Up come these 6x6 trucks and there was a lot of yelling. Next thing I know, I was packed on that sucker like a sardine. I was so squashed that I actually went to sleep standing up. I remember the exact date because the radio guys were hollering, "President Roosevelt died!" as we went down the road. We gave them a nice one finger salute. But after about the third time, we got serious. Yes, turned out he had died. That was the same day we were hauled up to the Motobu Peninsula. There wasn't any time to think about it. We were flopped out into a bad situation, that needed us. We started crawling up these miserable six-foot terraces.

Tom Shields, 93, Sixth Marine Division: On Mount Yaedake up on the north end of the island, we lost about sixty percent of my company in fifteen minutes. We ran into a hornet's nest up there. Our company commander and executive officer were sitting with the radioman—and the Japs got all three of them at one time.

During the five-day contest for the Motobu Peninsula, the Sixth Marine Division lost 207 killed and 757 wounded. On April 19, 1945, General Simon Bolivar Buckner, the commander of the Tenth Army on Okinawa, ordered a full-scale offensive against Japanese defenses in the south. Preceded by a devastating barrage of American artillery and naval shelling, Army troops from the Seventh, Twenty-Seventh, and Ninety-Sixth Divisions pressed forward, but were quickly met by a wave of overwhelming Japanese fire from mutually supporting hillside positions. At Kakazu Ridge alone, twenty-two out of thirty Sherman tanks were destroyed by enemy field guns. As the offensive stalled, the First Marine Division (soon followed by the Sixth) was called south to relieve Army units embroiled along a defensive perimeter known as the Shuri Line.

William Darling, 98, First Marine Division: We were told we were going to be transferred down to the south because the Twenty-Seventh Army Division wasn't making any progress. So our company—K Company, Third Battalion of the First—went down to relieve George Company of the 165th. When we got there, they were already walking out of their positions; put a nice big gap in the line. We rushed in to take over.

Tom Charlton, 95, First Marine Division: Our squad leader, "Red," crawled up to me and said, "We're going out on a forward patrol, and we'll be back at daylight. Our password is 'Franklin.'" Daylight came and they still weren't back. I told Rardin, "They must have run into trouble or something." We moved forward the next day. We hadn't gone half a mile—and there was a little knoll up ahead. As we approached it, we could see debris and stuff on the hillside. That patrol had been ambushed. The first thing I saw was Red's head. Most of the Japanese officers had swords, and they had just cut his head off. Even now, that's fresh in my memory. We never had any mercy for the Japanese, and they never had any for us.

Eldon Cedergreen, 96, Sixth Tank Battalion: We were up against a very vicious people. Their soldiers were indoctrinated. We read about the atrocities they committed and that didn't make us feel very good. We didn't have any empathy for them.

Eugene Thomas, 92, First Marine Division: It felt good killing those guys. If you killed them, that meant you lived.

Russel Nelson, 98, First Marine Division: If you saw a Japanese, you just shot him. I don't know how many we took prisoner on Okinawa. A lot of them would come out of the caves and hold their hands up. But sometimes they'd send a lady out with hand grenades under her arms. She'd come out and greet everybody. Then she'd open her arms, and we'd lose a couple guys.

Eugene Thomas, 92, First Marine Division: I saw one prisoner being carried down a ridge. It looked like he was wounded. The guys with me started making comments and laughing at him. Finally, the stretcher team dumped him into a shell hole and shot him.

Tom Charlton, 95, First Marine Division: I usually carried a little Japanese carbine over my shoulder. When we'd stop to take a break, I'd take it off because it was awkward to sit with. One day Gelderman yelled, "Tom, that Jap's alive!" He pointed at a guy laying against the bank, up along the road. I looked at the Jap. I can still see his eyes—they were really dark brown. I pulled up my carbine and shot him. Just shot him and kept going. I think about that: He was fighting for his country, and I was fighting for ours. I never liked any of them, but they were doing their duty. He had a mother and dad at home thinking: *I sure hope he gets back*. And I shot him. Stuff like that bothers me really bad.

Eugene Thomas, 92, First Marine Division: One afternoon, me and another guy went down to fill our canteens with water. We passed through the mortar platoon, which was set up behind us. They were taking it easy, and their lieutenant was taking a bath in a little stream there. I had left my BAR back in the foxhole and carried with me a Jap rifle. We were walking this little path the Okinawans used and, having hunted at home a lot, my instinct was to survey the trail and bushes around me. I looked over the edge to where the water was and didn't see anything, so we went down and filled our canteens and came back.

I was looking over the side of the same area we'd gone by—and I seen a shoe. My eyes ran up the body of a Japanese laying there. Thinking he was dead, I picked up a small rock, threw it, and hit him in the chest. But he was alive! The Jap jumped up and the man I was with took off for the rear. The Jap rifle I had was on "safe," so I leaned back to take it off. When I looked back up, the Jap had a grenade out. I shot him and the grenade went off at the same time and tore open his body. The lieutenant who was taking a bath, and others nearby, came up very alive. That Jap had probably been waiting there for a few days.

David Fusinato, 97, First Marine Division: One suicidal Jap came out of nowhere and threw an explosive charge—we called them satchel charges—at the tracks of my tank. Luckily it bounced off and we shot the guy. I saw a lot of dead Japs, but that was actually the only living one I ever saw from the tank.

Eldon Cedergreen, 96, Sixth Tank Battalion: Sitting in the tank, we didn't see all the mud, blood, and grime. The infantry saw the whole horrible thing, but we were spared that.

Ernie Ferguson, 98, First Marine Division: At one point, we were drawing sniper fire from the ridge across the valley.

I looked to my right, and I saw two or three people jumping into a bomb crater. I went down into a kneeling position, but the sniper spotted me before I spotted him. I got hit in the leg. I hopped into a nearby bomb crater for cover. We didn't have any corpsmen in the area, so the sergeant shot me with morphine, put sulfonamide powder on my wound, bandaged it as best he could, then called for a stretcher. After fifteen minutes, a stretcher showed up. I crawled down, got on the stretcher, they took me back to the jeep and down to the first aid station. Because I didn't have a corpsman tag, they hit me with morphine again, then they cut my clothes off. From that point on, I was out of it. I woke up on a hospital ship in a cast from my toe to my thigh.

Tom Charlton, 95, First Marine Division: We were going across a valley, but there was heavy sniper fire and we couldn't knock them out. So they had tanks come in, all the way across the valley, staggered. We'd run from tank to tank: I'd go first, then Rardin, and the rest. When I was running, I could see dirt kicking up from heavy Japanese fire.

We got to the second tank and a young replacement named "Curley" from Ohio—nice, good-looking young kid—came in behind us. He was just scared to death; you could see it on his face. We yelled at him, "Stagger your run, Curley!" But he just took dead aim and ran straight forward. He got hit, and he collapsed. Rardin and I ran out and pulled him back to the tank, but he was dead.

I saw Sergeant Johnson get it, too. We had a tank shooting into a cave—napalm. There was a sniper in there and he was trying to knock it out. We were probably fifty feet away. Sergeant Johnson got on a microphone in the back of the tank and was guiding him in. But Johnson stepped out too far and they shot him. He just dropped—and he was dead.

Eugene Thomas, 92, First Marine Division: We came across a railroad track and a sniper hit my squad leader. He was carrying his Thompson with one arm, with the weight on his hip. The bullet hit the stock of the gun, passed through his arm, and hit a second man behind him in the chest, killing him instantly. A third Marine, we called him "Old Man" because he was twenty-eight, cracked up after seeing this.

We had three tanks to support us, but two were knocked out before they got to the railroad tracks. I followed the third tank to the base of the hill we were attacking. But when the tank started to back up to get behind us, it was also knocked out.

Donn Thompson, 95, Sixth Marine Division: That whole island was just caves underneath the ground. We'd have Japanese come up behind us and beside us. It was just terrible.

Carl Scott, 98, First Marine Division: One day, we got stuck on a cliff and started taking fire from our left rear. The Army was supposed to be on our left, but we somehow got ahead of them. The Japs started throwing mortars at Third Platoon, to our right, and hit a lot of people. Finally, someone said we were moving back. My sergeant said, "Run across this open area and we'll be safe on the other side." Three of us started running together. Once I got across, I realized I was the only one left. The other two were wounded really bad; one was my squad leader. We got the wounded out—and they both lived. But each got hit in the hip and leg, and they were in the hospital for a long time. Bob Price lost part of his hip, and for the rest of his life, he called himself the "half-assed Marine."

Eugene Thomas, 92, First Marine Division: We moved out and set up across from Wana Ridge. I had a new replacement as my fifth "foxhole buddy"; a young man. At about 0400, we attacked Wana Ridge under the cover of our water-cooled .30 caliber machine guns. We set up a defensive position for the night, fifty percent watch, on guard.

At around 1900, it was getting dark. I started my first watch. About one hundred feet ahead of me, three Japanese started over the crest of the hill, on the skyline. I opened up with my BAR, but I didn't know if I hit anything because I couldn't see very well. During the night, you could hear them crawling around out there and hitting their rifles on the rocks. I woke up my young foxhole buddy and told him he was to stand guard. I looked up in about fifteen minutes and—*there he was*—sleeping! I went up and told him if he was going to sleep, to get back in the foxhole. I stood guard all night. I couldn't trust his watching with my life!

The next morning, early, 0500, we attacked the ridge. When I looked around, this foxhole buddy was nowhere to be seen. We didn't know what had happened to him until about a month later. The graves registration asked us to come and view the unidentified bodies. He was not among them. Much later, I heard that he had cracked up and gone through the battalion and regimental hospitals before being identified. He was listed as the worst crack-up case they received. And he had only been in our company a day and a half.

In the attack on the ridge, I was firing my BAR into a cave. I threw in a white phosphorous and fragmentation grenade. Then I went up on the skyline to where I had seen three Japs the night before. I could see I had been shooting too high because the dead one I found had been hit in the back of the head, having gone through his helmet. Why I wasn't shot that morning as I went over the skyline to see that body lying there, I'll never know. I moved into a little shell hole back on our side of the ridge. They knew I was there, and they threw hand grenades in front of me. I put my arms around my helmet, but no shrapnel touched me. Then a Jap came out of that cave behind me. I swung around and fired on him as he rounded the corner and hit him. We were there for about the next ten days, raining all that time, mostly.

Joe Harrison, 98, Sixth Marine Division: In all that combat, we were never in tents. We were always outside, with rubberized ponchos and a helmet. At nighttime, it got pretty cool, so you wrapped a blanket around yourself. But we still got wet.

Chuck Meacham, 96, Sixth Marine Division: We'd been down almost across the equator for months. Now we were up by Japan—and, for us, it was cold.

Bob Ehrlich, 94, First Marine Division: Toward the end, it was miserable; it rained all the time. You slogged around in the mud and dirt. Oh God, it was pitiful.

Donn Thompson, 95, Sixth Marine Division: We were on the front line for eighteen days straight, and it rained for all eighteen of those days. We were soaking wet. I remember taking my boots off, pulling my socks down, and both my feet were just wrinkled and white, almost to the point of being sore.

Gordon Black, 94, First Marine Division: One guy said you could put an empty Coke bottle out there and fill it to the top with rain. Maybe an exaggeration, but they were pretty heavy showers.

Russel Nelson, 98, First Marine Division: The water came right over the bank and filled my foxhole.

Carl Scott, 98, First Marine Division: We kept moving south, taking hill after hill. We got a new captain who had been on Guadalcanal. He sent a squad forward, then sent my squad after them. When we got to the top of the ridge, the first squad was pinned down. Our lieutenant got wounded. He sent word for me to come up. I don't know why—there was nothing I could do for him. But I started crawling over top of these Marines that were hiding in a ditch. I guess my head was too high because a bullet went through my helmet and grazed my head. When the corpsman finally got to me, my ear was bleeding, and my face was bleeding. A little later, I even found a scratch on my eyelid. A piece of my helmet had ripped off and hit me in the right shoulder. The corpsman thought I was hit in the head and started giving me morphine. He put me in a pup tent that night. The next day, four of us carried a Marine who had been shot in both legs down to the beach on a stretcher. The corpsman sent me to an Army doctor. He looked at me and said, "I'm going to send you back to Guam."

Donn Thompson, 95, Sixth Marine Division: We went out on a reconnaissance patrol over the crest of a hill. The officer in front of me went by a spider hole, and this Jap popped up and shot him in the head. The guy behind me picked the Japanese off. Our officer hit the deck and I thought, *God, they blew his head off!* There wasn't any blood on his helmet, head, or anything. The bullet went into the helmet, shredded the maps he stored between the liner and the steel pot, and all it did was knock him out.

Victor Rainey, 97, First Marine Division: One time, the lieutenant came up to our tank and said, "There's an infantry company on the other side of this ridge that's pinned down. They can't get out and we need to put some smoke shells over there."

Why they picked our tank, I don't know. But we loaded up with smoke shells. Roger Behling and I fired a round a minute for an hour and ten minutes. They finally said, "Hey! The infantry company got out okay!" so we stopped firing. But we couldn't hear anything for three days.

Tom Charlton, 95, First Marine Division: We were pulling off the line, going back for three days' rest, when Lieutenant Fitzgerald said, "Charlie, show this Army lieutenant where your machine gun is positioned." Richter was my first ammunition carrier, so I said, "Richter, run up there and show them." He dropped his ammunition cans and said, "How come I always get the crappy deals?" I thought, *How come I just didn't go?* Richter went up to where the Army lieutenant was—a mortar hit and blew him down the side of the hill.

I rushed down there, and an Army medic ran, too. We got there about the same time. He said, "Help me get him out of the brush." I put my arm under Richter—it was just like sticking my arm in a bowl of Jell-O. We pulled him out of the brush. I knew he was dead the minute I touched him. The Army lieutenant's leg was barely held on by the skin. I don't think he made it, but I don't know.

Norlyn Dossey, 100, First Marine Division: We were moving the company out and there was an ole sniper in a sugarcane patch. The leaves were dead and had fallen over, and he was underneath there with a light machine gun. He got me. I caught three bullets. But they weren't in critical spots: I got two of them in my thigh and one of them pretty close to my groin. I could walk some, but it eventually got to where I couldn't walk. They put me on a little old ambulance—well, what we called an ambulance—it was just a fixed-up jeep. Then they took me out to a hospital ship.

William Darling, 98, First Marine Division: We were finally relieved and moved into a rear area about a hundred yards back. We reorganized and got some more people in. I ran across my best buddy; we were in the same platoon, different squads. He had been wounded. The lieutenant told me to help him to the aid station. When we were going back, a mortar shell landed, and my buddy got hit in the wrist with a piece of shrapnel. He yelled, "Bill, take it out!" so I took the shrapnel out. It was a big, long piece. I said, "You don't play golf, do you?" He said, "Occasionally I do." I said, "Well, you'll never play golf with that wrist." I put him on the ambulance and returned to my unit. I didn't hear from him again for twenty years.

Chuck Meacham, 96, Sixth Marine Division: I was on light duty with a temperature of 102. The next day it was 104—and by that night it went up above 105. I don't remember anything from there on. How they were able to get me off that hill, I don't know. When I awoke, I saw a Navy captain and I sat up. He said, "Son, stay down!" That's the last thing I remember. The next sensation was a beautiful, beautiful smell and a screaming noise in my ear. I opened my eyes—and there stood a flight nurse. I thought I'd died and gone to heaven!

Jim Palmieri, 103, Sixth Marine Division: I had many encounters at night with Japs. They fought at night, the same as day, and it was hell. I shot one at three o'clock in the morning. How that Jap got through our lines, I don't know. But he ended up behind our foxhole. There were three Marines with me. Thank God for the flares—it was just bright enough for me to see the Jap's silhouette. He had two hand grenades, one in each hand. And he was crawling on his hands and knees. When they shoot a flare, you usually don't move. But

I grabbed my rifle. He was at a disadvantage because he was on his hands and knees. That was the first Jap I shot all by myself.

Russel Nelson, 98, First Marine Division: A Japanese soldier infiltrated our position at about four o'clock in the morning, one night. When he came at us, I turned my back. His bayonet hit my radio's steel jacket and went into the ground. My lieutenant killed him. We think he may have been wounded because of the way he fell into our foxhole. We just lifted him up, tossed him away, and went back to sleep. That's what you don't want to tell junior high kids; they don't need to know the gritty part.

Joe Harrison, 98, Sixth Marine Division: During the night, an Okinawan woman came down the trail, between my foxhole and the bank. When she started making a little noise, some guy on our machine dropped a grenade within four feet of my foxhole. I ducked and my buddy shoved his head down. The explosive went off and didn't hurt either of us. I hollered to the other guys to stay in their damn foxholes. I never did find out who threw that grenade. After that lady went past us, someone shot her. At least, I heard a shot.

Tom Charlton, 95, First Marine Division: During a banzai attack, with flares up, you could see them coming. I usually fired my pistol, but I don't know if I ever hit anyone or not. One night, Gelhar said, "Tom, if they pull another banzai attack, just sweep that area with your machine gun." The Japanese knew where we were—and they were coming. That night I just turned the elevation mechanism loose and swept the area right in front of us. It stopped them.

H.C. Beck, 99, First Marine Division: I was with a guy named Valaitis. He was from California, and he had a tobacco sack about half full of gold teeth. He would kill a Jap, step on his chin, split his jaw, and get gold teeth. We were out one evening and we could hear a racket out front in the bushes. He said, "I'm gonna go out and get me some more teeth." I said, "You'd better stay in here. We'll get 'em later on." But he didn't do it. He got up, went out about ten feet—and I saw a Jap raise up above the bushes. Valaitis pulled his rifle out and killed him, hit him right between the eyes. The Jap fell forward, and he had a hand grenade in his hand, plug already pulled. It exploded—and knocked Valaitis's leg off. I didn't see Valaitis anymore after that. But that saved my life. If Valaitis had stayed in the foxhole, the Jap would have thrown the grenade in the foxhole and got me too.

William Darling, 98, First Marine Division: When I got back to the front, they sent me out on patrol. We'd been held down by a machine gun inside a little hut and they wanted me to go back there and clear that hut. I took my squad out, but by the time we got near, the Japanese were gone. We returned to our position, and a shell suddenly came down. All I saw was something smash into the ground—and I dropped. I woke up, and the guy in the foxhole near me said, "Here, take this," and gave me some pineapple juice to drink. Then I passed out again. The lieutenant came down with some guys and they carried me up to his foxhole.

When I woke up, he said, "How about a cup of coffee?" I said, "A nice hot, black cup of coffee would really taste good." I took a couple of sips of that, then everything I'd eaten the week before came up—all over the lieutenant. He said, "We're going to send you back," and they put me on a hospital ship. It was the same hospital ship I was evacuated from Peleliu on.

Tom Charlton, 95, First Marine Division: We were under two heavy artillery attacks. They were zeroed in and vicious. There was nothing you could do. It felt like my mouth was full of cotton and my ears were ringing. Rardin was thrown clear out of the foxhole. I was lifted out and leaning over the other side. Someone yelled that Grimes was hit. I crawled out and put my hand on him—I knew he was dead. The corpsman got there about the same time. He said, "Is he dead?" and I said, "Yeah." I crawled back and Gaffney was dead, too.

George Bradbury, 98, First Marine Division: One time, we were facing a knoll, and we could see the Japanese stacking ammunition about a mile from us, getting ready to counterattack. That night, we had a mortar barrage. Fifty some mortars landed in an area about the size of a football field near our forward guns. I had fixed a nice foxhole, put wire across it and a poncho overtop, because it was hard to find a dry place to sleep. But a mortar landed about ten feet from me and blew me out of my hole. The first thing I did was reach down to see if I still had my legs. I did, I was okay. But we lost several Marines that night. Even our cook got killed.

Bob Ehrlich, 94, First Marine Division: It was like hellfire. Oh, that scared you to death, scared you to death. Especially when you couldn't find a place to go.

Victor Rainey, 97, First Marine Division: Some of the Japanese guns were inside caves, mounted on railroad tracks. They would run them out, fire, then go back inside and shut the doors. We usually couldn't see where the shots were coming from because they were camouflaged. One day, we were sitting against a wall, and this gun kept firing at us. For some reason, our lieutenant said he couldn't get a fix on it. There was a ridge surrounded by fields, with an Army or Marine observation post at the top.

The lieutenant said, "Go up there and ask them if they can get a fix on that gun so we can shoot them." I started out walking across the field, when the Japanese gun saw me. He started putting shells over where I was, so I started to run. When I got past the exposed point on the ridge, back where they couldn't see me anymore, a shell landed in the muddy ground behind me, about ten or fifteen feet away, and exploded. Man, it felt like I'd been hit in the rear end by a bunch of rock salt fired from a shotgun.

The people on the outpost were watching me come across. When they saw the shell knock me down, a corpsman came over. He said, "Here, let me take a look at you." He laid me over the hood of a jeep, took down my pants, got some tweezers, a little scalpel, some alcohol, and started picking fragments out of my butt. It blew mud *right* through my pants, into my rear end. After he got all the mud picked out, I pull my pants up and said, "I guess I'll get the Purple Heart for this." He said, "For mud in your butt? I don't think so."

Tom Charlton, 95, First Marine Division: You know who I had the most admiration for? The corpsmen. No matter how heavy the fire was, you'd yell, "Corpsman!" and they'd go. I've seen quite a few of them get killed. That was a tough job.

On May 12, 1945, the Sixth Marine Division encountered a small hill, no more than fifty feet tall and three hundred yards in length. The modest rise, later nicknamed Sugar Loaf Hill, would become the focal point of Japanese resistance along the western portion of the Shuri Line throughout mid-May.

Jim Palmieri, 103, Sixth Marine Division: I remember every minute of it. I can never forget. Before we got to Sugar Loaf, we had been fighting for about five days because the Japanese had drawn a perimeter that they called the Shuri Line. It was terrible. The Japs were in spider holes and bunkers, everywhere. They were ready to commit suicide; they were never going back to Japan.

My outfit was one of the first to hit Sugar Loaf. Boy, were we surprised! The Japs were dug in for months. The first day, G Company attacked and *man*, did they get beat up. The second day, Fox Company attacked, and in a couple of hours, they must have had forty percent casualties. It was awful. My company—Easy Company—was supposed to attack that afternoon. But when we got there, Fox Company was in the way. We said, "What the hell are you doing here? You're supposed to be up there on the hill." They couldn't move because there were land mines and bunkers everywhere.

That night, we were bedded down, and scheduled to attack at eight o'clock the next morning. There was a voice that said, "Anybody that wants to receive communion, get behind me in the line." Lo and behold, there was a Catholic priest up there giving us communion. And this was the *front line!* So I received my last rites that night. Fortunately, I made it the next day. But we still did not capture Sugar Loaf.

Eldon Cedergeen, 96, Sixth Tank Battalion: The casualties really built up there. Not so much for our tanks, but for the poor infantry. We went out every day like we were going to work. I was a loader, and my focus was keeping the shells ready, and keeping the machine guns loaded. I didn't see much of the damage or the casualties. But I'm sure we did our share of damage. A time or two, I had to jump out with my asbestos gloves and replace the barrel of the machine gun because they'd get too hot. I was fortunate, not getting hit. One day, we went around to the backside of Sugar Loaf, and we were able to fire right inside the cave entrances. I remember that portion because they'd come running out of there. That was quite a day.

Donn Thompson, 95, Sixth Marine Division: We had trouble trying to take that hill. It was out in the open, and the Japanese had their mortars and machine guns on the surrounding hills facing Sugar Loaf. Our group was in the fifth push, and we went up and secured the top. I figured we had everything going our way and there weren't going to be any more problems. But after I settled down in a shell hole, the Japanese started firing big guns at us again. One shell landed not too far away from me. I dove into a hole, but my fanny was sticking out. A water can, that had apparently been used and was empty, came down and hit me in the butt. And I thought I'd bought the farm for sure! I reached around but *nope*. It was sore but there was no blood.

Lester Penny, 98, Sixth Marine Division: I was attached to Fox Company, and we were making a strategic withdrawal—that's better than saying retreat—when a mortar shell or artillery shell exploded nearby. I got a piece of shrapnel in my rear end. According to the citation it was "the left buttocks area." Nothing real serious.

Tom Shields, 93, Sixth Marine Division: That's where I was a casualty. I got blown up by an artillery shell. I didn't get any shrapnel out of it, but I got a concussion. I don't remember anything. I was probably unconscious for a couple of days. When I gained consciousness, I was at the 204th Army Hospital on Guam. They didn't know I was a Marine; had no idea. I didn't have an ID, no Marine clothing, nothing. I didn't have a damn thing. When I was conscious, the doctor came around and said, "What outfit are you in?" I told him. He said, "You're not supposed to be here." They put me on a plane and flew me to Aiea Heights, which was the Navy hospital on Oahu. I stayed there for about a month, then they flew me to San Francisco.

After eleven assaults, Sugar Loaf finally fell to American forces on May 18, 1945. More than two thousand Marines were killed or wounded during the battle. One battalion, thrust into the action again and again, suffered more than four hundred casualties. After weeks of bitter fighting, the Japanese withdrew from Shuri under a protective shroud of bad weather to prepare for a final stand on the Kiyamu Peninsula. Thousands of Marines, soldiers, and sailors had been killed or wounded assaulting a network of intricate caves within the Shuri complex. On June 4, 1945, the Sixth Marine Division performed a shore-to-shore landing on the tip of the Oroku Peninsula, while the First Marine Division sealed off the promontory from the opposite end. Within ten days, the peninsula was under American control. Resuming the drive south, the Marines fought a hard battle for Kunishi Ridge before collecting at the southern terminus of the island.

Eldon Cedergreen, 96, Sixth Tank Battalion: During an advance, we found some buildings alongside the road, so we decided to get out and take a look: It was full of Japanese soldiers that had committed suicide. It was a terrible sight. It was getting near the end, and they were deciding whether they were going to surrender or kill themselves. Many of them just jumped off the cliffs and killed themselves.

James Rosenmiller, 99, First Marine Division: It wasn't a pleasant sight to see a young Japanese soldier hold a hand grenade against his stomach and discharge it. That was common. They didn't believe in surrender—they believed in hara-kiri. How can I describe it to you? You'll have to use your imagination on what a hand grenade against your stomach will do. But that's the way we found a lot of them. They just *would not* surrender.

Donn Thompson, 95, Sixth Marine Division: The Japanese told the beautiful people on Okinawa that we were a bunch of rapists. Some of their families had actually taken their daughters down and pushed them off a cliff because they didn't want them abused by us. It was nonsense—*it would never happen*. Sometimes the Japanese would use those people to come through our lines.

Keith Tucker, 100, Second Marine Division: The Japanese and the civilians got pushed down to the tip of the island and were trying to sneak back through our troops. At night, there were flares going up and you'd see people running. You didn't know who they were.

H.C. Beck, 99, First Marine Division: One night, we heard some talking. It kept getting closer to us, so we called for a flare. When the flare opened up, we opened up with machine guns and M1s. We don't know how many we killed, we don't know who we killed; whether they were Okinawans or whether they were Japanese. But one of them laid there and groaned and carried on for about an hour.

Tom Charlton, 95, First Marine Division: One time I was firing at a cave and three people came out of the brush below the mouth. I lowered my aim just a hair and killed them. When we went up there, it was three women. I don't know whether they were Okinawan women or nurses for the Japanese. I don't know, but I think they were probably Okinawan girls.

Gordon Black, 94, First Marine Division: I remember going through a graveyard and seeing an Okinawan lady laying on her back: She'd been shot. I don't know what happened there. It was the first time I'd seen a woman shot and die. I still recall that girl.

Thomas Fitzmaurice, 100, Eighth Anti-Aircraft Battalion: I hit Okinawa about the second week in June, so I was really involved with the cleaning up process with the Third Amphibious Corps. We were digging out Okinawan people and the last remaining Japanese; people reluctant to surrender. From the end of June until the early part of August, we were gathering Okinawans and taking some Japanese prisoners. Or killing those that would not surrender. There were quite a few that would not surrender on Okinawa. Whether they were informed of the end of hostilities or not, I don't know. But some of them continued to actively resist.

Okinawa was finally declared secure on June 22, 1945. In eighty-two days of combat, American forces had suffered nearly fifty thousand casualties, including the Tenth Army commander, General Simon Bolivar Buckner. On June 18, 1945, just days before the battle's conclusion, Buckner had been killed by shell fragments while inspecting an outpost near the front line. He would be the highest-ranking US officer to die as the result of enemy fire during the war. Like in previous engagements, Japanese losses were immense: the final number soaring north of one hundred thousand. The civilian population, often unwillingly employed as ammunition carriers or combatants by the Japanese military, lost as many as 150,000 people.

17 ★ ★ ★ ★ ★ ★

DOWNFALL

Operation Downfall, the planned invasion of mainland Japan, was set to begin in November of 1945. The first phase, code-named Olympic, would see fourteen divisions landed on southern Kyushu to seize harbors and airfields in preparation for Coronet; an operation designed to strike industrial and political targets on Honshu in 1946. The two-pronged assault would be one of the largest battles in human history, involving roughly five million Allied troops and millions of Japanese defenders (buttressed by untold civilian conscripts). The initial casualty estimates, provided by the War Department, indicated that the Allies would lose more than one million servicemen. Resigned to their fate, the survivors of Iwo Jima and Okinawa limped back to their rear-bases, received replacements, and began preparing for combat in the home islands.

Don Pilcher, 95, Third Marine Division: I was seasick all the way back to Guam. We got a week or two of taking it easy, then we started training for the landing on Japan.

Lucien Jandreau, 99, Fifth Marine Division: I left California the first of April of '45 and went to Hawaii. That's where

I met the Fifth Division. They were coming back from Iwo Jima, where they got the shit beat out of them. They had lost over one-third of their men, so I was a part of the replacements. We did some advanced training there before we left for the invasion of Japan.

John Marx, 97, Third Marine Division: I wouldn't have survived Japan. I didn't think we had a chance because we were going to be in the first wave.

Mike Ladich, 96, Fifth Marine Division: I figured my luck had run out. You only get so many chances, then you're gone.

Kenneth Luttrell, 99, Fourth Marine Division: You feel like the odds are building against you.

Harold Rediske, 94, Fourth Marine Division: I was really thinking, "How can I get out of this?"

Gordon Black, 94, First Marine Division: Thank God for the atomic bomb.

Eldon Cedergreen, 96, Sixth Tank Battalion: A guy came through in the middle of the night and told us what happened at Hiroshima. It kind of reminded me of Paul Revere.

Donn Thompson, 95, Sixth Marine Division: I thought, *There's nothing that potent. There's nothing that could do something like that.* I still didn't believe it after we dropped the second one.*

* The bombings of Hiroshima and Nagasaki were both launched from Tinian in the Mariana Islands (captured by the Second and Fourth Marine Divisions).

W. Lee Robinson, 97, Fifth Marine Division: There's a debate about the atomic bomb today. But to my way of thinking, Truman made the right call.

Robert Hall, 95, Marine Administrative Command: I was thankful for the A-bomb, naturally. I think Truman saved—Who knows? It's all speculation—maybe hundreds of thousands of Americans and millions of Japanese by doing it.

Ray Garland, 96, V Amphibious Corps: That saved a lot of lives. It killed a lot of Japanese, but it saved a lot of lives.

John Haney, 98, Sixth Marine Division: I wouldn't be here today if it wasn't for that.

Francis Stanger, 92, First Marine Division: The Japanese wouldn't give up. It took two atomic bombs—that's how tough they were. If the Americans had invaded, Japanese women, children, and men would have fought with weapons and pitchforks; killed a lot of our boys.

Elwin Hart, 93, Second Marine Division: I'm neutral about it. The people who made the call had a lot of guts. They knew what it was going to cost in lives. I give Truman a lot of credit for what he did. I don't think anybody's proud of what happened. I just hope we don't have to do it again.

Eldon Cedergreen, 96, Sixth Tank Battalion: Shortly after, word came down that Japan had surrendered. We were whooping it up: "We're done with war! It's over!"

Faris Tuohy, 96, Sixth Marine Division: There wasn't a sound. Everybody was just shocked.

Bob Ehrlich, 94, First Marine Division: I was relieved. I didn't cry, but I was happier than heck. If I could've danced, I would have.

Art Perez, 96, Third Marine Division: I was in a hospital in Chicago when it ended. They locked the gate, and we couldn't go on liberty. Everyone was having a helluva good time in downtown Chicago—from what I heard on the radio and saw in the paper. Having a great time. But they locked the gate on Great Lakes Hospital. I said, "All these guys who probably didn't see anything are celebrating with the women!" Which is always the case.

Hattie Kelley, 98, Women's Reserve: I was in New York. It was full of people screaming and yelling and hollering: "It's over! It's over! It's over."

Genevieve Lashaw, 95, Women's Reserve: When we got the news, I was working a five-to-eight shift. Everybody heard before we did and started coming into the PX. We told them, "Go home! Get outta here!" The band started marching up and down the street. Finally, Red went over and shut the door to the PX. We went to church to give thanks. It was a happy day.

Burt Withee, 95, Second Marine Division: We were stationed on Saipan after the fighting was over. When peace was declared, all the ships started firing. It was like World War II all over again. Pandemonium! The officers were getting drunker than hell. Guys were driving jeeps all over, smashin' into stuff. It was pandemonium for about ten hours.

Robert Rakestraw, 100, Sixth Marine Division: Everybody started running up and down the company street. I was in the band and our tuba player, who was from Virginia, was yelling: "The war is over! The war is over! Japan just surrendered!" We didn't get much sleep that night.

Bob Ehrlich, 94, First Marine Division: We went down to the airfield on Okinawa, where the whiskey was seventy-five dollars. We each bought a fifth—and sat around on old water drums. I got so stewed that I just passed out.

Robert Hall, 95, Marine Administrative Command: I was in a big barracks, on an upper bunk, when the word came in. There was a lot of yelling. We were really quite happy. Eventually my outfit had a party—and I don't want to discuss the details.

Keith Tucker, 100, Second Marine Division: I got home on a Sunday and by Tuesday, the war ended. I took my girlfriend out to the farm and woke her family up. She said, "Keith and I are getting married!" Her dad said, "I told you that you're not getting married while the war is on." She said, "The war is over!" The next day, we went to see Reverend Smith at the Lutheran church. He said, "The marriage will be this Sunday because I'm going to Minnesota fishing for two weeks." We said, "We'll take Sunday, then." The war ended on a Tuesday, and we got married that Sunday.

In August of 1945, Marine combat units began landing in Japan to reestablish order and disarm the military. The Fourth Marine Regiment, filled with combat veterans from Guam and Okinawa, spearheaded the assault by striking Yokosuka just before dawn on August 30, 1945. The Fifth Marine Division and Second Marine Division, supported by various amphibious units, arrived in the following months.

Lucien Jandreau, 99, Fifth Marine Division: We landed in Sasebo, Japan, on Kyushu—the southern island. We landed like the war wasn't over because we didn't know what to expect!

Donald Brown, 95, Fifth Marine Division: We had to march about five miles to the barracks. We passed some small towns. You could see the women open their curtains, watching us. They were scared to death. We didn't see many men.

Bill Gropp, 97, Fifth Marine Division: I went with the occupation forces into Sasebo in September, approximately the same time we were supposed to land if the war hadn't ended. We destroyed some weapons and dumped a lot of stuff into the ocean. Then I was transferred to Nagasaki, and, of course, that was still pretty hot with radiation.

Burt Withee, 95, Second Marine Division: The whole area was levelled and the only thing still standing was a barbershop sink. In that whole area—just rubble. We took over a woman's university in downtown Nagasaki that was operated by American women before the war. Nothing worked: all the plumbing was blown out, there was no running water; it was real primitive.

Ken Brown, 95, Fifth Marine Division: I saw the worst horrors of the war: I saw the worst things the Japanese could do on Iwo Jima, and I saw the worst thing the United States could do, in dropping that bomb. Of course, I happen to be one of the people who was very grateful for the bomb. I wouldn't be here today. It would have been terrible if we had invaded.

Burt Withee, 95, Second Marine Division: All day long and all night long, a line of Japs would walk by our compound—both ways. Our guys would sit on the brick wall nearby and barter with the Japs. They loved soap, toothpaste, chocolate: "Chokoreto! Chokoreto!" They loved our chocolate.

Bert Rutan, 95, Fifth Marine Division: I was walking down the street one time when a Japanese family waved me into their house. They gave me this little delicate ball of candy. I put it in my mouth and began talking with them. But I soon realized, once the outer shell of the candy was sucked away, I was eating raw fish. I kept it in the corner of my mouth and bid a hasty goodbye. I sure made a fool of myself, but I didn't want to embarrass them by spitting it out.

Marvin Strombo, 95, Second Marine Division: The Marine Corps taught the Japanese and us how to get along. Like I said—some of the guys still hated them. But, oh no, we got along really well. I had real good friends there in Nagasaki before I left.

Robert Schultz, 102, USS *California*: Everybody was surprised that the Japanese were so friendly because a month or two before we were trying to kill them!

Charles Pase, 99, Second Marine Division: We came to a barbershop and these ladies were in there shaving people. It cost about fifteen cents for a complete shave. This one Marine, Steve, said, "It's time for me to get a shave," so he motioned to the girl that he wanted the next spot. She bowed, very sweet and peacefully, then put him in a chair and took out a razor about seven inches long. She stood next to him, tilted his head back, showed his throat—and she shaved him! We were shocked! What if we had killed one of her brothers? Or her mother? Or burned her daddy to death? Word got around: "Steve's the bravest man in the whole damn Second Division!"

Bob Ehrlich, 94, Twentieth Amphibian Truck Battalion: The Japanese were nice and friendly, and we got along with them fine. They used to invite us over for beef steak. But I think it was dog because I never saw a cow around. It was good tasting, whatever it was. I had a girlfriend, and her mother ran a hotel. She invited me over quite a bit.

Bill Gropp, 97, Fifth Marine Division: I enjoyed Nagasaki—and made friends with the families. I've got pictures with the little kids. I've got good memories there.

Ken Brown, 95, Fifth Marine Division: I saw the true Japanese spirit. Their comeback from the terrible things that had happened to them was amazing. It wasn't long before they became an industrial power.

Ray Garland, 96, V Amphibious Corps: The Japanese had a big munitions base for Navy ordnance and my job was to take inventory. I had a Japanese lieutenant commander with me, and after ten days, we got along pretty well. When I told him that I was going home, he came to work with a bottle of sake. He said, "I've hidden this for a long time." We sat down between two great big Japanese torpedoes and had a couple of drinks together. After that, I boarded a troop transport, went to San Diego, and I was discharged from the Marine Corps.

Meanwhile, additional elements of the occupation force landed in China to repatriate Japanese soldiers, nationals, and Korean laborers. After nearly a decade of brutal occupation, China was in the process of establishing independence; a prospect that turned violent as tensions rose between communist and nationalist factions within the country. Marines from various divisions, officially neutral, were in a precarious situation as a civil war ignited at their feet.

Eldon Cedergreen, 96, Sixth Tank Battalion: You went home on the points system. How many points did you earn? How long were you in? Did you get a Purple Heart? Some of the really old veterans got to go home, but the main portion of the division got sent to Tsingtao, China, for occupation duty. We spent four or five months over there, waiting for my turn to go home.

Russel Nelson, 98, First Marine Division: Guys with twenty-four months overseas went back to the States, and the rest of us went to China. It was Peking then, but it's Beijing now. We had an old house to live in. My friend from Wisconsin and I kept radio communications in China. We were always watching for communist saboteurs, too. They were putting bombs on railroad tracks because the nationalists were hauling oil back and forth. We'd take turns on watch. My friend would take one day, and I'd take the next day. We'd ride the train, go up three miles, then come back. It was good duty in China.

Walter Spuck, 95, First Marine Division: We would stand guard at ammunition dumps. You had to be careful that one of those Chinese didn't sneak up and wring your neck with a wire.

Lucien Jandreau, 99, First Marine Division: At night, the Chinese would come in and steal ammunition; grab whatever they could. I was the sergeant of the guard one night, when we heard a lot of commotion out in this field. We called battalion to tell them what was happening. They said, "Don't let anybody get close." We had a .30 caliber machine gun at the gate, between the two guards, so I got on the gun and opened up—but I don't know if I hit anybody.

Faris Tuohy, 96, Sixth Marine Division: During a patrol in the foothills, we chased a bunch of Chinese bandits into a coal mine. Somebody climbed over the entrance and swung dynamite into the opening. When it went off, a few of us entered: There was a lot of dust from the explosion. I fell into a hole and broke my left foot. After the dust settled and my squad got everybody killed, our lieutenant came by with a flashlight. He looked in and said, "Tuohy, what the hell are you doing down in that hole?" I said, "Damned if I know, Skipper." The corpsman got me out and put my foot in a cast. They didn't have a hospital facility there, so they flew me and a bunch of other guys to Shanghai where the Navy had a big hospital ship anchored in the bay.

Glenn Ferguson, 99, Marine Scout Bombing Squadron 343: One day we had a show of force over Tientsin. The lead pilot turned up a canyon, but the weather kept lowering, so he tried to climb over the mountains. He accidentally wiped out the bottom half of the squadron. One of the pilots, who lived in my house, bailed out, and he never flew again because it scared him so bad. He went belly to belly with another plane. There were three TBMs—we called them "Turkeys"—that had been shot down by the communists earlier. We buried thirteen men in a mass ceremony. I had to help identify the dead. How do you recognize someone who's been in a plane crash? All I saw was a big, big bundle of sand—no arms, no legs.

Donn Thompson, 95, Sixth Marine Division: We went to Tsingtao, China, to accept the unconditional surrender of a Japanese tank battalion. That's what we did: We disarmed them, signed the peace documents, and they got to go home. They housed us in an old German high school or college. The whole area was surrounded by a big wall. They didn't want us to have anything to do with the Chinese population. Our commanding officer armed us with slingshots so we could keep kids from crawling up the walls. They told us, "The communists are in the hills all around Tsingtao. We don't want any of you to go into town by yourself. Go in couples." When we did, we'd just go to a restaurant or whatever.

Tom Charlton, 95, First Marine Division: They gave us a couple of days off once. We walked out and looked across the street. The sign said, "American Hamburgers." Rardin and I made a beeline and got a hamburger. The next time we got leave, I said, "I'm going to get another hamburger!" We looked over and the place was closed. They had a new sign that said, "Closed due to the use of dog and horse meat."

Don Pilcher, 95, Third Marine Division: We went from eighty-five-degree weather in the Pacific to midwinter in Tientsin. We were stationed in the old American compound which had been there since the Boxer Rebellion. The barracks were great. We had fairly good chow and nice quarters. We were on the second floor and one of the balconies overlooked "racetrack road," a major thoroughfare. There were always Chinese bringing in goods to sell. We'd go out on the balcony and talk with them. Some had never seen white people before. They thought we had big noses. We had one guy in the platoon that really had a "Jimmy Durante nose." He was out on the balcony, and they'd stop and yell, "Da bizi, da bizi!"—big nose, big nose.

Donn Thompson, 95, Sixth Marine Division: I stepped out of the jeep—and here was this little Japanese girl. She came over to me, looked up, and said, "You Gary Cooper?" I think she had seen a movie with Gary Cooper, and I resembled him because I was tall and slim. From then on, all the guys would say, "Here comes Gary Cooper!"

Don Pilcher, 95, Third Marine Division: There were little boys, about twelve, that looked like they'd slept in a coal bin. They'd come along in rickshaws and say, "No momma, no pappa, no flight pay! Oh, my aching back! Yen?" They wanted yen, Japanese cash.

Francis Stanger, 92, First Marine Division: My friends would give me a beer while I was on duty, and I'd report half-drunk sometimes. I got in trouble once: We were drinking whiskey and I had to report for duty as a cook the next day. I went back to the barracks, but I didn't wake up on time. The corporal turned me in. I got in front of the captain. He said, "I'd put you in the brig and give you a summary court-martial, but we're going home. I'll just give you bad duty aboard the ship on the way back." I pulled guard duty on the bow for the entire ride back.

18 ★ ★ ★ ★ ★ ★

HOME ALIVE BY '45

On September 6, 1945, the War Shipping Administration began the monumental task of returning eight million American servicemen, spread across fifty-five theaters of war, on four continents, back to the United States. Operation Magic Carpet, one of the largest combined air- and sealifts in human history, would deposit 22,222 veterans home every day for a full calendar year. Selection for the journey was determined by a "point system," which awarded credits for service length, decorations, campaign participation, and dependents under the age of eighteen. Accumulating eighty-five points was the minimum requirement for transfer home and discharge from the service.

Harold Rediske, 94, Fourth Marine Division: They took us back on an aircraft carrier, the old men in the division. If you stuck with it for all four landings, you got to go home first. We bunked where the pilots usually lived. That was the first time I'd been under sheets in two years.

Bob Ehrlich, 94, Twentieth Amphibian Truck Battalion: I came back on a ship that only had three other Marines on it. The rest were sailors—those dummies. God, they used to gripe me. They'd get drunk and throw cots and stuff over the side. I could never figure out why they were doing that, but they did. They were guys from—I think it was a cruiser. All they did during the war was go up and down the coast of Japan for months, until it ended. They were crazier than loons. I didn't like to be around them; they were really something. They were a bunch of characters.

Roy Mays, 99, USS *Idaho*: We used to say, "Golden Gate in '48." But we got there a little below it.

Robert Beale, 97, USS *Bennington*: We were going under the Golden Gate Bridge in San Francisco when I noticed all the factories along the bay had painted "Welcome Home!" on their rooftops. And there was all this patriotic music being played. It brought tears to my eyes. I thought, *I'm home! I'm home! I'm home!*

Donn Thompson, 95, Sixth Marine Division: When we came into the bay, we noticed a nice boat coming out: It must have had twenty or thirty girls in bikinis aboard. It came up to one side of the ship, and everybody went over to look. The captain got on the intercom and said, "For God's sake, will some of you guys get to the other side of the ship before you capsize us!" The small boat went around, and everyone followed. They finally realized they were causing more problems than anything, so they took off and left us out there. Being home again—it brings tears to my eyes. It did that to a lot of tough guys: nothing like love of country.

Robert Brutinel, 100, Fifth Marine Division: We came into San Diego. The thing that was odd about coming home was—you'd be on deck, and you'd see a ship's lights, off in the distance.

You never saw that before the surrender because you'd get torpedoed.

Charles Pase, 99, Second Marine Division: Our troopship landed in San Diego and the men piled out of there like a bunch of rabbits. Some of them were down on the ground, pounding their hands, some kissing the ground.

W. Lee Robinson, 97, Second Parachute Battalion/Fifth Marine Division: In San Diego we landed at about eleven o'clock at night. The mess halls were all closed, but they brought out bread, milk, butter, and raspberry jam. We feasted on that. I have never enjoyed a meal such as that, even in the fanciest restaurants.

Donald Bishop, 98, First Marine Division: When we got back to the States, there was nobody in my group old enough to buy a beer. We fought for thirty-one months, and we weren't old enough to buy a beer when we got back.

Frank Wright, 96, Third Marine Division: January 21, 1946, was a Sunday. The main discharge office was closed. Therefore, you could not get your discharge papers until January 22. I had to stay in for another day after my enlistment date. They were getting all the duty they could out of me, I guess. They tried to talk me into shipping over. They said, "We'll give you a sergeant's promotion and give you a platoon." Sounded awful sweet. I really wanted those stripes. But I didn't; I chose not to ship over—and that was the end of my military career.

Ben Carson, 96, Second Raider Battalion/Fifth Marine Division: Anything was better than being in the Marine Corps, especially after the war was over. All these aspiring generals, who were PFCs at the time, were doing their damnedest to raise their head above the gang and get picked for the new OCS programs. That made it even more stinking. I was so glad to get out.*

Grant Duncan, 100, Provisional Force Signal Battalion: They asked me if I wanted to go into the Reserves. I asked, "Are you out of your *blank-ing* mind?"

Hattie Kelley, 98, Women's Reserve: I didn't want to go home after the war, but my adopted mother was dying of cancer, so I needed to. I had a good experience in the Marine Corps. I never had anybody treat me rude or nasty. And I never had anybody try to make me do anything I didn't want to do. I didn't expect it and I didn't get it.

Eldon Cedergreen, 96, Sixth Tank Battalion: As soon as I got mustered out in San Diego, I grabbed the first Greyhound bus headed for Portland, Oregon. The bus hit Portland five minutes late and I missed my connection to Forest Grove. I phoned my younger brother and told him I was hitchhiking. He said, "Okay, I'll be down on the street corner waiting for you." My parents had moved into town because my dad had a farming accident, so I didn't know *exactly* where home was. I took off. When I was halfway up "Suicide Bridge," a car stopped. The driver was a young fella, just out of the service. He drove me right down into Forest Grove—and there was my younger brother sitting on the ground below a light pole.

We had a happy reunion. We walked to the house, then a couple of my sisters got up, and we sat there at one o'clock

---

* Officer Candidate School (OCS) is a military program designed to train officers.

in the morning and had strawberry shortcake. I was so emotional that I could hardly eat. But that was my homecoming.

Bob Bennett, 100, First Marine Air Wing: My wife had a picture of me up on the wall of her apartment—and when I opened the door, she was holding my daughter. My wife said, "Oh, this is Daddy! This is Daddy!" And my little baby pointed over to the wall, where my picture was, and said, "No, Dadda. Dadda back there!" She didn't think I was the same guy from the picture.

Robert Beale, 97, USS *Bennington*: When I was finally discharged, I got on a train and I got off in Philadelphia; North Philadelphia station, which is only two miles from where I lived. I threw my knapsack over my shoulder and said, "I'm going to walk." I saw all the different places I grew up as a kid. I got to my front door, knocked, and my mother answered. She didn't know I was coming. I was finally home.

Donn Thompson, 95, Sixth Marine Division: When I got off the bus in Spokane, there was my dad, a very stoic guy, with tears coming down his face. I thought, *You don't really know how tough it is on parents.*

Russel Nelson, 98, First Marine Division: My mom cried . . . and I did too.

Clyde Lacquement, 95, Second Marine Division: My folks had moved away while I was gone. I had to walk for a long time to find out where they lived. They were still poor, in a little trailer house. I only stayed for a few days before I moved to college. I was independent—and didn't need my parents to care for me anymore.

Richard Nelson, 98, First Marine Division: My mother lived in a one-bedroom apartment, so I had to sleep by the radiator. Then I got a job with the phone company in 1946.

Billy Byrd, 98, Fifth Marine Division: My momma and my little siblings lived in a housing project that used to be an old air base for fifty-seven dollars a month. After I got back home, I stayed there for a while. I couldn't find a job—and I went hungry for a bit. I got down to about 135 pounds before I finally found work. See, I didn't know a trade or anything. The government didn't help me in that time, so I went hungry. And my momma and my two little siblings got hungry, too.

Robert Riechman, 98, Fifth Marine Division: When I came back, nobody cared. "Oh, yeah? You're back? Fine." No big celebration, because in those days, everybody was at war. Every family had a husband, wife, or child in the service. Or they'd given up their gasoline, sugar, or coffee.

Mike Ladich, 95, Fifth Marine Division: I heard one guy went back to Indiana, carrying a seabag full of half a dozen skulls. His dad, who was a minister, said, "Son, what are those?" He said, "Well, those are Japanese skulls." His dad replied, "You know what, son, you don't belong here anymore. You go back to the Marines."

Eugene Thomas, 92, First Marine Division: I got a letter from my wife while I was on occupation duty, saying she wanted to go to the movies with another guy. I wrote to her and said, "Please don't." When I got home, she met me at the train platform with our twenty-four-month-old son (who I hadn't seen yet). I got down and she told me she had something to say. I could hear her brother yelling from the car, "Don't do it!

Don't do it!" But I didn't know what he was talking about. I looked at my wife and she told me that she had been going with another man for the past nine months. I asked how she could do that. She said, "I was lonely." I said, "You don't think I was lonely?" I kept my seabag packed for the first two weeks I was home; thought I might have to leave. But every time I looked at my son, I remembered what my father told me: "She might be a sore, but once you marry her, she's your sore," so I stuck it out and stayed.

In June of 1944, in the climactic years of the war, President Franklin D. Roosevelt signed into law the Servicemen's Readjustment Act of 1944 (also known as the GI Bill of Rights). Often heralded as one of the most important pieces of legislation in American history, the GI Bill was a wide-ranging act designed to provide benefits and assistance to returning veterans.

W. Lee Robinson, 97, Second Parachute Battalion/Fifth Marine Division: The GI Bill was a godsend. When the war was over, there were hundreds of thousands of veterans that would have been pushed back into society. Unemployment would have been rampant. But the Bill gave me a start through college. Many other people went to college, vocational school, or started a business. It was a broad-scope program.

Russel Nelson, 98, First Marine Division: If you went back to the job you left before the war, you were entitled for employment. So I went back to the Army warehouse. We packaged and shipped batteries for jeeps and all kinds of materials to various Army bases.

Chuck Meacham, 96, Third Raider Battalion/Sixth Marine Division: My dad and I were sitting around one afternoon, having a beer. I said, "I think I'm going to take the next year off with all my buddies." I explained to him the 52-20 program. The GI Bill allowed twenty dollars a week for fifty-two weeks, for one full year. I said, "I think I'll do that." My dad looked me in the eye and said, "Son, you take that welfare and you're not welcome in my house." January 2, I was in school. It was a real blessing.

Donald Harr, 100, Marine Night Fighting Squadron 534: I was discharged in November and, when January came around, I went back to Kansas State to reenroll and continue my education. After spending so much time with all these varied personalities in the Marine Corps, I took a strong interest in how and why people function. I consulted with a counseling psychologist and told him of my dilemma about switching fields (my previous major had been electrical engineering). He suggested that I get into psychiatry. I said, "What is that?" I had no idea what he was talking about. He explained that I would need to go through medical school first, get my MD. Then I'd have to take specialty training. I did that—and I eventually took residency in Kansas that included both neurology and psychiatry, before getting into active practice. I did that for around sixty years.

Robert Beale, 97, USS *Bennington*: I got out of the Corps in March of '46 and the next month I was at spring football practice at Temple University. I wasn't even enrolled at school—but, of course, I enrolled in classes for September. I played football at Temple for four years; I was a quarterback. I graduated in 1950 and got a job after in Fort Lauderdale, Florida, as a football coach and a phys ed teacher. I coached and taught for eleven years. Then they made me a "Dean of Boys" in charge of attendance and discipline. I only lasted five years in that job before they made me an assistant principal. Then they made me a principal at a brand-new high school in Fort Lauderdale. I was an educator in those different capacities for over thirty years: 1950 to 1987 in Broward County, Florida.

Clyde Lacquement, 94, Second Marine Division: After the war I went to a Christian college, and I surrendered to the Prince of Peace. I've been a Bible teacher since I was twenty-four and a schoolteacher. That's what I did for fifty-some years.

Hattie Kelley, 98, Women's Reserve: When I went home, I got my job back as the deputy city clerk at City Hall. I wrote the whole tax record by hand, collected garbage fees; didn't do anything very exciting. But that's what I did.

Ken Brown, 95, Fifth Marine Division: When I got out of the service, I worked on the farm. It didn't take long to get back to civilian life again.

Melvin Gribble, 95, Fifth Amphibious Reconnaissance Battalion: I went to work in the woods, sawing logs. I did every job they had—finally wound up in the sawmill.

Milton "Red" Cronk, 98, Third Raider Battalion: I went to work for the post office as a mailman and I worked for them for about thirty years.

Chuck Meacham, 96, Third Raider Battalion/Sixth Marine Division: I went to school for four years, three double summer sessions, straight through. I got out with a degree and two sons.

Stew Lahey, 97, Second Separate Engineer Battalion: I gave up two and a half years of my time in the Corps—then I had to go back and finish high school, before I went to college. You know the toughest part about it? These kids were seventeen and eighteen. I'm twenty-one. And they acted like a bunch of juvenile jerks—it just upset me. There was no discipline. I'd come from such a disciplined life as a Marine. You do anything the sergeant tells you. It was, "Yes, sir!" and you snapped to. The kids didn't give a darn. They got away with murder.

Mike Ladich, 96, Fifth Marine Division: I thought civilian life was innocuous. Ordinary people didn't know what the fuck was going on in the world. I grew up in Superior, Wisconsin, where they shipped iron ore. I did the next best thing to joining the military: I joined the merchant marines and got on with an ore boat. I did that for four years after the war, just to shake myself lose.

Ernie Ferguson, 98, First Marine Division: I wasn't short-tempered, but I had a short fuse. I opted not to go back to school. I wouldn't have fit in. That was before computers, so I had to take correspondence courses. I studied for a contractor's license and started my own business.

Joe Harrison, 98, Sixth Marine Division: I learned to be a master brick mason. I did a lot of work around Redlands, Beaumont, Yucaipa, Riverside, and a job or two out on the base.

Jack Rasmussen, 94, Third Marine Division: Someone once asked why I wanted to work digging in the dirt as a geologist. I said, "Well, it's much better than digging a foxhole!"

Many survivors of World War II elected to remain in the military or reenlisted after the war for financial or personal reasons.

Art Perez, 96, Third Marine Division: I wanted to stay in, but my folks wanted me to come home and help them. They had just bought a tavern and a dining hall. I thought, *Damnit, get somebody else to help you.* But I finally got out just to see what was happening. I stayed out for almost four years. Then, one day, I said, "The hell with this!" I went back in the Marine Corps in 1949.

Bob Ehrlich, 94, First Marine Division: I went home and started working at a place that made truck parts. The owner had a baseball team—and I didn't do anything but play ball for him. During my workday, he'd give me parts and say, "Here, put this together." Hell, I didn't know how to do it! You'd have to have an engineering degree. Instead, I sat in the bathroom and smoked cigarettes all day. But I finally got tired of that and reenlisted. I went home and told my wife. I don't know if she was happy or sad.

Luther Hendricks, 96, Fifty-Second Defense Battalion: I wanted to get into the Reserves when I got out: "We don't take colored men in the Reserves." Hell, man! I just came back from fighting! And you don't want me in the Reserves? One of my bosses, after the war, used to say, "We worked like niggers last night." Why would you want to use a word like that? You shrug it off and go on with the day, but you say to yourself: *Why did I risk my life for the same old thing?*

Robert Hall, 95, Marine Administrative Command: The Marines were having a campaign to get people into the Reserves, and I thought, *Why not join the Reserves?* Then I could still have some contact with the Marines. Wouldn't you believe it—in two or three weeks, the North Koreans invaded

South Korea. They were looking for bodies to send over there because we weren't ready for a war in 1950.

Ray Garland, 96, First Marine Division: I joined the Reserves to pay my house payment. When the war started, I was called up. That's where I went—*Korea*. I was married, and I had two boys. I said, "You don't have to worry. I'll probably teach demolitions in San Diego." But when I got there to report in, they said, "Pack your seabag." I knew what that meant. I called my wife—she came down, and we spent two or three days together. I had no idea what was going to happen; nobody did. At that time, Korea was a real mess.

Marvin Strombo, 95, Second Marine Division: I fought in Korea—that dumb war. They're all dumb.

Tom Charlton, 95, First Marine Division: They called me back for the Korean War. I went straight down to Camp Pendleton, and I was there for three months. I was about ready to launch off to Korea when the captain came by and said, "You're going home." I was glad to get out of it.

Ray Garland, 96, First Marine Division: I got aboard ship and landed at Inchon. We got rid of the North Koreans there, reloaded, and went around to Wonsan. We got as far as the Chosin Reservoir, way up there. We thought we were going to be home by Christmas. That's when the Chinese came. That was baaaddd, bad news. The Chosin Reservoir was nasty. It seemed like you were going to be shot or frozen to death—one or the other. It was worse than World War II, to tell you the truth. I was an older man then, in charge of a lot of younger guys.

Jack Becker, 99, First Marine Division: We had the Koreans beat—they were surrendering by the division. But that was before we heard from the Chinese. "Oh, we'll be home for Christmas easy!" When wintertime set in, it got cold, cold, cold, cold. We had snowpack shoes, but they didn't work. You'd open them up and the bottom would be filled with ice. MacArthur couldn't quite get the idea that the Chinese were coming in. They wore white uniforms and bullets would hit them and feathers would go flying. It was tragic, it was so funny. I was driving this truck—a 4x4—when we were leaving the Chosin Reservoir. I always had a shotgun driver, like an Old West wagon kind of thing. I said, "Look at these guys. I wonder what they're doing." One had a machine gun strapped to his back. He got close to the truck and let go. Luckily, he aimed too low, and the bullets went through the radiator; it didn't stop.

Somewhere along the line, a detachment of Marines got cut off by the Chinese. They were running low on ammo and had wounded. Someone asked for volunteers. I said, "I'm your guy." We loaded sandbags across the front of the truck and headed out. I'm driving, and tracers are going back and forth all over the sky. I didn't give a shit—I was just looking for something dangerous to do, just another crazy Marine. God, they were happy to see us, because they were on their last legs. That's how I won a Bronze Star.

Bob Ehrlich, 94, First Marine Division: Korea screwed my legs up—from the cold. It got way below zero and we didn't have any good winter clothing. They gave you some old boots that were rubberized, and—*shit*—they wouldn't stop anything. We had an overcoat—that was really heavy. But there just wasn't any good winter gear. They weren't prepared for anything like that.

Ray Garland, 96, First Marine Division: Coming out of Korea, I was assigned to the Seventh Marines. I lost an officer the first day, then, in the middle of the night, we lost another officer. I ended up in charge because I was the senior sergeant at the time. That was bad; got frostbite in both my hands and feet, then ended up with a bullet in my leg. I was getting out of a foxhole, and it felt like somebody kicked me in the shin. It was a ricochet. I didn't pay any attention to it because I couldn't take my clothes off to look for a week. About fifteen years after the war, it started aching. I went to the VA, and they said, "You've got a bullet in your leg." I didn't know.

Bob Ehrlich, 94, First Marine Division: The Chinese came down and we had a pretty good fight with them. We were going from the reservoir to Hungnam. I got shot in my foot. Shit, there were so many guys shooting at you. All you wanted to do was get out of there. And I did, I got flown out. I went down to some hospital in Japan, and I was there for two months.

Jack Becker, 99, First Marine Division: I made it to one of the big troopships at Hungnam. I had picked up this Czech rifle—*a beautiful thing*—and was carrying it up the cargo net. One of the Marines on deck said, "I can get rid of that rifle if you want me to." I didn't want to lug it around, so I sold it to him for thirty bucks or something.

Robert Hall, 95, First Marine Division: I was an old man among the young guys in Korea. I was twenty-six or twenty-seven; one of the old people. We fit quite well together though. I got there around January 1, 1951, six months after the war began. The remnants of the First Marine Division had just come back from the Chosin Reservoir and needed all kinds of replacements. I was one of them. For a few months, there was a lot of training going on. I met some fine people, and I heard a lot about the fighting that went on at the reservoir. I was honored to be among them.

James Shriver, 98, MAG-12: I arrived in Korea in February of 1953. February in Korea, with the wind coming down out of Siberia—you can't imagine. I had never experienced cold anywhere near it. That was cold beyond imagination. By that time, I was a buck sergeant. One day, somebody came into the armory tent and yelled out to me, "Hey, Shriver! The colonel wants to see you!" I thought, *What the hell does the colonel want?* He was the squadron commander of VMA-323. So I went back to my tent, put on a clean set of dungarees, and walked over to the headquarters. When I walked in, the sergeant major points down the hall and says, "The colonel's at the end of the hall. Go down there." I went down and reported in to him. He said, "I understand you were on Iwo Jima." I said, "Yes, sir." He said, "Well, I need a sergeant for a special assignment." I thought, *Oh, shit!* He said, "Go get your gear, get on the plane. They'll fly you down to K-1," which was the headquarters for the Marine Air Wing in Korea. I went down to K-1 and turned my orders in. The guy said, "Don't get out, just get back on the plane; they'll fly you over to Japan." So we flew over to Japan—and it turned out they were putting me in charge of the officer's whiskey warehouse! As you can imagine, I had a lot of friends in the Marine Corps! After that, I came back to the States to Treasure Island, and I got discharged from the Marine Corps—finally—in 1954.

Thousands of World War II veterans fought and died in Korea due to the sudden need for trained and experienced troops to defend against Communist aggression. Over three years of battle, some thirty-seven thousand Americans would die on the peninsula, fighting in what's often been classified as a proxy war in the larger struggle between the United States and the Soviet Union.

Ten years later, as the Vietnam War began to escalate in the 1960s, some veterans of the Pacific were still serving in the military, while others had sons and daughters in the conflict. It was an era of unrest and upheaval that placed generations at odds, and irreparably changed how Americans viewed war.

Art Perez, 96, Third Marine Division (World War II)/Third Marine Regiment (Vietnam): We went in by helicopter and landed just south of the DMZ, out in an open field, down near Dong Ha. I was there for a while, then we moved up to "Indian Country" over by the Rockpile and Mother Ridge (we always had pet names for everything). We got our tails saturated with mortar fire that first night. And they were accurate; they came right down the ridgeline and all the way around it. They had it zeroed in already.

We sent patrols out the next day to see what was going on near the other ridges. We stayed there for about a month or so. I got amoebic diarrhea from the water out there. I ended up in the hospital. Then they sent me to Guam. I came back and they made me the first sergeant in a medical company—Charlie Med. It was a big hospital in Da Nang. We took care of all the dead bodies because we had graves registration in the company. I was with them for several months, then they sent me to join two more medical companies up north.

I went to Phu Bai for a while, then broke off and went up to Dong Ha. I spent quite a while with them. I was all over the goddamn place! My captain was talking to me one time and he must have thought I was ignoring him. But he finally figured out that I just couldn't hear him. I ended up on a hospital ship, traveling back to the United States again, and ended up in Philadelphia. I spent two months in the hearing clinic there.

The doctor said, "You have significant hearing loss." There's nothing they could do about it because the nerves were dead. No operations, no nothing. You can't replace nerves. He said, "It will probably get worse." It has.

Keith Tucker, 100, Second Marine Division: I think it was tougher for me to have my son in Vietnam with the infantry than it was for him. I could think of all the things that could happen—*accidents*. Like when the guys were unloading LSTs in World War II: Hundreds of Marines lost their lives doing that. My son was always riding in helicopters, and so many guys were getting killed in helicopters. I made sure, every night, that I went out and stood on the patio, praying that he'd come home. And he did.

Donn Thompson, 95, Sixth Marine Division (World War II): You have to understand—guys were hated just because they went to Vietnam. That's a shameful, shameful thing. They were in a "bad war," and I happened to be involved in what was considered a "good war." But there are no "good wars."

19 ★ ★ ★ ★ ★ ★

LIFE AFTER WAR

Of the sixteen million Americans that served in World War II, more than half a million suffered some degree of psychiatric collapse due to combat related stress. During the battle for Okinawa alone, twenty-six thousand men were evacuated for some form of mental ailment. Millions more, afflicted by blast concussions or undiagnosed post-traumatic stress, were discharged into civilian life without support or counsel.

Mike Ladich, 96, Fifth Marine Division: Oh, Christ! Yes, I was having nightmares. For a long time. There were two: I'd dream that I was back on the beaches at Iwo Jima, getting shot at as I came in. Or I'd dream that mortar shells were coming down from above, and I couldn't do anything about it. They were just dropping like rain.

Keith Tucker, 100, Second Marine Division: I think everybody had that problem. You couldn't help it, couldn't help it. You just don't forget those kinds of events.

Frank Smith, 100, Fourth Marine Division: Anybody that's been in combat—you're never the same. It does something to the framework of the body.

Genevieve Lashaw, 95, Women's Reserve: I used to sleep in my husband's arms at night. One night, at two o'clock in the morning, I felt my head going over the foot of the bed. He had a dream that he was on the second floor of a building and the Japs were coming up. He was going over the railing, and he was taking me with him. I didn't sleep in his arms after that.

Frank Wright, 96, Fourth Raider Battalion/Third Marine Division: When I got married, I had problems sleeping next to someone. She'd have to go to the bathroom or something and I'd yell at her.

Chuck Meacham, 96, Third Raider Battalion/Sixth Marine Division: My wife, for the first couple of years, said she didn't dare touch me at night because I'd just flip out. But that went away.

Tom Charlton, 95, First Marine Division: I'd wake up and my wife would say, "What's the matter?" And I'd say, "Oh, nothing."

Ken Brown, 95, Fifth Marine Division: I'd go to bed at night, and I'd hear that machine gun rattle. Dreaming of that, night after night. Took quite a long time to get over it. But I don't think that was extraordinary or unusual. As far as I know, that was a common thing that happened to combat Marines.

Marvin Strombo, 95, Second Marine Division: I'd wake up sweating a lot of the time—or screaming.

Ray Garland, 96, USS *Tennessee*: When you close your eyes, it's there. I'd just stay up. It's not easy.

Tom Shields, 93, Fourth Raider Battalion/Sixth Marine Division: I had a little gal at the University of Louisville ask, "What did you do during the war?" I said, "I killed people." Her eyes got big as saucers. I said, "You had a choice, you killed them, or they killed you." It ain't hard to make that kind of decision.

Eugene Jones, 94, Fourth Marine Division: It's not like some goddamned movie.

Ken Brown, 95, Fifth Marine Division: My parents said I walked the house a lot. They could hear me stomping around at night. And I was really jumpy when someone would come into a room. I told them not to come over and touch me because I didn't know what I would do. Those things stayed with me for a long time.

Burt Withee, 95, Second Marine Division: I hadn't been home more than a day or two and my mother wanted to sit down and relive all that shit. I couldn't do it. I knew it upset her. I told her, "I'm through with all that shit. I don't want any more of it. Maybe in another couple years I'll talk about it—not now." She was disappointed because she wanted to hear more of the nasty stuff. I never did tell her. What little she did hear was so bad for her that there was no sense elaborating on it.

Russel Nelson, 98, First Marine Division: I worked at the mill right away. That was the worst, because I'd be tired going in every morning. I wouldn't get any sleep, or I'd lose a couple of hours because of the nightmares.

Howell Wheaton, 99, Second Marine Division: I think the worst time for me, after the war, were the three years I spent back in my hometown before my wife and I went to Purdue. They were bringing the dead home for military funerals, and they wanted someone from each branch of the service to act as a pallbearer. I was the only Marine there. I made too damned many military funerals right after I got home. I suppose that was one of the saddest times for me. I survived it okay, but it's still a memory that I have.

John Marx, 97, Third Marine Division: After the war, I went to jail for fighting, drunk driving, and driving with a revoked license. One police officer—who didn't like me—would pick me up for no reason at all. I tried to run away from him once, but they got a car ahead of me, and they got me. After that, they tried to take my kids away from me. They gave me a choice: Go to rehab for alcoholic treatment or we'll take your kids away from you and send you to jail. I chose rehab.

Les Anderson, 97, First Provisional Field Artillery Group: When I came back, I thought some of my friends would still be around. But they were all gone. That was tough—not having anybody that I could relate to. I helped my folks on the farm as much as I could. There was a girl that wrote me letters while I was in the service, and she lived in Sioux City, Iowa. I went back there by train. I spent a week with her and her family. But I just wandered the streets in Sioux City. I was lost.

James Boutin, 97, Fourth Marine Division: I couldn't sleep. I'd walk the streets of downtown Syracuse. I did that for two or three months. I fought the war every night. When I came back, I wasn't normal.

Jack Rasmussen, 94, Third Marine Division: When I got home, I had trouble hunting deer. I didn't see any sport in it. The only way I could do it was by scaring them first and making them run. It was only fun if they were on the move.

Howard Rieckers, 100, Second Armored Amphibian Battalion: It still kind of bothers me to hunt. When you shoot a rifle, you can smell the powder, and it brings back memories.

Lester Penny, 98, Sixth Marine Division: You see all these war movies—and some of them look pretty realistic—but they haven't been able to get the smell. The stench of death is just overpowering; the smell of decaying bodies and all of that. I don't think it's something you ever get used to. You just sort of suppress it and you don't think about it. But sometimes it just pops in my mind. I'll smell something particular, and it brings back a memory.

Luther Hendricks, 96, Fifty-Second Defense Battalion: I take stuff now that's supposed to calm me, but it doesn't do a thing. I hear planes flying, I hear shells exploding, I see people coming at me with knives. I have dreams that people are in the house, trying to hurt me. But there's nobody there. They've been working on my PTSD for two years, but they haven't fixed a thing. They talk a lot. It took them seventy years to figure out that the ringing in my ears came from the guns and explosions; seventy years to get me a pension. Where were they when I was thirty-five? Forty-five? Fifty? "Oh, you're crazy. You're just hearing things. There's nothing wrong with you." Hell, I'm ninety-six now. What do I have to do?

Bill Gropp, 97, Fifth Marine Division: I was so fortunate, I never did have nightmares. I've got some friends who had them until they died.

Donn Thompson, 95, Sixth Marine Division: I didn't have any problems, it was just like changing shirts to me. I've been very fortunate.

John L'Abbe, 97, Second Marine Division: I never had any trouble sleeping. I didn't think about—I just didn't think about the war.

Melvin Gribble, 95, Fifth Amphibious Reconnaissance Battalion: It didn't bother me. It never bothered me at all. I wondered about that, too: *How come it didn't?* But it just didn't.

Roy Mays, 99, USS *Idaho*: Thinking about them and knowing they happened are different things. When you're home—that's it. It was time to move on.

Wallace "Wally" Hamlin, 99, Second Marine Division: That's one thing I didn't have any trouble with. I worked in the woods all my life and I immediately went back to work; it didn't bother me a bit. I could forgive the Japanese. I never held any grudges.

Ben Carson, 96, Second Raider Battalion/Fifth Marine Division: I don't have any bad feelings against the Japanese. A helluva lot of what happened was brought on by their leadership. The Japanese people had no hand in it at all: They just got dragged along.

Donn Thompson, 95, Sixth Marine Division: It's taken me a long time to get comfortable being around Japanese people, even though they're no different than we are.

Marvin Strombo, 95, Second Marine Division: We used to have arguments: Half the guys used to say they hated them. But I never did. I always felt—either I killed them or they killed me. But there was no hate. You had to respect them because they were good soldiers, they fought hard.

John Marx, 97, Third Marine Division: I hated their fuckin' guts. I do to this day.

Eugene Thomas, 92, First Marine Division: I don't like Japanese—I never will like 'em. Hunting Japs was just about like shooting coyotes for me. No different.

Robert Beale, 97, USS *Bennington*: I despised the Japs. *But* do I despise them today? No, no. I don't despise anybody. If I want God to love me, I have to love everybody.

Mike Ladich, 96, Fifth Marine Division: I got over that a long time ago. I realized they were just victims of their fuckin' system, too.

Paul Frederick, 98, Third Marine Division: If you boil it down, they were doing the same thing we were doing. We were getting paid to kill them and they were getting paid to kill us. We have a big Toyota factory here, right out of Lexington. It's been in operation for several years now. But there were some guys who would never even touch a Japanese car; you couldn't give them one. I was never like that.

William Darling, 98, First Marine Division: I went back to Peleliu in 2014 on a tour with about six other people. I spent almost a week there. On the anniversary of the landing, the guide said we were going up to the school for something. I didn't think too much about it. When we got to the school, there was a Marine band and a bunch of chairs. About half the population of the island was there. The governor of the island was conducting the event and he introduced me. He told me to stand up. Then he started talking to somebody on the other side of the room and this little Japanese guy stood up—a veteran of the battle.

We walked towards each other, and we stopped. Then we saluted each other, reached out and shook hands. Finally, we pulled into a clinch. The whole room exploded in applause. I thought he was a real nice old guy. Didn't speak any English but we could talk through an interpreter. It turned out, at one point, on the second or third day of the battle, we were about six hundred yards from each other. We might have even shot at each other! He was one of the holdouts when the war was over, and didn't get home until sometime in '46 or '47.

I enjoyed his acquaintance. I would like to have spent a lot more time with him. I had no hard feelings towards the Japanese anymore. Why should I? Just because one of them killed my best friend? It could have been me killing someone else's best friend.

Jim Palmieri, 103, Sixth Marine Division: Even today, talking to you, I can see the first Jap I killed. I was only three feet from him, he was about my age. He was fighting for his country, and I was fighting for mine. People made fun of the Japs: "They have eyes like they come from Mars." They don't have eyes like they come from Mars. "They have teeth like groundhogs." They don't have teeth like that. "They have bowed legs." Are you kidding? They were the toughest sonsabitches I ever saw. And people back home made fun of Japanese soldiers. They oughta meet one—they'd change their minds. I never fought in Europe, so I don't know about Germans, Russians, Italians, or English. But the Japs were fighters.

John L'Abbe, 97, Second Marine Division: I'm still glad we weren't in Europe. I would've had a helluva time shooting Italians. That would have been a terrible war, fighting someone you knew. I grew up with Italians—and I couldn't have done that.

Harmon Hunter, 101, First Marine Division: I didn't want to be in the European War, over there fighting the Germans. You'd see little kids and women getting killed. This way it was mostly men.

Gordon Black, 94, First Marine Division: That would have been hell, to sleep in a foxhole in a foot of snow. One thing about the South Seas—it rained pretty hard, but I'd rather be there than in the cold European weather.

Melvin Gribble, 95, Fifth Amphibious Reconnaissance Battalion: I'm glad I didn't go to Europe.

W. Lee Robinson, 97, Second Parachute Battalion/Fifth Marine Division: The only problem I have now is sitting through movies: Something graphic—usually a battle scene—will happen and I just come apart. Otherwise, I'm fine. It's obvious that I still tear up, regurgitating everything that happened.

Genevieve Lashaw, 95, Women's Reserve: If the TV was on and it had anything to do with the war, it was off right away.

My husband would say, "Get that off of there or I'm getting out of here." A lot of the fellas wanted to come talk with him. He said, "You can come, but if you start talking about the war, there's the door." Some of the fellas would talk about it, but he wouldn't. It was that bad.

Ken Brown, 95, Fifth Marine Division: For fifty years, I never talked about the war. I don't know why, but I just didn't. As my family grew up, they knew I was in the Marines, but they didn't really know my account.

William Darling, 98, First Marine Division: Sometime after the war, I was taking down storm windows from the house and carrying them down to the basement and stacking them. Something happened and my mother yelled at me (which wasn't typical). I started throwing the windows down because I was mad. I got off by myself and thought, *They don't know what I've been through!* My mom called my dad, and my dad came home and said, "What's going on?" I made some dumb comment to him. Then I stopped and thought, *I've heard of guys doing this. I'm going to fight it. I'm not going to lose my mind,* so I put the war out of my head. For sixty-some-odd years, I put it out of my head.

Tom Charlton, 95, First Marine Division: I had the same doctor for about twenty years at the VA. She asked me, "Tom, anything ever bother you from the service?" I said, "No." She said, "Nothing bothers you?" I sat there thinking and I said, "Well, there's a few things that bother me." She said, "Well, tell me one of them." So I told her the story about Richter getting killed on Okinawa. She said, "Would you do me a favor? Would you go see a counselor?" I said, "Why?" She said, "I think it would do you good to talk about it." I took my wife, and we went up there. I liked the guy—he was an Iraq veteran. He said, "Tom, would you mind telling me your story?" So I told him the story. My wife had never heard it . . . and we'd been married sixty-five years.

Chuck Meacham, 96, Third Raider Battalion/Sixth Marine Division: The only time I discuss the war is when I go to reunions, just to get it out of my system. Then I wouldn't talk about it.

Eugene Jones, 94, Fourth Marine Division: When I went to the reunions, it was always a three-day thing: The first day was a meeting, the second day was a general making some bullshit speech, and the third day was for reminiscing together in a room. Everybody had scrapbooks and little inky-dinky black cameras. And there was nothing but people fucking crying in those rooms. They'd lay the albums out on a long bench, turn the pages, and say, "Here's Billy, you remember? He got killed the third day." The crying—and these were hard people, working shit jobs when they came back. And they were crying like babies. I took three years of that, and my wife and I said, "We can't bear it anymore."

Tom Charlton, 95, First Marine Division: I had an old cassette player, and a guy fixed it so I could record on it. I sat in the back bedroom, and I told my story. My wife, Ruth, came back one day to tell me lunch was ready. And I was just sitting back there crying. Ruth said, "What's the matter?" I said, "This is the hardest thing I've ever done in my life," bringing those memories up.

Frank Wright, 96, Fourth Raider Battalion/Third Marine Division: I've never discussed any of this stuff with my children.

I have three sons, but I'm ashamed of a lot of the stuff I did. I didn't want them to know that their dad had been killing people.

Tom Charlton, 95, First Marine Division: We weren't proud of ourselves.

Stew Lahey, 97, Second Separate Engineer Battalion: I bet half the guys you've talked to, their families don't know what they did in the service. Why? Because we didn't want to talk about it. My son doesn't know. My daughter doesn't know half the stuff I went through. I wanted to shield them from it. I thought, *They don't need to know; it's not going to help their lives any.* But now, young folks don't realize what they have because of what happened eighty years ago in World War II.

Ken Brown, 95, Fifth Marine Division: I was a college professor. When I started talking to some of the students—this would have been about the 1980s—they didn't know anything about that war. They didn't even know who was fighting. I had a sticker on the back of my truck: "Iwo Jima." I parked downtown and this college girl came around and saw the sticker. She said, "What's that 'Iwo Jima'? Is that some kind of a drink?" They didn't know anything about it, so I decided that I would tell my story.

Frank Wright, 96, Fourth Raider Battalion/Third Marine Division: It seems like every February they want to hear about Iwo again. Now I'm happy to tell them, so they know what their fathers did.

Harold Rediske, 94, Fourth Marine Division: This lady was tracing her father's service, and she got ahold of my name from somebody. She called me and wanted to know what I knew about him. I didn't tell her the truth—I didn't tell her how he looked after he was killed. He was just burned up.

Donald Brown, 95, Fifth Marine Division: I had one buddy named George Burrows. He got killed on Iwo Jima. After the war, I went down to southern Illinois, and I stopped to see his folks. They wanted to know if he was in any pain when he died. I said, "No, he died right away."

Lester Penny, 98, Sixth Marine Division: My brother, who was three years older than me, was also on Okinawa. But he was in the Seventy-Seventh Army Division. He was killed. The only reason I found out was because one of my letters was returned to me. "Deceased" was written on the outside. That was in April of 1945, and I got the letter back in May.

At the end of the battle, after the island was secured, I got permission from my CO to go to the Seventy-Seventh Division. I located his company, talked to his company commander, and found out how he was killed. The company commander told me he had put my brother in for a Distinguished Service Cross, which is the second highest medal for bravery. Charles was killed on a little island off the coast: Ie Shima. Apparently his company was pinned down by a Japanese machine gunner and they couldn't find it, so he volunteered to ride a tank toward where they *thought* the machine gun was. But in order to direct the tank, he had to expose himself to fire. And they killed him.

After I got home—it was in 1948, I think—I hadn't heard anything from the War Department about his award. I wrote to them, and they said, "Yes, that's right. He's entitled to a Distinguished Service Cross and a Bronze Star." My wife and I went to a ceremony at Camp Meade in Maryland, and they gave us the medals. Then I got a notice from the War Department that the island where he was killed was sinking; they were going to move all the bodies. They asked me where I wanted to send him. I said, "Well, if you're going to move the body, bring it back and I'll have him buried at Arlington National Cemetery." And that's—that's where he is.

Howell Wheaton, 99, Second Marine Division: I had a dear friend, who was younger than me, that came from a very poor coal mining family. He was essentially my little brother. He spent a lot of time at our house, out on the farm. He joined the Marines, I'm sure, because I did. He was killed on Iwo Jima. I suppose that's my worst memory of the war.

Bert Rutan, 95, Fifth Marine Division: My best friend, Stan Shofner, was a really great guy. He wanted to go back and play for the Louisville Colonels; and I think he was good enough that he could have. But he was killed right next to me when we landed on Iwo Jima. I wrote his parents and told them what a great guy he was—and how much I loved him. And they wrote back and wanted to know all the details. I never could answer them. His back was just splayed open, and I could see his lungs. The skin was all gone. I was standing right next to him. It could have been me.

Harold Rediske, 94, Fourth Marine Division: It kind of bothers me sometimes. I get to thinking, *Why me?*

Ken Brown, 95, Fifth Marine Division: Survivor's guilt. I had some trouble with that. I couldn't understand how I'd made it when all these other guys, with a lot more going for them, didn't.

Robert Schultz, 102, USS *California*: We had three or four guys that committed suicide from our ship. One was a very good friend of mine, a guy named KV Johnson from Chicago. KV never acted like the war bothered him any more than I did. He went home, got married, but never had any kids. We kept in touch. I found out—*later*—that his parents had died, and his wife had cancer and was in the hospital. The combination, plus whatever he was dreaming about with the war, and he killed himself. He did it on his parents' grave. I thought, *Oh, geez. KV, you've got more class than that.* I had another good friend in Detroit. I didn't get the whole story, but he committed suicide. And another one in the St. Louis area, Richardson. I got the word that he had killed himself, too. Anyway, there weren't a lot of them. But out of ninety Marines on the ship, it was quite a high percentage.

Harmon Hunter, 101, First Marine Division: Wouldn't you think we would have learned from that experience? But we haven't learned a damn thing. Everybody's willing to take on a war, no matter who starts it. It's unbelievable.

Elburn Cooper, 95, Fifth Marine Division: If there's any way to avoid a war, I think we oughta do it.

Ray Kempf, 90, Fourth Marine Division: When will we ever learn that killing each other will never solve our problems? It will only destroy us.

Les Anderson, 97, First Provisional Field Artillery Group: I still don't know, to this day, why so-called civilized nations don't find a better way to solve their problems. I pray every day that Ian, my little boy in the Marine Corps, doesn't have to fight.

Genevieve Lashaw, 95, Women's Reserve: We had five daughters. My husband did not want a son. What Clem went through, he did not want a son to go through. When Iraq started, our grandson was over there, and they'd have it on the TV every morning. After the fourth day, my husband ended up in the hospital from stress, not knowing where he was.

Eldon Cedergreen, 96, Sixth Tank Battalion: I don't wish war on anybody. If you haven't been through the experience, you have no idea what it's like—*not really*. To experience it is something else.

James Rosenmiller, 99, First Marine Division: I can still see the first Japanese I ever killed. It's no pleasure to kill another man. No pleasure at all. That's the truth—I've shot a few of them, but I don't *ever* gloat about it. You do what you have to do. Either you kill, or you get killed. That's the way it is. That's the way war is.

Milton "Red" Cronk, 98, Third Raider Battalion: I wish they didn't have to fight anymore. It's a losing battle no matter who's fighting. It just doesn't make any sense. But someone gets it going and they just fight, fight, fight. War is hell.

Les Anderson, 97, First Provisional Field Artillery Group: They're glorifying Iwo Jima today. That's one of the main whoop-de-doos for the Marine Corps. They think it's the greatest place in the world.

Elburn Cooper, 95, Fifth Marine Division: There were Marines who spent their whole life in the Corps. We called them "Gung Ho Marines." I was never one of those. To me, the idea of having an organization that's there to kill people, it hits me the wrong way.

Donald Brown, 95, Fifth Marine Division: Some guys hated the Marine Corps, but I didn't hate it. I thought it was a very good branch of service to be in.

Don Browning, 95, Flag Allowance: I wouldn't want to go into the service again, but I wouldn't take a million dollars for my memories.

W. Lee Robinson, 97, Second Parachute Battalion/Fifth Marine Division: I have a little great-granddaughter who calls me Papa Lee. She says, "My Papa can do anything because he's a Marine." She was only three or four at the time, but she was convinced that there was nothing like a Marine for being tough.

Art Perez, 96, Third Marine Division: They were the best fighting force in the world.

Bill Gropp, 97, Fifth Marine Division: I was proud to be a Marine.

20 ★★★★★★

IN THE SHADOW OF WAR

In the years following World War II, the United States saw a drastic surge in birth rates, now known as the Baby Boom. In 1946 alone, 3.4 million Americans were born, a 20 percent increase from 1945. The "Baby Boomers," 73 million strong, would inherit the stories, legacies, and traumas of World War II.

Bob Ehrlich Jr., son of Bob Ehrlich: When I was young, my parents had a trunk downstairs that I'd get into every once in a while. There was a blood-stained Japanese flag inside and what I *thought* were bullet casings. I took the casings to school for show-and-tell one year. My teacher called my mother and said, "Do you know what your son brought to show-and-tell?" Turned out they were gold-plated teeth from a dead Japanese soldier. I got into a lot of trouble for that. And that's when I first realized Dad had been in a war.

Terese Rasmussen, daughter of Jack Rasmussen: When I was about eight or nine, I found his photograph album in the basement. It had a few really gory pictures inside: One showed a native holding the head of a Japanese soldier. There were others where the whole ground was covered with bodies. That scared me to death when I found it. He'd never shown it to me, it was just hidden down in the basement. I knew he'd been in the war, but I couldn't believe the number of bodies. About that time, he started telling stories every now and then. I remember him talking about this one guy named "Pinkie," who was a friend of his. I said, "Well, what happened to 'Pinkie'? How come I don't know him now?" He said, "Oh . . . he stepped on a land mine. We never found his body."

Maurina Ladich, daughter of Mike Ladich: When I was about ten years old, we were rummaging around in some boxes in our parents' attic and came across this little record. Our mom played it for us: It was a recording of our father's voice. He was talking to his own mother, just before going into battle. For us, it brought the war home; we realized our father had participated in this massive event, that he'd been a Marine, that he had a life before us.

Howard Rediske, son of Harold Rediske: I remember, as a young child, seeing dad's Silver Star and Bronze Star in a drawer. But I didn't understand the significance. And they were never on display. My mother would always refer to him waking up with bad dreams, but I never saw that either. I do remember him sitting on the side of the bed, smoking Lucky Strikes at night.

Sandra Williamson, daughter of Marvin Strombo: I had the room next to my dad and he had a lot of nightmares. I remember it. I think because my dad was a single parent, he shoved everything down and kept his nose to the grindstone.

He didn't drink or suffer from panic attacks. But he did have nightmares. As a little kid that was unsettling because he was our only parent, and he was suffering. None of us knew what to do.

Joe Withee, son of Burt Withee: We didn't ask much about the war and he didn't seem to want to talk about it. *Did you kill people?* I never said that to my dad. I've always felt, in war, bravery and cowardice is a fine line. If you jump out of your foxhole, grab somebody's arm, then pull them inside, you could get killed. Do you do that or not? Do you stick your head up and fire three times or do you stay down to avoid getting shot? But then you've got to live with it your whole life. Maybe you think you were a coward on a few occasions. That's probably hard to live with.

Bob Ehrlich Jr., son of Bob Ehrlich: Dad had so much depression when he came home from Korea, thinking: *Why was I one of the people who survived?* He had a terrible time trying to figure why God kept him and not everyone else.

Sandra Williamson, daughter of Marvin Strombo: When I was about twelve years old, Dad got a phone call. He was asleep because he was working nights. I went in to wake him up, but when I shook him, he jumped out of the bed and knocked me across the room. He felt terrible about it, but told me, "You can't wake a Marine like that. Always announce yourself at the door." It was really a powerful moment, realizing that he had fought and lived like that.

Joe Withee, son of Burt Withee: When my mom would clank a pan, drop a pan, or make a loud noise in the kitchen sink, Dad would react every time: "Jesus Christ! Goddamnit!

What the hell's going on over there?" He'd get really upset. I guess it brought back memories of shelling and shooting from World War II.

Maurina Ladich, daughter of Mike Ladich: We never talked to our father about the period after the war; it's a lost decade. All we heard were scant stories from his family, saying he was a really angry young man. We can only speculate: *What was he doing?* We don't know. What helped him was meeting our mother, who was a very calm person. She spent a lot of time reassuring him because he would have anxiety about things. I can still hear her saying, "Mike, Mike, it's going to be okay."

Howard Rediske, son of Harold Rediske: When I was older, probably in my forties, we were watching a program on the History Channel that did a segment on Saipan. They showed footage of people throwing themselves into the sea. Dad said, "I was there . . ." and he started to cry. Then he said, "Why did they do that?"

Marcia Rutan, daughter of Bert Rutan: I didn't fully understand Dad's involvement in the war until I was in my fifties. He really didn't want to talk about it, but he definitely carried a sorrow from watching his friends die. I think the grief was too big. Maybe, in a way, he felt it was inappropriate to discuss. I don't know. My mother and father went through the University of Minnesota together in three years on the GI Bill. They both majored in philosophy because they didn't have enough money for two different sets of textbooks. It was a whirlwind. We grew up in Alaska and that was a world apart from the mainstream culture of the country; we were removed, recovering from the war. He was very busy, becoming an active and loved minister. He ran all kinds of groups, activities, and programs; he was always in meetings and was the chair for a new hospital. Dad was very, very active. I don't know how other veterans responded. There was probably a tremendous number of different responses; maybe a different one for each person. But the way Dad chose to handle the war was to engage with family and work. Yet those feelings and memories were still there.

He finally gave them a chance to emerge around 1958 or 1959. That was the first memory I have of it. We drove to Anchorage every week to meet with a counselor to work some of that out. That was an important thing to do. But *honestly*, he still didn't talk about it after that. It wasn't until 1995 when he finally opened up about it. He and three other men, who had all been on Iwo Jima, connected through the church. Their meeting was featured on the front page of the *Seattle Times*. From then on, my father has talked about it openly.

Leslie Rutan, daughter of Bert Rutan: What switched after the article? I'm not sure I have the answer. Maybe it was the distance of time. Maybe it was the comradery. Maybe, as we grew older, we could relate to him as an adult, and he felt like he could share things he couldn't share with young children. Maybe, over time, some of the trauma eased. I'm not sure.

Maurina Ladich, daughter of Mike Ladich: In 1990, I attended a reunion with my mother and my father. All the guys were relatively young—late sixties and healthy. But it was sobering to sit there and listen to their stories. There was one guy, Adolph Fang, who sat at our table and explained how our father had saved his life. I remember my father crying because he didn't know Fang had survived the war; all he remembered was dragging Fang's bullet-riddled body to a corpsman. I was riveted because my father hadn't told us any of it.

I could see the bond they shared after all these years. And it wasn't all trauma and sorrow. They joked and laughed; they had married, had children, and lived fine lives. It was a joyful experience. They were so happy to be together because they understood what they'd gone through in a way none of us ever could.

Sandra Williamson, daughter of Marvin Strombo: Joe Tachovsky, the son of Dad's commanding officer, came to see Dad when he was on his deathbed. He was in and out of consciousness, but when Joe got up to leave, the last thing Dad said was, "Joe, Semper Fi." That showed me how important those people were to him. You have your family, but you also forge deep bonds with all the men you fought with. And their descendants as well. They were all family to him, even to his last moments.

Terese Rasmussen, daughter of Jack Rasmussen: Dad was always glad to be a Marine and proud to have fought for his country. He got really patriotic in his last few years. Much more so than when I was growing up; more demonstrative. Every time the opportunity to speak about freedom arose, he was always there, with something to say.

Colleen Mussetter, daughter of Harold Rediske: Dad still hated when people would say he was a hero. He would get very upset: "I am not a hero. The heroes are the ones that never came home."

Maurina Ladich, daughter of Mike Ladich: Eventually, I think Dad came to the conclusion that you have to live a good, moral life. That's how you make sense of it. You can't let horror and destruction define you; you have to find a way to move on and find good in the world. By telling his story and passing on strong values, he showed us that you can have a good life in spite of the horror. That was how he coped with it. He wanted to be a good person who tried to do good and show compassion, to live the opposite values of hate and war.

Diana Kempf, daughter of Ray Kempf: Dad always felt like he owed his community and his country something. He was always very involved. He was just an outstanding, stalwart man. After living through the battle as a nineteen-year-old kid, trying to sort out what it meant, I think he was just grateful and wanted to contribute. And he did.

Sandra Williamson, daughter of Marvin Strombo: My dad also fought in Korea. And because of what happened in Korea, he had a different view on war. He felt there was a disparity about what they had done in World War II, as opposed to Korea. So when Vietnam came along, my dad would get very upset about what was going on. He felt it was wrong and shouldn't be happening. He had people tell him, "Love it or leave it." It really bothered him because he said he fought for everybody's right to speak—including his own.

Marcia Rutan, daughter of Burt Rutan: Because I was of the generation that protested the Vietnam War, in my mind, it lumped all wars together—war is bad. It wasn't until later, in the last ten years, that I've come to appreciate the importance of World War II. I recently read that less than two percent of the veterans are still alive. I now have this big hunger to learn, appreciate, and honor my father. It's been a surprising journey for me as a descendant. It's an increasing desire to not have World War II be lost or forgotten. It would be easy for fascism to reclaim the world again and we must take a stand against it.

APPENDIX I

Marines who contributed to the book:

1. Leslie Anderson (HQ Battery, First Provisional Field Artillery Group)
2. Jesse Arney (Company B, Third Tank Battalion, Third Marine Division)
3. Thomas Baker (VMFA-112)
4. Robert Beale (USS *Bennington*)
5. Harlan "H.C." Beck (K Battery/4/11, First Marine Division)
6. Jack Becker (Marine Barracks, Pearl Harbor)
7. Robert Bennett (HQ Squadron, First Marine Air Wing)
8. Gilbert Berg (HQ/2/7, First Marine Division)
9. Donald Bishop (K/3/1, First Marine Division)
10. Gordon Black (Eighth 155mm Gun Battalion)
11. Louis Bourgault (K/3/21, Third Marine Division) & (B/1/21, Third Marine Division)
12. James Boutin (Wpns/23, Fourth Marine Division)
13. Loyd Brandt (Fifth Amphibious Reconnaissance Battalion)
14. George Bradbury (A Battery/1/11, First Marine Division)
15. Donald Brown (H/3/27, Fifth Marine Division)

16. Kenneth Brown (HQ Battalion, Fifth Marine Division)
17. Donald Browning (Marine Detachment, CINCPAC)
18. Robert Brutinel (E Company, Second Parachute Battalion) & (H/3/27, Fifth Marine Division)
19. Bill Byrd (D/2/28, Fifth Marine Division)
20. John "Bob" Carlson (VMB-433)
21. Ben Carson (2BE) & (E/2/26, Fifth Marine Division)
22. Eldon Cedergreen (Sixth Tank Battalion, Sixth Marine Division)
23. Thomas Charlton (B/1/1, First Marine Division)
24. Joshua Clark (Fifth Motor Transport Battalion, Fifth Marine Division)
25. Elburn Cooper (Fifth Marine Division Band) & (HQ Battalion, Fifth Marine Division)
26. Milton "Red" Cronk (3MHQ)
27. William Darling (K/3/1, First Marine Division)
28. Anthony DeMarco (A/1/8, Second Marine Division)
29. Norlyn Dossey (B/1/5, First Marine Division)
30. Grant Duncan (HQ Company, Provisional Force Signal Battalion)
31. Royal "Roy" Earle (First JASCO, Fourth Marine Division)
32. Robert Ehrlich (Third Armored Amphibian Battalion) & (Twentieth Amphibian Truck Battalion)
33. Robert Evans (I/3/1, First Marine Division)
34. Ernie Ferguson (B/1/5, First Marine Division)
35. Glenn Ferguson (VMSB-343)
36. Thomas Fitzmaurice (Second Defense Battalion) & (Eighth AAA Battalion)
37. Edgar Fox (Sixth Defense Battalion) & (H&S/2/13, Fifth Marine Division)
38. Paul Frederick (M/3/21, Third Marine Division) & (L/3/21, Third Marine Division)

39. James Freel (Third Parachute Battalion) & (D/2/28, Fifth Marine Division)
40. Willis "Bill" Friberg (VMF-212) & (VMF-511)
41. Howard Frye (L Battery/4/12, Third Marine Division)
42. David Fusinato (First Tank Battalion, First Marine Division)
43. Ray Garland (USS *Tennessee)* & (V Amphibious Corps)
44. Conrad Gillette (Ninth Defense Battalion)
45. W.R. "Bill" Gropp (HQ Battalion, Fifth Marine Division)
46. Melvin Gribble (Fifth Amphibious Reconnaissance Battalion)
47. Robert Hall (HQ Battalion, Fleet Marine Force)
48. Billy Hall (VMSB-141) & (VMF-121)
49. Wallace Hamlin (L Battery/4/10, Second Marine Division)
50. John Haney (Service Company, Service Battalion, Camp Pendleton)*
51. Donald Harr (Marine Night Fighting Squadron 534)
52. Joe Harrison (2H) & (Wpns/4, Sixth Marine Division)
53. Elwin Hart (HQ/2/8, Second Marine Division)
54. Luther Hendricks (Fifty-Second Defense Battalion)
55. George Hirschkamp (HQ Detachment, American Embassy, Peiping, China) & (Prisoner of War)
56. Harmon Hunter (B/1/5, First Marine Division)
57. Blair Hyde (H&S/21, Third Marine Division) & (K/3/21, Third Marine Division)
58. Lucien Jandreau (B/1/26, Fifth Marine Division) & (C/1/5, First Marine Division)
59. Eugene Jones (HQ Battalion, Fourth Marine Division)
60. Hattie Kelley (Women's Reserve)

* John Haney fell ill en route to the Sixth Marine Division and was transferred to Base Hospital #18 on Guam. After three months of convalescence, he was shipped back to the United States for further treatment.

61. Ray Kempf (First JASCO, Fourth Marine Division)
62. Aaron Levin (VMO-155)
63. Frank King (VMFA-112) & (VMTB-131)
64. Richard Kolodey (VMTB-233)
65. Herman Kulla (B/1/9, Third Marine Division)
66. John L'Abbe (F/2/8, Second Marine Division)
67. Clyde Lacquement (L/3/6, Second Marine Division)
68. Dean Ladd (B/1/8) & (C/1/8, Second Marine Division)
69. Mike Ladich (Second Raider Company, Raider Battalion) & (F/2/27, Fifth Marine Division)
70. Stewart Lahey (Company C, Second Separate Engineer Battalion)
71. Genevieve Lashaw (Women's Reserve)
72. Raymond Lewis (HQ Squadron, MAG-15)
73. William "Ken" Luttrell (First JASCO, Fourth Marine Division)
74. John Marx (Pseudonym, Third Marine Division)
75. George Mason (Wpns/7, First Marine Division)
76. Roy Mays (USS *Idaho*)
77. Charles "Chuck" Meacham (3K) & (K/3/4, Sixth Marine Division)
78. Jonathan de Sola Mendes (VMSB-151)
79. David Mertell (USS *Monterey*)
80. William Morgenroth (B/1/26, Fifth Marine Division)
81. Dennis Meyer (G/3/28, Fifth Marine Division)
82. Richard Nelson (G Battery/3/11, First Marine Division)
83. Russel Nelson (HQ/1/5, First Marine Division)
84. Melvin Ogg (A/1/19, Third Marine Division)
85. James Palmieri (E/2/22, Sixth Marine Division)
86. Charles Pase (H&S/2/10, Second Marine Division)
87. Lester Penny (HQ/2/29, Sixth Marine Division)
88. Arthur Perez (G/2/21, Third Marine Division)

89. Donald Pilcher (HQ Battalion, Third Marine Division)
90. George Poppe (H/2/5, First Marine Division)
91. Larry Pressley (F/2/24, Fourth Marine Division) & (F/2/2, Second Marine Division)
92. Donald Procter (H&S Battery/1/11, First Marine Division)
93. Clayton Narveson (HQ/3/6, Second Marine Division) & (HQ/1/23, Fourth Marine Division)
94. Walter O'Malley (First Raider Company, Raider Battalion) & (E/2/27, Fifth Marine Division)
95. Victor Rainey (First Armored Amphibian Battalion)
96. Robert Rakestraw (HQ/22, Sixth Marine Division)
97. Jack Rasmussen (L/3/9, Third Marine Division)
98. Harold Rediske (B/1/24) & (H&S/24, Fourth Marine Division)
99. Burt Reynolds (C Battery, Eleventh 155mm Gun Battalion)
100. Raymond Rice (E Battery/2/11, First Marine Division)
101. Robert Riechman (First Parachute Battalion) & (H/3/26, Fifth Marine Division)
102. Howard Rieckers (Second Armored Amphibian Battalion)
103. Bobby Robinson (Marine Barracks, Puget Sound Naval Shipyard)
104. W. Lee Robinson (Second Parachute Battalion) & (D/2/27, Fifth Marine Division)
105. Augustus Rogers (L Battery/4/14, Fourth Marine Division)
106. James Rosenmiller (I/3/5, First Marine Division)
107. Richard Russell (E/2/7, First Marine Division)
108. Bert Rutan (Fourth Parachute Battalion) & (HQ/1/27, Fifth Marine Division)
109. Carl Sampson (B Company, Third Armored Amphibian Battalion)
110. Carl Scott (B/1/7, First Marine Division)
111. Dave Severance (Third Parachute Battalion) & (E/2/28, Fifth Marine Division)

112. Donald Raasch (D/2/26, Fifth Marine Division)
113. Donald Shedd (A/1/5, First Marine Division)
114. Thomas Shields (4P) & (G/2/4, Sixth Marine Division)
115. James Shriver (I/3/28, Fifth Marine Division)
116. Robert Schultz (USS *California*)
117. Ralph Simoneau (Second Raider Company, Raider Battalion) & (D/2/27, Fifth Marine Division)
118. Frank Smith (H&S/24, Fourth Marine Division)
119. Walter Spuck (H&S Battery/11, First Marine Division)
120. Francis Stanger (H&S/7, First Marine Division)
121. Gladys Stevens (Women's Reserve)
122. Marvin Strombo (D/1/6) & (H&S & Wpns/6, Second Marine Division)
123. Eugene Thomas (Pseudonym, First Marine Division)
124. Donn Thompson (H&S/22) & (Sixth JASCO)
125. Keith Tucker (Second Motor Transport Battalion, Second Marine Division)
126. Faris Tuohy (Pnr/22) & (H&S Co., Sixth Service Battalion, Sixth Marine Division)
127. Howell Wheaton (E/2/6, Second Marine Division)
128. James White (G/3/29, Sixth Marine Division)
129. H. Lloyd Wilkerson (A/1/7, First Marine Division)
130. Burton Withee (Second JASCO, Second Marine Division)
131. Burt Workman (MAG-22, Fourth Marine Air Wing)
132. Frank Wright (4DQ) & (H&S/21, Third Marine Division)
133. Paul "Bill" Town (Marine Detachment, US Naval Center, Farragut, Idaho)

APPENDIX 2

SILVER STAR

Harold R. Rediske

"The President of the United States of America takes pleasure in presenting the Silver Star to Private First Class Harold R. Rediske, United States Marine Corps Reserve, for service as set forth in the following citation: For conspicuous gallantry and intrepidity while serving with Company B, First Battalion, Twenty-fourth Marines, FOURTH Marine Division, in action against enemy Japanese forces on Namur Island, Kwajalein Atoll, Marshall Islands, on 1 and 2 February 1944. Although sustaining painful wounds, Private First Class Rediske repeatedly exposed himself in order to maintain fire against the enemy. Unmindful of his own danger in his efforts to aid casualties lying in the field of fire, he fearlessly crawled forward under withering small arms fire to bring one man back to safety, to aid another in returning to the beach and to direct corpsmen with stretchers in the evacuation of several others, thereby contributing materially to the saving of many Marines who otherwise might have perished. By his fortitude, dauntless spirit of self-sacrifice and steadfast devotion to duty, Private First Class Rediske rendered valiant service and upheld the highest traditions of the United States Naval Service."

SILVER STAR

James L. Rosenmiller

"The President of the United States of America takes pleasure in presenting the Silver Star to Private First Class James L. Rosenmiller (MCSN: 850170), United States Marine Corps, for conspicuous gallantry and intrepidity while serving as an Acting Fire Team Leader in a platoon of Company I, Third Battalion, Fifth Marines, FIRST Marine Division, in action against enemy Japanese forces on Peleliu and Ngesebus, Palau Islands, 29 September 1944. Advancing forward of the lines in the face of almost certain death from a withering barrage of Japanese artillery fire, Private First Class Rosenmiller unhesitatingly went to the rescue of a comrade who had fallen critically wounded during a fierce attempt to destroy an enemy fieldpiece and, despite the grave hazards, brought the wounded man to a place of safety. When the advance of his platoon was halted by deadly hostile automatic and sniper fire from a well-covered cave during an attack on one of the low ridges on Ngesebus later the same day, he boldly crept over precipitous terrain and, reaching an advantageous position, completely routed and destroyed the concealed enemy. By his daring initiative and relentless fighting spirit, Private First Class Rosenmiller contributed essentially to the success of his unit in securing that section of the island and his great personal valor in the face of grave peril was in keeping with the highest traditions of the United States Naval Service."

SILVER STAR

Robert C. Brutinel

"The President of the United States of America takes pleasure in presenting the Silver Star to Private First Class Robert C. Brutinel (MCSN: 818418), United States Marine Corps, for conspicuous gallantry and intrepidity while serving as a Demolition Man and Flame Thrower Operator of Company H, Third Battalion, Twenty-seventh Marines, FIFTH Marine Division, in action against enemy Japanese forces on

Iwo Jima, Volcano Islands, 12 March 1945. When his company was held up by an enemy pillbox, Private First Class Brutinel made a direct frontal attack on the hostile emplacement, firing his flame thrower until the fuel supply was exhausted. Returning to the company dump, he refilled his weapon and, advancing again on the Japanese position, attacking the pillbox until it was completely silenced. His courage and devotion to duty reflect the highest credit upon the United States Naval Service."

COMMENDATION

Donald Bishop

"For meritorious service, on 26 December 1943, while the Third Battalion, First Marines was engaged with enemy Japanese forces at Cape Gloucester, New Britain. Private Donald Jay Bishop, U.S. Marine Corps, and another Marine, acting as stretcher-bearers, were carrying a wounded man to the rear when suddenly attacked by five of the enemy. Placing the wounded man on the ground, Private Bishop and the other Marine killed the five enemy with their rifles, and then continued to the rear with the wounded man. The fact that the wounded man's life was saved may be attributed to Private Bishop's high degree of courage and quick thinking. The above act was one demanding great personal bravery and fortitude and was in keeping with the highest traditions of the Naval Service."

SILVER STAR

Bertram Rutan

"The President of the United States of America takes pleasure in presenting the Silver Star to Corporal Bertram H. Rutan (MCSN: 804290), United States Marine Corps, for conspicuous gallantry and intrepidity while serving as a Squad Leader of Company C, First Battalion, Twenty-seventh Marines, FIFTH Marine Division, in action against enemy Japanese forces at Iwo Jima, Volcano Islands, on 28

February 1945. When his company's advance was held up by a heavily fortified hostile emplacement of four heavy machine guns and two light machine guns, Corporal Rutan courageously volunteered to lead a tank across a fire-swept area to a position in front of the lines from which it could deliver accurate fire on the enemy emplacement. Although he sustained a painful wound while guiding the tank, he remained in his hazardous position to direct the fire of the tank and aided greatly in destroying the hostile emplacement and in enabling the assault companies to move forward in that area. By his aggressive fighting spirit and initiative, Corporal Rutan upheld the highest traditions of the United States Naval Service."

APPENDIX 3

One of the most unique and little-known units to serve with the Marine Corps during World War II was the 121st Naval Construction Battalion. Activated on May 10, 1943, at Camp Lejeune in North Carolina, the battalion worked briefly constructing buildings on base, before being reassigned to the Third Battalion, Twentieth Marine Regiment of the Fourth Marine Division at Camp Pendleton, California. Although still officially sailors in the United States Navy, the construction workers—known as "Seabees"—were issued Marine fatigues and tasked with providing shore party duties and engineering capabilities to the Fourth Marine Division. Thomas Cooper, 100, was a rifleman with H Company, and one of two known survivors of the unit when he was interviewed in 2024.

Thomas Cooper, 100, 121st Naval Construction Battalion: Telling you a story about a war is difficult because there's so many pieces to it.

I dropped out of high school. Well, I didn't drop out, I stayed out. At the end of my junior year, I went to work at a shipyard with my dad. I had a good job, worked ten hours a day, six days a week, and made a lot of money. When I turned eighteen, I knew the draft was coming, so I went down to the recruiter the day after Christmas in '42. He talked to me about the Seabees. I really knew nothing about them, but he said maybe my experience in the shipyard would get me a stripe, so I took it. I joined. Thirty days later, I was on a bus heading to New Jersey for a train trip down to Camp Peary. Camp Peary was a fairly new base. We were only there about five weeks and did the usual things you do in boot camp: We learned how to march, got our shots, and did a little bit of training.

After five weeks, my name was listed on a bulletin board with orders to be ready at eight o'clock the following morning. That's when they took us over to Camp Lejeune, a Marine base. They said, "Send your Navy gear home, keep your blues." So, I kept my dress blues and everything else went home. I wore a Marine uniform until the end of the war. We were trained as a beach party. The Marine Corps needed to be supplied up front, and that was our job.

We joined the Fourth Marine Division at Camp Pendleton in California. There were no distinctions between Seabees from the 121st and the Marines. We wore the same uniform, ate the same food, did everything the same. The only difference was our job. During our training, we rode in trucks down to San Diego, loaded into APA ships, and attacked San Clemente Island. When we finished, the landing craft would take us up to the shoreline, and we'd march back to camp. It was only eleven miles! We did that twice, made two round trips. But the third time we went to San Diego, you could tell it was real; there was more activity, and it was more somber. We left on the thirteenth of January in '44.

In February of 1944, we hit the island of Roi-Namur in the Kwajalein Atoll in the Marshall Islands. It was my first action. I was frightened, of course. We landed in a little LCVP (Landing Craft, Vehicle, Personnel); they drop the ramp down and a guy says, "Go!" and you don't know what you're running into. But we didn't run into very much. It was easy for us. There were so many dead Japanese around—a bulldozer would scrape a spot, move bodies inside, and put a sign up with a number followed by "ED," enemy dead. Eating was a problem because of the flies. It was flies galore, landing on all our rations. At one point in the battle, a building with Japanese torpedoes stored inside exploded. It was a fantastic explosion! Concrete was hailing down all over the place. We lost a couple men, and the Marines lost quite a few. It was really something.

After Roi-Namur, we went back to the island of Maui. We thought it was going to be a rest base, but it was no rest base! It was a retraining and refit base. Maui was a pretty pleasant experience actually—lot of rain, and the food wasn't so good—but the people treated us very well, and they kind of adopted the Marines.

From there, we went to Saipan. I landed in an amphibious tractor: We went up forty or fifty yards, made a right turn parallel to the beach, and got off on the seaward side for protection. I had a Browning automatic rifle and an ammo carrier with me. We jumped into a ditch. I took a peek to see what was going on, and a bullet went by my ear. I shot at some movement ahead, but I don't know whether I hit anything. Some of our guys got into actual firefights with the Japanese because there were always stragglers between us and the Marines on the front. Marines—my hat's off to those guys. Rifle companies had to chase the Japanese and get them out of their holes. When you're fighting people who don't value their lives, it's a tough battle.

As soon as we got ashore, Hank Gebhardt got it. A shell killed him . . . a great guy. We used to play catch together; we were both from Long Island. That was the first person I was close to that got killed. I really didn't believe it, so I left my post and went down and lifted the poncho covering him. That's real. That makes the war real to you.

Around the fourth day, we went up to the airstrip. It was pockmarked and beaten up badly. We got it cleaned up pretty fast, the guys made brooms from brush, and we got 2,500 feet cleared. Pretty soon, we had airplanes coming and going. They were loading them up with gas from barrels brought up from the beach. The skillset we had in Seabees was interesting: We had excellent officers; these were not "ninety-day wonders."* These fellas came in with degrees in civil engineering and they did their jobs well. I can't say enough about the people in the outfit. I had no skill, but we had guys with every skill you could think of. They just had the ability to make things work. For example: there was a small railroad on the island used for the sugarcane industry. They fixed up the broken tracks, got three of those trains going, and we were hauling hundreds of thousands of pounds of material up to the front where it was needed.

The next island we hit was Tinian. We set up bivouac next to a cane field and, every time the wind blew, the cane would rub. We thought the Japanese were sneaking up on us! I'm pretty sure we shot up a water tank one night! Our outfit was left at Tinian; we did not go on to Iwo Jima with the Fourth Marine Division. Supposedly, our commanding officer asked if we could stay and get started on the layout of the airfield. Tinian was a beautiful little island with a lot of agriculture. But—all of a sudden—it had the world's largest airdrome on it. It was a masterpiece! I sat and watched hundreds of B-29s go out early in the morning, then twelve hours later we'd

* "Ninety-day wonder" refers to graduates of an abbreviated officers' training course established during World War II. The term is derogatory in nature because many of the graduates lacked practical combat experience.

watch them come back. Some came back on fumes and some didn't make it. Eventually, they took us off that duty and sent us back to Saipan.

On Saipan, we were back with the Third Battalion, Twenty-Fifth Marines, waiting for a ship to take us to Okinawa to stage for Operation Coronet. Our Fourth Division would have been involved in the invasion of Japan, along the plain near Tokyo, in 1946. But the war ended, and I went home. I had to go back to high school! Ten days after I separated from the service at Long Island, I went back to my old high school; there were about forty of us. We were welcomed back; we were heroes. School—I enjoyed it, and I did well. I had to make a decision about where to go to college. I had two schools in mind: Adelphi in New York and Seattle Pacific. I applied to both, and Seattle Pacific answered first, so I came out to Seattle. I got my master's and doctorate at Columbia University in New York. I'm a CEFP, which is Certified Educational Facilities Planner, that's my title. So, I've been a school planner—and it's been fun.

By the end of hostilities in 1945, the 121st Naval Construction Battalion boasted one of the finest service records of any Seabee unit in the war. They had participated in three major combat assaults, provided vital logistical support to the Marine Corps, prepared thousands of feet of runway for the Air Force, and constructed numerous military facilities across the Pacific. For their efforts, on February 25, 1945, the battalion was awarded a Presidential Unit Citation alongside the Fourth Marine Division. For years after the war, the bond between the Seabees and the Marines remained so tight, men from 121st would attend national Fourth Marine Division Association reunions every summer until the group's disbandment.

A NOTE ON SOURCES

Each veteran interviewed for this book was vetted and verified via US Marine Corps muster rolls. I used hundreds of books to craft the historical narrations that intersect the veteran accounts, the most notable of which were three publications released by the Marine Corps: *The History of US Marine Corps Operations in World War II*, *US Marine Corps Monograph Series*, and *Marines in World War II Commemorative Series.* Each is available online for free. Additionally, I relied heavily on *The Old Breed: A History of the First Marine Division in World War II*, *Follow Me! The Story of the Second Marine Division of World War II*, *The Third Marine Division*, *The Fourth Marine Division in World War II*, *The Spearhead: The World War II History of the Fifth Marine Division*, and *History of the Sixth Marine Division*; all splendid unit histories. Richard Frank's *Guadalcanal* is a must for anyone interested in World War II's defining moment in the Pacific. In the same vein, *Utmost Savagery* by Joseph Alexander is an incredible, in-depth study of the fighting on Tarawa. Oscar Peatross's hard-to-locate *Bless 'Em All: The Raider Marines of World War II* is a dense, thorough account of the Marine Raiders' contribution to the war. Ian Toll's trilogy—*Pacific Crucible*, *The Conquering Tide*, and *Twilight of the Gods*—is arguably the finest account of the Pacific War, from start to finish, ever written. I would be remiss if I didn't cite Eugene Sledge's *With the Old Breed: At Peleliu and Okinawa*; an inspiration for this work and a piece I have often championed as the greatest memoir to emerge from World War II. I also drew inspiration from *Bringing Mulligan Home: The Other Side of the Good War* by Dale Maharidge; a dark, singular exploration of combat trauma. I also enjoyed Richard Tregaskis's *Guadalcanal Diary*, Chuck Tatum's *Red Blood, Black Sand*, and Richard Wheeler's *The Bloody Battle of Suribachi*. The *Unauthorized History of the Pacific War* podcast hosted by Seth Paridon and Bill Toti was also a welcome companion as I finished work on this book.

ACKNOWLEDGMENTS

I wish I could recognize every individual that contributed to this book or shared encouragement along the way, but after ten years of work, the list would simply be too long.

I would, however, be remiss if I did not acknowledge the veterans that invited me into their homes, answered phone calls, shared stories, and treated me like family. I only wish more of them could have lived to see the publication of this book to receive the recognition they often shunned, but so richly deserved. I'd also like to extend my thanks to their families, who were incredibly gracious, often facilitating interviews, digging up old photos and memorabilia, and allowing me to tell their loved ones' stories.

Thank you to my parents, who fostered and supported my interest in World War II, no matter how strange it may have seemed. To my mom, my first editor, who read every iteration of this book. If there's ever a medal awarded for reading bad rough drafts—she's earned it. To my brother and sisters: Sam, Emily, and Megan. And to my Grandpa Wayne, a veteran of the Korean War, whose enthusiasm for this book never wavered.

I owe a huge debt to Jon Bozak, who recognized the merits of this project from the start, and whose advice helped transform this from an idea into a book. Thanks to Jocko for giving this project the green light. I'd also like to thank my agent, Jennifer Joel, and her team at Creative Artists Agency for their work. And last, but certainly not least, thank you to Marc Resnick and the team at St. Martin's Press for taking a chance.

ABOUT THE AUTHOR

Alex Moses

Scott Davis is a historian and journalist based in Spokane, Washington, with a degree in history from Gonzaga University. He runs a popular YouTube channel on the Vietnam War, *The Vietnam Experience*, which has amassed more than 200,000 subscribers and over 100 million lifetime views. His writing has appeared in *Naval History*, *Army Magazine*, and many other publications. Over the last decade, he has interviewed more than five hundred veterans of World War II, Korea, and Vietnam.